READING UP

READING UP

Middle-Class Readers and the Culture of Success in the Early Twentieth-Century United States

AMY L. BLAIR

 Temple University Press

PHILADELPHIA

Temple University Press
Philadelphia, Pennsylvania 19122
www.temple.edu/tempress

Copyright © 2012 by Temple University
All rights reserved
Published 2012

LIBRARY OF CONGRESS CATALOGING-IN-PUBLICATION DATA

Blair, Amy L., 1972–
    Reading up : middle-class readers and the culture of success in the early twentieth-century United States / Amy L. Blair.
        p.   cm.
    Includes bibliographical references and index.
    ISBN 978-1-4399-0667-5 (cloth : alk. paper)
    ISBN 978-1-4399-0668-2 (pbk. : alk. paper)
    ISBN 978-1-4399-0669-9 (e-book)
    1. American literature—Appreciation—United States—History—20th century.   2. Popular literature—United States—History and criticism.   3. Books and reading—United States—History—20th century.   4. Middle class—Books and reading—United States—History—20th century.   5. Success in literature.   6. Literature and society—United States—History—20th century.   7. Mabie, Hamilton Wright, 1846–1916—Knowledge—Literature.   8. Ladies' home journal.   I. Title.
PS228.P67B63   2011
306.4'88097309041—dc22

                                                                    2011015287

        Printed in the United States of America
        2 4 6 8 9 7 5 3 1

THE
AMERICAN
LITERATURES
INITIATIVE

A book in the American Literatures Initiative (ALI), a collaborative publishing project of NYU Press, Fordham University Press, Rutgers University Press, Temple University Press, and the University of Virginia Press. The Initiative is supported by The Andrew W. Mellon Foundation. For more information, please visit www.americanliteratures.org.

Contents

Acknowledgments   vii

Introduction: Cultivating Taste in a Mass-Market World   1
1   Mr. Mabie Tells What to Read   23
2   The Compromise of *Silas Lapham*   61
3   James for the General Reader   99
4   Misreading *The House of Mirth*   137
5   The Comforts of Romanticism   171
    Epilogue: Reading Up into the Twenty-first Century   195

    Appendix A: The Mabie Canon   205
    Appendix B: "Novels Descriptive of American Life"
    (November 1908)   209
    Notes   211
    Bibliography   227
    Index   241

Acknowledgments

Now that it is my turn to try to acknowledge the profound intellectual and emotional gifts I have received during the many years of this book's conception and production, I hardly know how to begin. At Cornell University, I had the honor of working with inspirational and generous teachers and mentors: Shirley Samuels, whose intellectual and personal generosity and unflagging faith have been a pillar of my career; Mark Seltzer, Laura Brown, and Shelley Wong, who were all inspirational teachers and constructive readers and critics of the best kind; and Lois Brown and Mark Dimunation, who introduced me to the joys of the material text and taught me how to navigate the archive. During the peripatetic stage of my academic career, many people along the way offered important advice and support that nurtured and shaped this project. Kevin Ohi has been an incisive reader and a dear friend. Natalie Friedman, Heather Dubnick, Karen Halil, and Javier Rodriguez formed an ideal writing group at Boston University. The History and Literature Program at Harvard University was a wonderful space for teaching and collegiality; Steve Biel, John O'Keefe, Megan Nelson, Katherine Howe, and Andy Muldoon were particular friends and insightful readers of my work. My student Catherine Shoichet taught me much about Edith Wharton, and I feel very fortunate to have worked with her. Colleen Lanick's friendship has maintained me across careers and miles. Eliza Richards, Mary Loeffelholz, Melissa Homestead, Faith Barrett, and Alice Rutkowski all offered guidance and constructive criticism that have helped me focus my inquiry.

Philip Goldstein and James L. Machor have my everlasting gratitude for the energy and perseverance with which they have shepherded the Reception Studies Society (RSS) into existence. I must thank them both for their support of my projects throughout the years, and thank particularly James Machor for his insightful reading and profoundly helpful comments on this project. I have met a number of kindred spirits through the RSS, foremost among them Barbara Hochman, whose work I deeply admire and who has been generous with her time, her counsel, and her wonderful sense of humor. Charles Johanningsmeier, Barbara Ryan, and Emily Satterwhite, fellow fans of other people's mail, have been wonderful resources and offered key suggestions as I researched and revised this project. Other scholars have read and commented on portions of this text in various capacities; I am beholden to Eric Lott, Priscilla Wald, and Mary Chapman for their constructive criticism and support of the project at various stages. Helen Damon-Moore was generous with her expertise about the *Ladies' Home Journal*, and for this I owe her a debt of gratitude. An anonymous reader for Temple University Press offered many key suggestions for strengthening the project.

I feel incredibly fortunate to have landed in the English Department at Marquette University, where I have found a supportive institution and the most generous and sympathetic friends and colleagues imaginable. Tim Machan and Krista Ratcliffe, as chairs of the department, have been paragons of humane leadership: unflaggingly supportive, unselfish with their time, and generous with financial support for research and writing. I must particularly thank John Curran, Heather Hathaway, Diane Hoeveler, Al Rivero, Angela Sorby, and Amelia Zurcher, who are exemplary senior colleagues. John Su, Jodi Melamed, Rebecca Nowacek, Cindy Petrites, and David Nowacek are persons who defy categorization: colleagues, dear friends, and adoptive family, this book simply would not have been possible without their critical readings, their sympathetic ears, and their fellowship.

My research assistants, Kathleen Burt, Robin Graham, Linden McBride, and Abby Van de Walle, were instrumental in building a database for working with the compendious columns of Hamilton Wright Mabie. I simply could not have done this project without their hard work. Janet Francendese at Temple University Press has been a gracious and patient editor, and I will always be thankful to Micah Kleit for introducing us. Charles Ault at Temple, and Tim Roberts and Jane Lichty at the American Literatures Initiative, have made the production process a pleasure.

For material support at various stages of the project, I am grateful to the following: the Olin Foundation, for a graduate Olin Fellowship; Marquette University, for two Summer Faculty Fellowships; the Graduate School at Marquette University, for a travel grant to pursue research; and the Klingler College of Arts and Sciences at Marquette University, for a Junior Faculty Fellowship. The archivists at Yale's Beinecke Library, Harvard's Houghton Library, and The Mount were tremendously helpful as I researched this project, and thanks are due to these institutions for permission to cite from archival materials. I must particularly thank Jennie Rathburn at the Houghton and David Dashiell at The Mount for their assistance to a geographically bound researcher. I thank Amy Beckwith for her gracious permission to quote from Edith Wharton's letter to Francis Kinnicutt and the anonymous poem that was interleaved in Wharton's first edition of *The House of Mirth*. An earlier version of chapter 4 appeared as "Misreading *The House of Mirth*" in *American Literature 76*, no. 1 (March 2004).

Last, and at long last, I must try to find the words to express the profound gratitude I owe to my family. I count myself the most fortunate of people to have gained Takeko, Masaaki, Dan, and Kentaro Toyama as parents and siblings through marriage. I will never be able adequately to express my love and gratitude to my parents, Anna and Neil Blair, for their enduring faith in me and for their physical and spiritual support. My daughters, Eleanor and Abigail, and my husband, Haruki Toyama, have sacrificed the most for this project—their love and patience are the condition of possibility for this work, and it is dedicated to them.

Reading Up

Introduction: Cultivating Taste in a Mass-Market World

Popularity, it must be remembered, has never been popular with the unpopular.

—HAMILTON WRIGHT MABIE,
"ARE THE BEST-SELLERS WORTH READING?"
(NOVEMBER 1911)

The first page of the February 1902 issue of the *Ladies' Home Journal* proudly announced a new feature in response to "several hundreds" of readers' requests to "tell us which among the books of to-day are really worth reading, and something of their authors." The magazine's editor promised that "[f]rom all that is published, Mr. [Hamilton Wright] Mabie, with his ripe judgment, will give each month his careful and competent advice as to which books are best worth while, and why." The editor "confess[ed] to a special degree of pleasure" in making the announcement because Mabie was "one of the best-read men in the world of books," a judgment supported by even "the most conservative literary critics."[1] The *Journal* readers were clearly going to be well served. Presumably, Mabie would not recommend books too radical for his audience but would offer the requested guidance in navigating "the great flood of books currently issued by the publishers," a flood in which "the average reader is totally dazed and swamped."[2] While the request for advice suggests that the *Journal*'s audience recognized book reading as a desirable activity, it does not indicate that reading was regarded as *inherently* important or "worth while." *Journal* readers hungered for books that would repay attention and time, but not necessarily those that were aesthetically superior. Indeed, the language of aesthetics has no presence in this announcement, and in its place we find only the language of economics. Worth, profit, and usefulness have become the markers of a good book.

A similar logic of literary value operates in a famous fictional scene of readership penned in the years just before this *Journal* issue appeared: the closing scene of Theodore Dreiser's *Sister Carrie* (1900). In this scene, Carrie sits at a window in a lavish suite at the Waldorf hotel reading Honoré de Balzac's *Père Goriot*. Until now, she had read only popular historical romances or sensation novels, but she does respond, in her distinctive way, to *Goriot*: "It was so strong, and Ames' mere recommendation had so aroused her interest, that [she] caught nearly the full sympathetic significance of it. For the first time, it was being borne in upon her how silly and worthless had been her earlier reading, as a whole."[3] Carrie feels that Ames is "far ahead of her" (*SC*, 257). She knows (it is her "saving grace," insists Dreiser) that Ames is "better educated than she [is]—that his mind [is] better" (*SC*, 256). And so, any book recommended by this "far-off" man, whose thoughts were "the right thing[s] to think," would necessarily be "better" in some inchoate way than the books she has already been reading, popular novels like Bertha M. Clay's *Dora Thorne* and Albert Ross's *Moulding a Maiden*.[4] Carrie's appreciation of *Goriot* does not seem to extend to Balzac's social critique; she barely registers a response to the content of the novel. The strength of the novel resides almost exclusively in how it makes her perceive her other reading, which she now condemns as "silly and worthless." As Dreiser's insistent use of the language of finance—worth, interest, and profit—suggests, Carrie has dutifully followed Ames's recommendation because she is interested in the novel in the same way she is interested in fashion or in money itself: it is an outward sign of, and a means to, upward mobility.

For Carrie, as for the *Journal* readership, a trusted intellectual's advice opens the path to books. For both, the language of economics is superseded by the language of aesthetics in determining the literary text's "worth." Furthermore, neither Carrie nor the *Journal* readership reads solely, or even primarily, for comprehension of a particular work. Instead, the fact of having read the "best books" is in itself supposed to confer status upon the reader. That is, this new sort of reading is not intrinsically good; it is good because it is "better" than reading works that have no status and, thus, elevates the reader in a cultural and social hierarchy. The elision of aesthetic and economic value terms is common to both scenarios; in the logic of reading advice, economics masquerades as culture. The tacit promise is that some texts, like some mysterious alchemical lore, can make the reader wealthier; by demonstrating knowledge of these texts, one can trade on that knowledge to achieve wealth and elevated status. When a reader approaches a text because experts have deemed it "the best" thing to read and reads in the interest of self-interest, that reader is "reading up."

When reading up, one is reading the "right books," dutifully, but not necessarily in the "right way." For example, a reader might identify with characters not intended as the central figures of a text or might reject aspects of the text that do not reinforce the upward striving that brought the reader to the text in the first place. The entire nexus of literary culture at the beginning of the twentieth century looks different in light of the nascent logics of reading up. These logics also help explain the most intractable paradoxes that vex current scholarship about American literary realism. In the first place, the concept of reading up enables us to understand why some texts became popular best sellers despite their critique of, or even contempt for, popular tastes and ambitions. When reading is a means of upward mobility, readers might well respond idiosyncratically to elements in a text that are inconsistent with their assumptions and ambitions. The concept of reading up also helps us unpack the ways that criticism shifted under the dual pressures of a burgeoning middle-class reading audience and an increasingly stratified market for fiction. Although popularity seems antithetical to the world of elite literature, unpopularity usually brought economic ruin to publishers and writers. Elite authors and cultural arbiters saw that wooing larger audiences could ensure their own continued publication and employment, and playing into desires for cultural capital answered this necessity nicely.

If the reading up phenomenon I am describing sounds a lot like an element of "middlebrow culture," as described by Joan Shelley Rubin and Janice Radway, that is because it is the leading edge of what would become, by the 1920s, an unapologetically middling aesthetic. Reading up evinces among the middle class a status anxiety that would not be fully exorcised until the postwar period, when elitism became antithetical to respectability. Because reading up was so invested in the maintenance of cultural hierarchies, rather than in the blanket repudiation of disinterested and exclusive elites, it also helps us better understand the plasticity of the term *realism* as it was variously deployed in the American context. While it is certainly the case that various authors aligned themselves with or against the term to one degree or another throughout the late nineteenth and the early twentieth centuries, American literary realism was by no means an organized aesthetic project. And yet the notion of realism in literature had considerable cultural purchase, becoming a shorthand means of positioning oneself relative to a variety of aesthetic assumptions. When it comes to the goals of reading up, however, all that mattered was the cultural capital accorded to works variously aligned with realism. In other words, "realism" from the perspective of reading up is an empty signifier. It is a brand and, ultimately, a term that signals a moment in the rhetorical production of a culture of taste within the culture of success in the newly industrializing United States in the beginning of the twentieth century. This culture of taste created a set of incentives for everyone involved—middle-class readers, who desired economic and social success; cultural arbiters, who hoped to remain relevant in the world of the mass media; and authors and publishers, who hoped to retain elite literary status for their works but who also, frankly, hoped to sell books. Each of these claimants had an ideological and material investment both in perpetuating the tensions at the heart of realism and in maintaining the apparent contradictions between realism and mass culture.

The Canny Advisor and the Desiring Reader

In any library that still holds dusty books from the 1880s through the 1910s on its shelves, the "bibliography" stacks house a dizzying array of volumes with titles like *Books and Reading; or, What Books Shall I Read and How Shall I Read Them?* by Noah Porter (1881); *What I Know about Books and How to Use Them*, by George C. Lorimer (1892); *Books, Culture, and Character*, by J. N. Larned (1906); and *Open That Door!* by Robert Sturgis Ingersoll (1916). Redeploying the rhetorics of upward mobility commonly associated with success manuals, the authors of reading manuals such as these counseled their middle-class audiences that all reading should redound to the benefit of the reader. During a time when self-help books like Orison Swett Marden's *Pushing to the Front* could go through twelve printings in a year and Horatio Alger's novels were enjoying a popular renaissance, it is hardly surprising that reading advice should also come to incorporate the material and social goals of success culture.[5] By this point, the institutionalization of reading advice from intellectual experts already had a long history; guides for "young gentlemen" building their libraries, for college hopefuls, and for the moral education of young ladies date back at least to the second half of the sixteenth century, if not before.[6] But the reading advice of the late nineteenth and the early twentieth centuries differed in its direct appeal to a new generation of literary novices, people whose education had toppled the barrier of literacy but who had not been able to breach the barrier of taste. The advice that appeared in book form, and therefore required a certain degree of familiarity with the bookstore or library, was targeted towards those who were financially stable, relatively well educated, and possessed of some leisure time within which to pursue the habit of reading. The audience, in other words, comprised members of a growing "professional-managerial class," which Richard M. Ohmann characterizes as the increasingly well-defined middle class of industrial managers, who "hired employees who . . . managed money, the law, education, government agencies, and other key institutions of the new society" after 1900.[7]

As Hamilton Wright Mabie would write in his own contribution to the genre, *Books and Culture* (1896), the goal of reading manuals was to support and nurture the would-be reader's conviction that "the great service [books] render us—the greatest service that can be rendered us—is the enlargement, enrichment, and unfolding of ourselves."[8] To purchase one of these manuals, or even to seek it out in a library, one would already need to be convinced of the worthiness of the reading enterprise and would certainly be prepared to dedicate considerable resources (time or finances) to improving one's reading practice. How, though, might a casual reader, or even a nonreader, reach this advanced stage in the pursuit of literature? To answer this question, I suggest that we look at reading advice that someone might encounter incidentally, in the midst of other pursuits, as in the pages of the most widely circulated, most influential women's lifestyle magazine of the early twentieth century, the *Ladies' Home Journal*. It is in such locations that the persuasive rhetorics of reading up become the least opaque, and the workings of ideology most clearly revealed. Though he has been lost to literary posterity, Mabie, the *Journal*'s reading advice columnist for a decade at the beginning of the mass-cultural era, is the direct ancestor of latter-day literary maven Oprah Winfrey. The reading attitudes Mabie fostered and helped codify were the condition of possibility for book series like Everyman's Library and buying services like the Book-of-the-Month Club. His work has become part of the fabric of aspirational middlebrow culture, and his relative anonymity preserves the appearance of reading up as a natural inclination towards literature, even into the twenty-first century.

In the pages of the *Ladies' Home Journal*, Mabie was reaching a much larger segment of the population than any book would, and his audience differed from a book audience because it included large numbers of the literarily uninitiated. He was certainly still writing to the group that would be interested in the reading manual (in fact, he frequently recommends that his readers seek out essay collections by William Lyon Phelps, Arnold Bennett, and others), but he was also writing to people who did not yet have the wherewithal, or the time, to access the more genteel reading advice published in book form and available from bookstores and libraries. Mabie's columns would do double duty: first, as an advertisement for the reading habit, and second, as a guide to the book selection process for those already convinced of the desirability of frequent reading. In the latter capacity, Mabie spoke directly to the status anxieties in the new groups of readers who were caught by the wide net of the *Journal*'s ubiquity and whose lives were increasingly framed by American consumer culture. Desire for consumable goods was "pumped into the American discourse at all levels" by the owners of department stores and by manufacturers; in the widening array of billboards, illustrated mail-order catalogs, and display windows; and, of course, in the pages of mass-market magazines like the *Ladies' Home Journal*.[9] Even if Mabie never made any explicit concessions to the consumer mindset, his readers would very likely have read his recommendations in the light of the other editorial and advertising content of the magazine. For example, in the February 1902 issue, where his upcoming columns were announced, readers were presented with the life story of the actress Helena Modjeska and the lavishly illustrated "Summer Homes of Famous People."[10] They could learn the proper form for party invitations and then what sorts of fashionable entertainments could be offered at a Valentine's Day party (and they were happy to hear that advice from "The Lady from Philadelphia" [34]). They could likewise learn in "Correct Speaking and Writing" the answers to numerous questions including whether it is appropriate to say one is "sick" or "ill" or whether it is redundant to write "limited to men of fashion only" (35). They might read both "What a Girl Does at College" (24) and "Why Bread Dough Sometimes Falls" (28). Fashion, though relegated to the back of the magazine, was a significant feature, represented by beautifully detailed illustrations in "The New Spring Bodices" (43) and "The Business Woman's Dress," but also in the practical article "Dressing Well on Small Means, Some Helps for the Woman Who Makes Her Own Clothes" (46).

The magazine's dominant ideal, in short, was respectable display, and it was this goal that Mabie had to address with his approach to reading advice. Mabie was charged by the *Journal* with guiding his readers to a taste that would confer the same kind of respectability that proper writing and speech, proper dress, or proper manners would, even to a taste that would enable his readers to appear as if they were denizens of the highest cultural precincts of the time. And, indeed, in the columns he produced over the next ten years, literature would exist on a continuum with these other practices. As we shall see in the first chapter, "Mr. Mabie Tells What to Read," Mabie was not the first books columnist for the magazine, but his tenure was by far the longest; he became a fixture in the magazine because he situated reading so successfully within the *Journal*'s zeitgeist.

Middlebrow Reading, Reception, and Identification

Reading advice in popular magazines, as one might expect, was somewhat different from that published in book form, primarily because the mass-market periodical was much more highly mediated by the consumer culture of success. In her history of the Book-of-the-Month Club, Janice Radway examines a number of reading manuals to describe the process by which elite desires to shore up the difference between "commercial books" and "literary books" led to the development of "a new genre of writing . . . that was devoted to the issue of how and what to read," but one that finally, and ironically, "did so not by linking ['literary books'] with leisurely meditation and reverent appreciation but by associating them with a more instrumental view that emphasized the benefits they conferred on the reader."[11] Focusing closely on Noah Porter's *Books and Reading* (1881), Radway finds the older ideals of concentrated, responsive reading giving way to a model of rigorous reading for the purpose of information gathering. But "information gathering," while useful, does not satisfy the pleasure principle on which so much of consumer society is predicated. The reader who turns to books because they offer information is not going to form the "reading habit," an easy and automatic rapport with books that makes reading the default option for a leisured hour.[12]

Radway's work, along with Joan Shelley Rubin's *The Making of Middlebrow Culture* and Gordon Hutner's *What America Read*, describes in large part the world that Mabie made. The attitudes on display in Mabie's *Journal* columns become the ideologies of the 1920s through the 1960s, when, as Hutner writes, the middle class deployed itself behind a notion of "standards" to protect against "avant-garde rebellion" on the one side and "the combined forces of aristocratic and mass culture to authorize status" on the other.[13] Hutner's and Rubin's middlebrow readers, sharing the same goals as Mabie's readers, turned against "elite" literature in favor of works like Booth Tarkington's, which celebrated middle-class life.

But they did so with the Mabiean mind-set: that reading literature would be improving and ultimately profitable. Just two decades earlier, Mabie and his readers were still comfortable with the highbrow as a category worthy of pursuit. At the same time, a growing body of literature—the very "Howellsian realism" that Hutner excavates in the twenties—intermingled with the highbrow offerings in uncomplicated and largely undifferentiated fashion in Mabie's pages. These *Journal* columns provide an essential prehistory to the postwar middlebrow explosion and the concomitant modernist rebellion against "genteel" literature of all stripes. Radway terms "the scandal of the middlebrow" the process by which literature was sold as "Culture, thereby baldly exposing its prior status as a form of capital—symbolic capital, to be sure—but capital nonetheless."[14] Careful attention to the case study of Mabie in the beginning of the century allows us to see the foundations of the strategy Book-of-the-Month Club editor Harry Scherman and his successors would pursue; they were simply monetizing what had already been explicitly marketed as symbolic capital by a previous cycle of cultural arbiters.

While we can know a good deal about Mabie, and about who Mabie and his editors in the *Journal* thought would be reading his columns, from the text of the columns themselves, discerning with any further certainty who those readers were and what they made of either Mabie's advice or the books they subsequently read is a trickier proposition. After the mid-nineteenth century, reading became primarily a private practice, performed silently by individuals and leaving very few traces that one can document historically.[15] The lives of most nonprofessional readers remain unpreserved by the archive. Still, as James L. Machor contends in his introduction to *Readers in History*, it is possible to learn something of these readers through a process of reconstruction that sees reception as "a product of the relationship among particular interpretive strategies, epistemic frames, ideological imperatives, and social orientations of readers as members of historically specific—and historiographically specified—interpretive communities." Literary texts also hold clues for historians of reception, Machor continues, because we can map "the way literary texts construct the reader's role through strategies necessitated and even produced by particular historical conditions."[16] Machor's model is particularly useful for my purposes because it allows for the recognition of the dialogic relationship among readers, texts, and critics that sustains the culture of advice.

Indeed, as we recognize the mutual influence of readers, texts, and advisers, we must continue to move beyond a simple notion of consumption as assimilation, in which, as Michel de Certeau phrases it, "'assimilating' necessarily means 'becoming similar to' what one absorbs, and not 'making something similar' to what one is, making it one's own, appropriating or reappropriating it."[17] To acknowledge the creativity of the consumer is not altogether to reject the notion that cultural formations may have an influence on the reader, but it does require us to recognize that within the nexus of cultural formations the reader is selectively, variously, and unpredictably influenced. This understanding is not unlike the one Jonathan Rose reaches in his study of working-class autodidacticism in Victorian-era England. But, while much of Rose's influential study relies on a caution against thinking of the working- or middle-class reader as influenced by elite cultural arbiters in the choice of reading material— what William J. Gilmore calls the "trickle-down" hypothesis—the idea that the working-class autodidact was able to "somehow . . . discover the classics on his own" seems to ignore the process by which the classics became the classics; they certainly did not do so without some help from tastemakers, and somewhere along the line Rose's autodidacts would need to have imbibed the notion of what the classics were.[18] At the same time, I take very much to heart the insistence that no reader of reading advice is going to follow a program of reading precisely as it is laid out by an expert, even a beloved and trusted expert. In other words, a more complicated picture must emerge, in which readers both explore on their own and are influenced by the cultural productions of the elites.

A dynamic that allowed for both obedience and creativity along these lines was the readerly process of identification. While the hermeneutics of "reading up" involve a process of identification akin to that of sentimentality, the requirements for the "reading up" reader's identifications are much more fluid. When we talk about identification in sentimental or romantic texts from the nineteenth century, we typically mean a process through which the reader identifies with a suffering character such as a woman in distress or a slave. Through such sympathetic identifications, the reader comes to an understanding either of the suffering figure's essential humanity or of his or her own capacity for fellow feeling. While there are nearly as many definitions of sentimentality as there are critics discussing Anglo-American literature of the eighteenth and nineteenth centuries, the process of sympathetic identification is always a part of any discussion of the mode. Anglo-American sentimentality, as June Howard explains, has its roots in the moral philosophies of Lockean thinkers whose attempts to explain the existence of benevolence in a rationalist world led them to sympathy, and sympathetic identification, as the location of virtue. Howard demonstrates that, in particular, Adam Smith's discussion of the imagination's role in identification paved the way for the mode of sentimentality in literature and for the use of sympathy as a training ground for the emotions.[19] But this sympathetic model of identification relies on the abjection of the subject being identified with and can very easily lead to what Saidiya V. Hartman terms the "violence of identification," in which the identifying reader/observer, "in making the other's suffering one's own," actually "occludes" that suffering, a process that ultimately leads to "the other's obliteration."[20]

The self-identifications of Hartman's self-centered reader are precisely the goals of the "reading up" reader. As Jesse Lee Bennett, the candid author of *What Books Can Do FOR YOU*, wrote in 1923: "The enjoyment which comes from fiction arises from this basic fact—one temporarily identifies one's self with the hero and has one's life vividly enlarged and clarified through his experience. If this identification does not take place there is no enjoyment."[21] A reader need not even identify with the hero of the novel; he or she might identify instead with an imagined author, as projected through "friendly authorial narrators" who "invited their readers to participate imaginatively in the life experience, the moral vision, and the aesthetic process through which they shaped the represented world of the text," as Barbara Hochman has found in her study of reading practices in the age of literary realism.[22] Such creative and self-interested misreading took place even among trained readers in the period before mass-marketed reading advice, as evidenced by Barbara Sicherman's study of the Hamilton family of Fort Wayne, Indiana. Examining the family's diaries and correspondence, Sicherman finds that the Hamiltons' intense involvement with reading "provided both the occasion for self-creation and the narrative form from which they might reconstruct themselves"; their reading led to career aspirations, and the women of the family were idiosyncratic with respect to the identifications they formed with the characters in the novels they read.[23]

Sicherman reads the Hamiltons as symptomatic of a Victorian reading culture in which women, in particular, "found in reading an occasion that, by removing them from their usual activities, permitted the formulation of future plans or, more generally, encouraged vital engagement with the world, a world many thought would be transformed by women's special sensibilities."[24] The Hamiltons favored Charles Dickens, Sir Walter Scott, the Brontës, and Louisa May Alcott, unsurprisingly— their tastes generally trended, as did the tastes of most respectable readers of the nineteenth century, towards the romance or the more genteel end of the sentimental canon. They enjoyed literary magazines, such as *Harper's*, and occasionally admitted to one another desires to read more sensational fiction, designated "trash," for the purpose of diversion. The Hamiltons, in other words, were creative misreaders despite their comfort with the texts they were reading and their enfranchisement in the world of letters. Their desires for sentimental identification were validated by the texts themselves and by the highbrow literary magazines to which they subscribed.[25] Their extended family functioned as a support network for their well-formed reading habit, and they were engaged frequently in social reading and in dialogue about the texts they encountered.[26]

How much more likely is it that a reader newly arrived to the realm of the novel, or more specifically to a highbrow novel to which he or she had been directed by a reading adviser, would perform whatever interpretive gymnastics necessary to assimilate that novel to his or her own motivations for reading it in the first place? In the pages that follow, I refer to this kind of work as "misreading," terming it thus as a nod to generally accepted readings that purport to follow the "intentions" of an author or the "truth" of a text. Stanley Fish, Steven Mailloux, Tony Bennett, and James L. Machor have all addressed the concept of misreading, in all cases asserting the contingent nature of reception and asserting the necessity of understanding reading contexts in order to discern and comprehend reception—for Fish, "interpretive communities"; for Mailloux, "rhetorical practices"; and for Bennett, "reading formations."[27] To talk about "reading formations," Bennett writes, is to "attempt to identify the determinations that, in operating on both texts and readers, mediate the relations between text and context, connecting the two and providing the mechanisms through which they productively interact in representing context, not as a set of extradiscursive relations, but as a set of intertextual and discursive relations that produce readers for texts and texts for readers."[28] The mutual imbrication of text and reader that emerges in Bennett's formulation is the phenomenon I hope to capture by retaining the term *misreading*—the notion that there is a proper reading of a text is never far away from either Mabie or his readers, nor do they attempt wholly to ignore or usurp it, but their own readings supersede that notion in their own practice and reception because of particular, material considerations and preferences. As a professional critic, I cannot help but be aware of the "proper" reading that is determined by my own reading formation; it is against such readings, and counter to readings offered by authors themselves, that I posit accounts of reading up. Bennett's notion of reading formations is also useful for this study because it acknowledges, and provides a means of describing, the material and disciplinary pressures at work in any act of interpretation, along with the historically contingent aspects of reception: "The relations between textual phenomena and social and political processes can be theorized adequately only by placing in suspension the text as it appears to be given to us in our own reading formation so as to be able to analyze the differential constitution and functioning of that apparently same but different text within different reading formations."[29] By reconstructing the reading formation that is produced by, and that produced demand for, Mabie's columns in the *Ladies' Home Journal*, we can access interpretive possibilities that are canny, strategic, instrumental misreadings of resistant texts.

Anxious Authors, Unruly Audiences

The authors whose works this study addresses were all aware of, and largely disdainful of, trends in the interpretations and reception of their work. At the beginning of the twentieth century, the most self-consciously highbrow literature, if not the most popular literature, tended to be produced by authors who identified or were identified with the aesthetics of realism. Recent scholarship, most notably Christopher P. Wilson's, has made great advances in our understanding of realism's imbrication with the burgeoning professionalization of the middle class; as I discuss below, realist authors largely thought of themselves as professionals in relation to their literary output, and their texts were intimately concerned with the dynamics of a culture of professionalism.[30] And yet that professionalization did not take the form of a comfortable embrace of popular reading; instead, realist authors were largely uncomfortable with the conditions of possibility for their profession: a large, and largely unprofessional, reading audience. Since Mabie's primary job in the *Journal* was to make reading "the best books" palatable to and profitable for his readers, he needed to render realist literature attractive and accessible despite its frequent hostility to the American consumer-driven culture of success. This would require ideological concessions from Mabie and practical concessions from his readers, as both parties were temperamentally inclined towards the modes against which realism strove to define itself: sentimentality and the romance. As we shall see, these concessions involved the strategic selection of texts and a degree of interpretive creativity or—as many realist authors would see it—misreading, even interpretive violence.

Given the frequent appearance of hand-wringing essays in genteel periodicals, Mabie and his ilk were having an impact. Edith Wharton, for example, was terribly concerned about the probability of her work being read improperly by an increasingly active mass of "sense-of-duty" readers, or people who had taken up the habit of reading in the same spirit as "such seasoned virtues as thrift, sobriety, early rising and regular exercise."[31] Wharton's 1903 essay "The Vice of Reading" disdains people who are not "born readers" when, under the tutelage of advice manual authors and columnists, they "renounce their innocuous dalliance with light literature for more strenuous intercourse" ("VR," 514). Wharton dubs this menace to literature the "mechanical reader," and her vituperative attack on the practice ("As grace gives faith, so zeal for self-improvement is supposed to confer brains" ["VR," 515]) suggests not only that it was widespread but also that she felt her own work vulnerable to readers of this type. "It is when the mechanical reader, armed with this high conception of his duty, invades the domain of letters—discusses, criticizes, condemns, or, worse still, praises—that the vice of reading becomes a menace to literature" ("VR," 515). The "mechanical reader" feared by Wharton has the audacity to respond to literature, to offer an opinion. This terrifies Wharton because, by virtue of their opinion's influence in the marketplace, mechanical readers could alter the shape of American literary production. Because they pursue "the book that is being talked about, and [their] sense of its importance is in proportion to the number of editions exhausted before publication," a book's potential popularity, its mass appeal, is more important to a potential publisher than its literary quality ("VR," 517). With publishers racing to the bottom to produce only the books that will sell the most copies to the mechanical readers, the "best in literature" is in danger of extinction, and the authors of the "best" books are in danger of irrelevance and even poverty.

Martha Baker Dunn, among others, shared Wharton's concerns that a lack of popular interest in literary realism and naturalism would lead to decreased interest on the part of publishers. In the facetiously titled "A Plea for the Shiftless Reader" in the *Atlantic Monthly* for January 1900, Dunn offers a pointed critique of the aesthetic disorganization that plagued the literary elites at the opening of the century. She ostensibly argues for the "common reader's" right to select his reading based on personal idiosyncrasy, and even to be unreflective about his preferences for literature, as in the case of a "simple farmer" whose unexamined passion for the works of Sir Walter Scott informs the most important moments in his life. He chooses his wife because she reminds him of a

Scott heroine; he joins the Union army because he is reminded of a line of Scott that encourages brave military service; and when wounded at Gettysburg, he draws comfort from remembering passages of Scott. As Dunn comments, "I doubt if it would have meant half as much to him if he had ever pulled it to pieces, to ask himself why it moved him, or if he had any rhetorical right to be moved by it at all."[32] By 1900, the *Atlantic* had already reconciled somewhat with Scott, so a preference for him was not in and of itself a problem, but Dunn suggests that the infighting of professional critics and authors that created the romantic revival in the first place had also created this plague of blissfully benighted readers. "It is perfectly legitimate for the humblest reader on earth to dissent from the judgments of authors, critics, and all other geniuses, however god-like, and recklessly, shamelessly, to form his own uninspired opinions, and stick to them,—all the more that the godlike ones themselves have been known to differ widely in their decisions."[33] The cultural mavens who read the *Atlantic* were therefore the only ones to blame if the "humble" readers wreaked havoc, reading the wrong books, or reading the right books in the wrong way.

Figuring out the right way to read the right books was, as Dunn demonstrates, one of the more intractable problems among the self-proclaimed partisans of realism. Defining the parameters of the mode, particularly in the American context, remains a critical conundrum to this day because realism was not actually a coherent aesthetic program. In Michael Davitt Bell's formulation, using the terms *realism* and *naturalism* was primarily a way for authors to "describe what they thought they were doing—or at least what they wished others to think they were doing."[34] Specifically, realism seems to have been a mode of reaction against sentimentality and romance, the two dominant literary genres of the nineteenth century. Scholars today generally agree that it was, as Nancy Glazener argues, a series of "relational assessments," in which realism was set in opposition to rival works of romance or sentimentality.

> [T]he construction of realism at mid-century as a uniquely democratic and modern form was simultaneously the construction of the romance as aristocratic and outmoded; the construction of realist authorship as professional authorship around the 1880s was simultaneously the construction of sentimental and sensational authorship as unprofessional; and the construction of realism as genteel and elitist toward the end of the century was simultaneously the

construction of the revived romance as a refreshingly transgressive form that bridged privileged and popular audiences.[35]

The crux of the conflict was both the relative professional status of the author and the critic and the relationship between the book and the reader, as well as the reader's freedom to engage with the text and the author. The readerly practice of identification, which was central to the work of sentiment and similarly inflected in the romance, became a key battleground in these taste wars.

While realism was, like sentimentality, committed to "deploying feminized capacities for observation and empathy," Glazener observes, realist literature did so with a "distance and decorum" that would short-circuit the addictiveness realists attributed to sentimentalism, and would therefore also avoid the messy elision of class and gender boundaries that was a danger of too-close identification in less "professionally" written texts.[36] Even the professionals could come under scrutiny, though, for lapses that took them too close to the sentimental fold. Balzac, whose *Père Goriot* becomes *Sister Carrie's* first foray into the world of literary realism, was actually one of the more hotly contested figures in the universe of American realist criticism because of his text's susceptibility to sentimental reading practices.[37] All of the figures Mabie would recommend as representative of American literary realism weighed in on Balzac, and it is not coincidence that his masterpiece is the representative highbrow text in Dreiser's novel. But, per Dunn's critique, there was nothing near a consensus among American realists about Balzac's success or failure as a practitioner of realism, despite a general agreement that he was at least a progenitor, if not the founder, of the move towards realistic representation in fiction. Just a brief look at William Dean Howells's, Henry James's, and Edith Wharton's relative assessments of Balzac gives us a good sense of realism's critical inconsistencies, particularly when it comes to the question of how a reader should identify with the characters in a novel.

In *Criticism and Fiction* (1891), Howells reproaches Balzac for works that share in a "sympathetic," as opposed to an empathetic, ethos. In the story of Cesar Birotteau, Howells claims that Balzac "felt obliged to construct a mechanical plot, to surcharge his characters, to moralize openly and baldly; he permitted himself to 'sympathize' with certain of his people, and to point out others for the abhorrence of his readers. This is not so bad as it would be in a novelist of our day. It is simply primitive and inevitable, and he is not to be judged for it."[38] Balzac is too present in his text—a criticism that resonates with the realist dynamic of authorial distancing described by Barbara Hochman. Balzac overdetermines readerly sympathies by projecting his own sympathies too strongly through the text, creating some characters who are, to Howells's mind, too self-evidently "good," and others who are too self-evidently "bad." *Père Goriot* is, for Howells, the most egregious item in Balzac's oeuvre: "[I]t is not worthy the name of novel . . . full of a malarial restlessness, wholly alien to healthful art."[39] While some of these issues are a function of Balzac's vanguard position, the fact remains that the novelist is too invested in certain characters. In a "healthful" novel, presumably, the reader must not be led by the nose, but must be given enough information to make the proper choice of identification for him- or herself.

Such authorial coyness, on the other hand, could lead to problems of misreading; as Phillip Barrish points out, Howells drew a distinction between readers who could properly appreciate the "rawness" of realist literature and those who, like Bromfield Corey in *The Rise of Silas Lapham*, tended to bend that rawness into "picturesqueness."[40] In fact, contra Howells's assertions about the explicitness of Balzac's text, such a bending seems precisely to be the move Carrie makes when she looks down from her Waldorf suite to the streets below and briefly wonders whether she and her sidekick Lola shouldn't be helping others out. When Carrie asks, "Isn't it just awful?" there are a number of possible references for "it": the awful "it" could be the man she sees falling, or his "sheepishness" in doing so; "it" could be the general situation of poverty and want; or "it" could simply be the heavy snow that will require Carrie and Lola to hire a coach to get to the theater (*SC*, 258). The falling man, admittedly looking "sheepish" rather than picturesque, is a mere abstracted presence for Carrie, not an immediate concern or a soul to be assisted. Her quasi-aesthetic appreciation of him is only a step away from the reaction that philanthropists predict Bromfield Corey would have to Italians in the slums: "[H]e would make them keep still to be sketched, and forget all about their wants."[41] The criticism, though, that Bromfield would forget about the "wants" of his philanthropic targets sounds much like current criticisms of the literature of sympathy: if the suffering of others becomes too aestheticized, action ceases to be the result of reading.[42] Carrie's reaction would seem to give the lie to Howells's critique of Balzac—clearly, she is able to resist all Balzacian heavy-handedness. By the close of the novel, when Carrie sits again, rocking, contemplating her desires for even more upward mobility, it seems clear that her sadness about Father Goriot will never stand in the face of her desires to stay out of the snow. In this moment she becomes a third Goriot daughter, unable to properly attend the elderly man's tragic end because she is too busy attending to her own social and financial elevation. Sympathetic identification has been usurped by an identification that is structurally similar but which has a different target: the striver.

The dynamics of identification were not as central to Edith Wharton's and Henry James's writings about Balzac, but both carefully differentiated Balzac from sentimentality in general, and in ways that suggest their concerns about the potential misplacement of readerly identification. In *The Writing of Fiction* (1925), Wharton names Balzac and Stendhal the "two dividing geniuses" in literature, praising Balzac especially because he "was the first not only to see his people, physically and morally, in their habit as they lived, with all their personal hobbies and infirmities, and make the reader see them, but to draw his dramatic action as much from the relation of his characters to their houses, streets, towns, professions, inherited habits and opinions, as from their fortuitous contacts with each other."[43] She also, tellingly, cites Balzac's self-differentiation from Sir Walter Scott, the paragon of historical romance and an idol of nineteenth-century American readers. Confessing that Balzac drew a line of influence from Scott to himself with regard to seeing his characters in relation to their contexts (supposedly the most "realistic" element of Balzac's innovation), Wharton continues that

> Scott, so keen and direct in surveying the rest of his field of vision, became conventional and hypocritical when he touched on love and women. In deference to the wave of prudery which overswept England after the vulgar excesses of the Hanoverian court he substituted sentimentality for passion, and reduced his heroines to "Keepsake" insipidities; whereas in the firm surface of Balzac's realism there is hardly a flaw, and his women, the young as well as the old, are living people, as much compact of human contradictions and torn with human passions as his misers, his financiers, his priests or his doctors. (*WF*, 8–9)

Wharton is less concerned than Howells about Balzac's allegedly heavy authorial hand, focusing her attention on the quality of Balzac's character descriptions. To her mind, he is antisentimental because he can portray female characters, in particular, as complex and contradictory "product[s] of their particular material and social conditions" (*WF*, 9). Balzac's achievement, to Wharton, was his melding of the novel of manners and the psychological novel into a more meaningful hybrid form.

While his characters had interiority, that interiority was also always refracted through a particular social lens. Presumably, such representations would thwart easy readerly identifications, because of the apparent specificity of the character descriptions—but as we shall see in the chapters that follow, this was never a real barrier to the determined "reading up" reader.

The potential misreader haunts James's 1905 discussion in "The Lesson on Balzac," in which he observes that a facility for identification is essential to the author but potentially detrimental to a reader. Balzac, James argues, had a preternatural ability to "get into the constituted consciousness, into all the clothes, gloves and whatever else, into the very skin and bones, of the habited, featured, colored, articulated form of life that he desired to present."[44] How else, after all, could Balzac have written so much in the span of twenty years—he had no time to gain such experiences for himself, he was too busy writing! And just as Balzac was able to enter into his characters' situations, so must the reader be able to understand characters "from their point of pressing consciousness or sensation—without [the reader's] allowing for which there is no appreciation" ("LB," 132). But by 1905, James would know, from personal experience, that readers could not be relied on to do the right things with the novels they read. Unlike Howells, James thinks that Balzac leaves the door open for readerly mistakes, willing "to risk, for the sake of his subject and its interest, your spiritual salvation" ("LB," 132). In theory, James finds it preferable to risk misreading than to overload any characterization with hints to the reader, as the detestable, "moralizing" William Makepeace Thackeray does. In practice, James would spend considerable energy trying to redirect reader reception in his New York Edition prefaces, and would bemoan the frequent misreadings of his texts in letters to his friends and family. For James, such was the risk of embracing the process of identification; he was all the more disappointed when his readers' identifications went awry.

The disagreement over Balzac centers on whether it is the author's fault or the reader's if a text is "misread." Howells and Wharton are both wary of identification, because of the possibility that it occurs only as a result of an unnuanced effusion of sympathy rather than a carefully considered assessment of the circumstances in the text. At least, this is what they claim vis-à-vis Balzac. As we shall see, in chapters 2 and 4, respectively, as authors of fictional texts Howells and Wharton have more sympathy for identification, and more desire to evoke it, than their critical arguments suggest. Such accommodations, I argue, are at least in some measure a concession to the material conditions of the literary marketplace of the early twentieth century. Just as the new mass market of readers needed to move away from previous preferences for sentiment and romance in pursuit of greater cultural capital, so did the realist authors need to satisfy—or at least acquire a healthy tolerance for—the impulse to sentimental and romantic reading practices in their readers. Those who did not, Dreiser among them, did not become the highbrow best sellers that Wharton, Howells, and, to a lesser degree, James were.

Janice Radway describes the judges of the Book-of-the-Month Club in the 1920s and 1930s as advancing "a reading experience that promoted interest in an object or situation beyond the self and that dialectically evoked in the reader a sense of being recognized by another." Like Mabie, the club's judges "steer[ed] clear of books that positioned their readers to feel certain negatively charged affects, including disgust, contempt, and shame."[45] But the focus on affect, and on a sense of connectivity with others, that Radway sees as a key to this orientation, which she terms "middlebrow personalism," must be seen in large part as a modification of the utilitarian, and largely affectless, identificatory practice of reading up that Mabie validates in his columns.[46] Radway describes her readers as searching for an anodyne for the "excessive rationalism and distance of the instrumental, utilitarian approach to life";[47] however, it was precisely this approach that Mabie had embraced, and rendered consistent with the apparently nonutilitarian world of reading, in his *Journal* columns. Mabie worked to make the book relevant to those who found the practices of Sicherman's readers too removed from a modern life; Radway's judges responded to the backlash against Mabie's readers' instrumentalism. All of these readers desired, and discovered, literature that would function as a guide to middle-class life. Mabie's readers simply had to do more interpretive maneuvering to assimilate resistant realist works to their material needs.

* * *

Reading Up: Middle-Class Readers and the Culture of Success in the Early Twentieth-Century United States examines the expectations of and for the upwardly mobile reader during the later phase of American literary realism. I begin in the first chapter by detailing the ways that elite literature was made both desirable and accessible to upwardly mobile audiences by one reading adviser in particular: Hamilton Wright Mabie in the *Ladies' Home Journal*. While Mabie worked to retain a sense of hierarchy in literary taste, and to uphold the genteel ideals of a refined taste, he also accommodated popular desires for texts that had happy endings, that narrated material and social success, and that offered few technical challenges to the novice reader. The elision of the languages of taste and finance in Mabie's columns signals his need to accommodate the desires of both his perceived audience and the commercial sponsors of the magazine. This chapter provides an analytic overview of Mabie's columns over his ten years with the *Journal*, paying close attention to his engagement with literary realism and to the rhetorics of success, profits, and progress that become more pronounced in his columns year by year.

Mabie's recommendations provide a framework for the remainder of the book, which addresses the dynamics of reading up in the cases of Howells, James, and Wharton and in a variety of regionalist works. I begin in the second chapter by exploding the notion that it was ironic for Mabie to recommend Howells's novel *The Rise of Silas Lapham* more frequently than any book besides Thackeray's popular romantic comedy of manners, *Vanity Fair*. Howells appeared in the pages of the *Journal* a decade before Mabie, and I show that his writings there evidence his complicity with the branding of realism as elitist, desirable cultural capital. After understanding the production of Howells as an intellectual ideal in the pages of the *Journal*, it is no longer surprising that Mabie came in his *Journal* columns to recommend *The Rise of Silas Lapham* even after he eviscerated the novel and realism in general in a famous 1885 review essay. The remainder of the chapter stubbornly reads *Lapham* and two other Howells novels, *The Lady of the Aroostook* and *A Hazard of New Fortunes*, as Thackerayan novels of manners, demonstrating that even the most violent misreadings are relatively simple to perform if one wants badly enough both to have read Howells and to remain comfortable in the mind-set of the U.S. culture of success.

Howells was a fairly easy sell for Mabie, particularly because of his previous appearances in the pages of the *Journal*. The early twentieth-century works of Henry James, on the other hand, posed a problem for Mabie because of James's eclectic late-phase stylistics, which Mabie could not countenance for his *Journal* audience. If James, the least likely of all authors at the time for general readership, was nevertheless necessary for cultural capital, what then were the imperatives for creating a readable James? In chapter 3 we see that Mabie directs his readers to James's earlier novels *Roderick Hudson*, *The American*, and *The Portrait of a Lady*, all works which, particularly before James revised them for the New York Edition, lent themselves to "misreadings" consistent with a romantic or sentimental sensibility. Mabie never acknowledged the publication of James's New York Edition—not surprisingly, as he utterly rejected late James stylistics—but the prefaces accompanying these three novels seem to speak directly to the readerly dynamic Mabie and his cohort were facilitating. James bemoaned the misreadings wrought on all these novels by critics and nonprofessional readers alike, particularly their attraction to the "diligent" minor characters, whom he saw as mediocre counterpoints to the striking, if tragic, protagonists of his novels. Mabie's success-culture "aesthetic" explains how a reader might find inspiration in Henrietta Stackpole or Sam Singleton instead of in Isabel Archer or Roderick Hudson.

Frustrated readers plagued Edith Wharton throughout her career, most particularly after the tremendous popular success of *The House of Mirth*. In the fourth chapter, we see that Mabie championed *The House of Mirth* even as he sought to ameliorate its bleakness by suggesting that the critique of society inhered only in one small "fast set" and that the remainder of society was still a functional ideal. His views about the "habit of reading," a phrase he first uses in the column in which he introduces Wharton to his audience, offer a point-by-point refutation to Wharton's essay "The Vice of Reading," in which she repudiates readers who misinterpret belletristic texts. Her concerns resonate strongly with the evidence of reception we find in a lengthy debate that hijacked the letters section of the *New York Times Saturday Review of Books* from November 1905 through January 1906. In letters that variously excoriated Wharton for misleading her readership about society, lamented the failure of Lily and Selden to connect, and dramatically misrepresented the text, readers demonstrated the unpredictability that Wharton thematized in *The House of Mirth* and bemoaned in her nonfiction and personal writings about audiences. The poem found interleaved in a first edition of *The House of Mirth*, next to a letter in which Wharton clearly indicated the intentionality of Lily's death, serves as a capstone to this discussion.

The recurring notion in Mabie's columns that there is a need for compensatory literature as a palate cleanser or as an anodyne to realism underscores Mabie's sense that his audience was uncomfortable with realism's tendency towards bleakness and highlights his persistence in accommodating his readers' desires both to read the right literature and to take away a validating message. The ideal solution for this conundrum was often found in regionalist literature or in the reemergent historical romance. From Mabie's inaugural column, which celebrated both new offerings and backlist classics by Sarah Orne Jewett, Mary E. Wilkins Freeman, and George Washington Cable, to the last installments he penned, we can see a tendency that remained consistent throughout Mabie's ten years at the *Journal*: Mabie loved to recommend regionalism as literary comfort food, ever emphasizing the sympathetic and romantic elements of regionalist writing. The conclusion briefly explores the pleasure principle in Mabie's championing of regionalism and historical romance and identifies, through close readings of some of the lesser-known works he mentioned most frequently, exactly what "use" such texts could be put to by the *Journal* reader whose time was money, and whose time was scant.

Finally, my epilogue briefly discusses the legacy of reading up in the highbrow best sellers of today. Briefly addressing popularizations of highbrow reading like Oprah's Book Club, I argue that such phenomena testify to the endurance of the reading up mentality as a way of justifying, and determining, what reading is really "worth while."

Mabie is barely remembered today, and primarily for his scathing review of *Lapham*, not for his work in the *Journal*. But this is precisely the point. Reading Mabie's columns, recognizing their contemporaneous influence, and noting his complete erasure from cultural memory allows us to see the workings of ideology. Reading up, as an orientation towards literature and the study of "difficult" texts, has become almost second nature to us today. We know that certain texts are "better," and are "better for us," even if we publicly deny the validity of such assessments. We know this because there were Mabies, and because they erased themselves, and were erased, from the history of canon production. Reacquainting ourselves with Mabie, we find that his compromises and accommodations sound very familiar to us, because they are foundational; at some point in our personal history, we have all probably been practitioners of reading up.

1 /   Mr. Mabie Tells What to Read

Hamilton Wright Mabie conducted young ladies into the suburbs of culture and left them there.

—FRANK MOORE COLBY (1917)

Hamilton Wright Mabie's authorized biography mentions the *Ladies' Home Journal* only once, in an aside, and then only because Mabie mentions it in a letter that the biographer cites in full for its rhapsodic description of the Adirondacks. This neglect is no small oversight: Mabie contributed ten full-page columns a year to the *Journal* over the course of ten years, mentioning in those compendious pieces more than two thousand discrete titles and nearly as many authors. The erasure of the *Journal* tenure from Mabie's biography was deliberate, a function of the desire to rehabilitate Mabie's reputation from dismissive assessments like the facetious one-liner from Frank Moore Colby that serves as my epigraph. Anecdotally, this eulogy was all that Colby, an essayist and humorist, was able to muster on the occasion of Mabie's death. Having been asked to write an appreciation by the editor in chief of the New York *Globe*, Colby agreed, but then presented no text for three days following the assignment:

> His chief inquired several times and Colby said, each time, that he was still writing it. The chief had visions of column after column on Hamilton Wright Mabie, taking up all the space he had reserved for editorials against Tammany and in favor of certain municipal improvements. He was in despair. Finally, on the fourth day, the chief said, "Frank, we can't give too much space to Mabie. Let's see what you have written. We may have to cut it to get it into the paper now." Colby handed him a sheet on which were written just these

words, no more, no less: "Hamilton Wright Mabie conducted young ladies into the suburbs of culture and left them there."[1]

By ignoring Mabie's significant relationship with the *Journal*, Mabie's widow and biographer hoped to recast him as "a torch-bearer on the difficult path leading to high ideals, attainable only through intellectual enrichment and spiritual enlightenment."[2] But it was too late—his contemporaries already knew him as a literary popularizer, and he eventually became a footnote to literary history, remembered only when critics wanted to mock the benighted old guard that could not appreciate the realism of William Dean Howells.

From 1902 to 1912, however, when he was writing for the *Journal*, Mabie was a household name and an incredibly influential cultural arbiter. He occupied the bully pulpit during a moment of significant transformations, both aesthetic and material, in the production and consumption of literature in the United States. As a growing number of readers entered the American literary marketplace at the beginning of the twentieth century, they found themselves overwhelmed by the sheer number of books—titles, editions, and formats were multiplying seemingly overnight. Governed by a sense that there must be some meritocracy to reading, and motivated by a culture of success that insisted that every action be directed towards upward mobility, these readers turned to a willing group of elite cultural arbiters for advice on what to read and why. These advisers, writing both in monographs and in the pages of elite and mass-market periodicals, were called on to popularize reading, but also to make accessible for their readers some of the more inaccessible literature of the day: American literary realism. Realist authors balked against both the American culture of success and the growing popularization of reading, but they depended on market forces to sustain their access to publication and therefore needed a good number of "common" readers to purchase their books—for whatever reason. And that reason, more likely than not, had very little to do with aesthetics, and more to do with the sense that reading could, by some mysterious alchemy, make one socially and financially successful.

Though a number of cultural arbiters disseminated their opinions in monographs or in more genteel literary periodicals like the *Atlantic* or the *Century*, the readers who could access such publications were already comfortable with the world of literature. The readers of a more truly mass-market periodical, like the *Ladies' Home Journal*, were more likely to be relative newcomers to the world of letters, especially to the high-cultural titles that were usually offered in response to requests for lists of the five best books published by American authors in the last ten years. By the time Hamilton Wright Mabie began his ten-year stint as the *Journal's* reading advisor, the magazine had already tried several times to provide a regular reading advice column. None was as successful, as regularly appearing, or nearly as long-lived, as Mabie's column, which would run ten times a year every year from March 1902 through April 1912. Mabie's column was successful because it achieved an ideal mix of prescriptive advice and permissive validation; Mabie told his readers what they should be reading, but he also told them it was okay to read what they wanted to be reading. Moreover, he refused to tell his readers what they should be getting from the books they read, leaving the door open for them to read what they "should" be reading the way they wanted to read it.

Joining the *Journal* when it was rapidly expanding its circulation, and when it was cultivating its appeal to men as well as to women, Mabie was uniquely positioned to affect the reading habits and cultural attitudes of a broad swath of the U.S. population. But his columns, in their persistent elision of the languages of aesthetics and economics, also *reflected* the larger American culture of "reading up." His work in the *Journal* could be termed a missing link in the evolution of an unashamedly middlebrow aesthetic, the place where the otherwise obscured connections between the arbiters of taste and the people who read become discernable. His simultaneous direction of and responsiveness to the reading public made him the longest-lived, most successful books columnist in the *Journal's* history.

Not Just for Ladies: The *Journal* at the Dawn of the Century

The *Ladies' Home Journal* was the uncontested circulation leader for all monthly magazines from 1903 until it was leapfrogged after World War I by its fellow Curtis Publishing Company title, *The Saturday Evening Post*, and it had reached a paid circulation figure of one million by January 1904. Mabie's tenure with the *Journal* coincided with this period of rapid expansion in that magazine's popularity and influence. Edward Bok had taken over the editorial reigns in October 1889 and immediately began transforming the already moderately successful magazine into a cultural juggernaut. Touting itself as a friend and counselor in the home, the *Journal* successfully positioned itself as the ultimate authority on all elements of domestic life, and from the 1890s on, the *Journal's* didactic,

department-driven style and copious advertising made it a lifestyle magazine for the new consumer society.

Indeed, it is difficult to overstate the impact the *Journal* had on U.S.
culture, particularly given its national reach and its universal appeal;
despite its name, it was not just for the ladies of the home. Though particularly targeted to "white, native-born, middle-class women, who lived
with the uncertain legacies of the nineteenth-century women's rights
movement and who tried to find a comfortable role in the rapidly changing world of the expanding middle class," the *Journal* was also a family
magazine, with a good deal of editorial content specifically directed towards men.[3] Particularly during Bok's editorial tenure (1890–1919), the
Journal ran columns like What Men Are Asking and Between Father and
Son.[4] Bok promoted these efforts through his editorial pages, as in the
November 1898 column marking the magazine's fifteenth anniversary:

> [The *Journal*] touches the people of every means, of every age, of
> both sexes and almost every clime. In city homes of easy accessibil-
> ity it is found, as well as in homes of almost complete isolation—in
> some cases two and three hundred miles removed from a railroad.
> To the young and to the old alike it seems acceptable. Although it
> was originally designed as a periodical for women, indications are
> constant and unfailing that it is read by thousands of men. It has
> been said by one that no magazine reaches so many young men.[5]

These young men, presumably the school-age and early teenage sons
of a subscribing family, were some of the important collateral readers
that each issue affected as it was passed among family members and
neighbors. Bok offers a degree of evidence for the secondary and tertiary
circulation of individual issues in this same anniversary editorial: "At
one time the *Journal* selected one hundred names at random from its
subscription list and wrote to each subscriber, asking how many persons
read his or her particular copy. From seventy odd answers received the
average appeared to be more than six." While the principal subscriber
might be the woman of the household, many of the other readers were
male; the pursuit of male readers was a central component of Bok's plan
to make the *Journal* indispensible and culturally ubiquitous. And, no
doubt, it was a key to the growing circulation numbers. A subscription,
which ran $1.00 per year in 1902, and went up to $1.50 per year by 1912,
was a fairly sizable discretionary expenditure for many of its readers.
If a family could afford only one magazine, it needed to be a magazine
that would appeal to all its members.[6] In the cases where the male of the

household held the purse strings, an appeal to masculine readers would be even more essential.

Just as the readers of the *Journal* were not exclusively female, they were also not exclusively middle-class, despite the magazine's contemporaneous reputation as a "handbook for the middle class."[7] The publisher, Cyrus Curtis, had initially harbored aspirations for a well-to-do audience. In 1893, for example, he tried to court the wealthy by sending "a prospectus of one issue's contents to all of the people listed in the *Blue Book*, or social register, in San Francisco, Boston, and Milwaukee."[8] Bok, however, was more comfortable with the middle-class characteristics of his audience, and Curtis finally acquiesced; by 1897, Curtis would describe the *Journal* as "in every sense a popular home magazine . . . appeal[ing] to the income of the many rather than the few."[9] During the first decade of the twentieth century, the magazine also seems to have made a decided appeal to readers in the lower financial strata of the middle class, as well as to women working outside the home.[10] The magazine frequently ran series such as "How We Saved for a Home," which told how, for example, a Minnesota family with "nine children and $800 a year" or families in which the husband made $7 a week could achieve the magazine's domestic ideal.[11] In the same vein, the magazine offered advice on how young girls could save enough money to go to college, how women could supplement their "pin money" by taking in laundry or seamstress work, and how women working outside the home were able to overcome daily exhaustion to find "joy in work."[12] Though the magazine was filled with advertisements for aspirational consumables, and one might be able to read the articles cynically as a part of a disciplinary project to produce happy buyers, a more sympathetic reading is possible in which the readers derive comfort and learn strategies from such articles, and the magazine becomes, perhaps unintentionally, an instrument for negotiating the burgeoning consumer society for which so many readers were woefully unequipped—a handbook *to*, as well as *for*, the middle class.

In short, it is difficult to generalize about the *Journal* readership, but it is possible to talk about the kind of reader the *Journal* imagined for itself and to speculate that the readership would look for itself in the wide-ranging contents of each issue. Bok acknowledged that the magazine's "vast audience represents every shade of taste," and the eclectic mix of the editorial content reflects a goal of casting a wide net for the sake of greater circulation.[13] At the same time, the *Journal* consciously constructed its readers as hungry for advice on matters material, social, and intellectual. In the adviser role, the magazine was certainly a taste *maker*, particularly when it came to the cultural acquirements that would make one a respectable member of the middle class. Importantly, middle-class respectability was not yet inherently a rejection of upper-class tastes and habits; this attitude would not predominate until the postwar period, about which Joan Shelley Rubin writes in *The Making of Middlebrow Culture*. The early twentieth-century *Journal* encouraged its readers to dress, act, and think like the more moneyed elite, and a key channel for such upwardly focused behavior was the pursuit of genteel, highbrow literature.

Early Attempts: Ramsey, Bok, "Droch"

Almost from its inception, the *Journal* made some gestures towards advising its readers in the literary realm. Most of these columns appeared only sporadically, and at first they were primarily focused on advice to readers who wanted to become writers, rather than on book reviews and reading advice. June 1889 saw the inauguration of a regular column authored by A. R. (Annie) Ramsey titled Books and Bookmakers. Ramsey promised that this new feature would be responsive to "the wishes of [my] vast army of readers all eager for the best, all anxious for 'more light.'" Ramsey sets forth three governing principles for the column, asserting first that "no review will appear in these columns of any book which has not been thoroughly read and reflected upon" and next that "in spite of all the mad rush after the 'latest thing out' I shall ever remember that in our literary Past, we have gems without whose luster no diadem is complete." Finally, Ramsey insists that she will respect the privacy of the authors she writes about, because they are simply "doing their duty in the sphere in which it has pleased God to place them." And yet, after paying homage to the inviolability of domestic space Ramsey has no problem assuring her readers that her columns will still provide juicy, gossipy tidbits:

> Therefore, when [authors] retire into their private lives and homes, and shut the doors between themselves and the outer world, pray let us leave them there, nor seek to penetrate the seclusion of their homes, as sacred to them as yours is to you.
>
> What they do in a public way belongs to the public, and you have a right to this as fast as I can gather it.

With only the transition of a carriage return, Ramsey launches into an intimate and detailed narrative of Robert Louis Stevenson's courtship and marriage, a description of his current ailments and the Adirondack retreat which they necessitated, and a thorough accounting of the advances and profits he has made from the sales of his latest serials, books, and forthcoming travel diary (more than $30,000 that could be readily determined; even greater sums are "whispered"). Ramsey continues in a similar vein in this first column, discussing the new vogue for literary teas in New York and the apparent trend for society women to take up the pen. Finally addressing a literary text, Ramsey laments the regrettable ubiquity of the "theological" novel, and the overexposure of Mrs. Humphry Ward's *Robert Elsmere* in particular. Despite her opening promise to help her readers attain "more light," Ramsey's column is concerned less with actual literary products than with literary gossip and the personalities of authors.[14]

Just before Ramsey was beginning her column, Curtis read and became interested in a syndicated literary "letter" appearing in newspapers and penned by a young syndicate chief named Edward Bok. Bok had worked as the advertising manager for *Scribner's Magazine*, the house journal for the publishing company of Charles Scribner's Sons and a distinctly highbrow publication affiliated with the *Atlantic Monthly*.[15] While at *Scribner's*, Bok had begun his own syndicate, the Bok Syndicate Press, specifically focused on content that would be appealing to women readers. In the mid-1880s, he began to write his own column of literary advice and gossip for the syndicate, and it was this column that Curtis invited Bok to produce exclusively for the *Journal*, apparently without concern for the potential overlap with a feature already in place.[16] Indeed, the first installments of Bok's Literary Leaves columns differed somewhat from Ramsey's in their address to readers who hoped to become literary producers themselves, but this angle did not become Bok's exclusive focus until much later in 1889. At first, Bok, like Ramsey, addressed only glancingly the content of recent literature, choosing instead to discuss expansively the personalities and habits of authors and editors. In his autobiography, he identifies the column as a "literary gossip" column, and it is in his unembarrassed embrace of the gossip genre that Bok differentiated himself from Ramsey. Where Ramsey writes from the perspective of a curious outsider, Bok places himself in the midst of the literati, self-aggrandizingly emphasizing his frequent social interactions with the most brilliant literary lights of the day. He parlays his intimacy with popular writers into insight for his *Journal* readers, as in this profile of Grace Greenwood from his sophomore column, printed in the September 1889 issue:

Sitting directly opposite "Grace Greenwood" (or Mrs. Lippincott, as she is known to her friends) not many evenings ago, I could not help noticing what a striking face this remarkable woman possesses. It is a face that at once impresses you, I think, as belonging to a woman of singular force of character. Shadows play upon it continually, as if in sympathy with the feelings which sway its possessor. The eyes that are so restless are deep and penetrating, and your very soul seems to be undergoing a thorough examination as they look at you. One moment the eyebrows will contract and almost completely hide the orbits underneath; another moment and the eyes are fastened upon you with a keen and searching brilliancy. The forehead is high and domelike in shape. Of late, the raven-black hair that fringes Mrs. Lippincott's head has shown silvery threads. I have always questioned whether we have a more truly brilliant writer in our literature today than Grace Greenwood.[17]

Bok's observations are not secondhand, and he shows none of Ramsey's compunction in offering intimate details—such as a writer's graying hair—to his readers. Also unlike Ramsey, who at least pays lip service to the preservation of an author's private life, when he reveals Lippincott's real name he completely dismantles the separation that the author had established between her private self and her public persona. He then renders his readers intimates of Mrs. Lippincott by using the real name, not the pseudonym, for the rest of the column. The logic of the sketch is precisely this obliteration of the public/private divide, as when he praises the way that his subject's face is—or at least "seems" to be—a perfect sympathetic mirror of her internal, emotional life. Echoing the prose style of the popular sentimental or sensation fiction of the day, Bok renders Lippincott a character straight out of a Grace Greenwood novel; if not a dewy-eyed heroine, she is the wise older mentor, exactly the kind of author a reader would want to place her trust in. Even more than a review of any specific book, this profile recommends Lippincott/Greenwood's fiction to the reader by confirming the sensitive insightfulness of the author. Anything arising from this magnetic woman's pen is necessarily worthwhile reading.

In August 1889, Bok's column Literary Leaves began appearing side by side with Ramsey's column, even sharing column space with Ramsey. By November 1889, Bok seems to have gained something of an upper hand, as the woodcut that had initially appeared over Ramsey's column was used as the heading for Bok's, with only a small notice that this column was Bok's Literary Leaves and not actually Books and Bookmakers. Bok's column had, by this point, come to address more exclusively the reader who wanted to become a writer, a focus that makes the reassignment of the illustrated banner even more confusing. While her column's marginalization was probably distressing, the separation of subject matter must have been a relief to Ramsey, who had spent the previous months being scooped by Bok. In September 1889, Bok reported that "Margaret Deland's new novel, 'Sydney Page,' will not see publication before the end of the present year or the beginning of the new."[18] Ramsey mentions this in her October 1889 column, with the editorializing comment that "[i]t is the best of signs when an author refuses to be hurried into hasty (and generally unworthy) work"; on the same page, Bok's column announces that "Margaret Deland put the finishing touches on her new novel at Kennebunkport, Maine—the same place where she completed the last chapters of 'John Ward, Preacher.'"[19] Bok was a step ahead of Ramsey when it came to literary gossip—probably as a result of his closer ties to the publishing industry—and Ramsey's columns had begun to look amateurish by comparison. Her peevish complaints about the lack of worthwhile fiction and the public fascination with religious novels seem all the more petty alongside Bok's revelation of the true identity of "The Duchess" or his portrait of George Washington Cable's domestic felicities.

Finally, by January 1890, Bok and Ramsey began to share space under the same heading, each of them contributing much briefer portions of a miscellany column on books and literature. The Duchess became a regular contributor of miscellany, as did Will Carleton, whose working habits were a focus of Bok's August 1889 column. In February 1890, the new multiply authored column was rechristened In Literary Circles, with Ramsey contributing the critical angle, Carleton offering insights into the world of the writer, and Bok talking about the business angle of writing and publishing. With Bok focusing on the work of literature, Ramsey had more latitude to focus on the offerings in children's literature, and to criticize the fans of Little Lord Fauntleroy, without looking trivial by comparison. The fracturing of the literary column into briefer individually authored pieces enabled the simultaneous publication of apparently contradictory pieces, as in March 1890 when an unsigned piece titled "Romance Reduced to Figures" appeared with a review of William Dean Howells's A Hazard of New Fortunes. The "Romance" piece looks, at first glance, to be a facetious critique of the formulaic nature of romantic novels:

There is an English literary man who at the end of each year pen-
etrates into the published fiction and extracts therefrom very often
some exceedingly interesting figures. The results of his researches
into last year's fiction are entertaining. Of the heroines portrayed in
novels, he finds 372 were described as blondes, while 190 were bru-
nettes. Of the 562 heroines, 437 were beautiful, 274 were married
to the men of their choice, while 30 were unfortunate enough to be
bound in wedlock to the wrong man. [. . .] The personal charms
of the heroines included 980 "expressive eyes" and 792 "shell-like
ears." Of the eyes, 543 had a dreamy look, 390 flashed fire, while the
remainder had no special attributes.

The enumeration of romantic clichés continues to plot-points (seventy-
one children were rescued from watery graves; "seven husbands had notes
found in their pockets that exposed 'everything'"). The humor, though,
is undercut with a sense that such quantification, while it exposes the
highly conventional nature of the romance, is not entirely fair—"And
thus is the romance of a year reduced to figures." Set alongside a review
of *A Hazard of New Fortunes* that laments Howells's decision to portray
the Marches from *Their Wedding Journey* as a "disillusioned" middle-
aged couple, and looks askance at the "requirements of Realism," the
tone of "Romance Reduced to Figures" seems more ambiguous than its
actual content would suggest.[20]

Perhaps the experiment with a single-authored literary column
was short-lived because Ramsey preferred to write travel articles (this
genre would be her new area of expertise in the 1890s), or perhaps it
was doomed by the interposition of a man the publisher was hoping to
name as editor. In either case, the column, even in its fractured form,
lasted only through May 1890. That the column was not long-lived does
not mean the *Journal* readership was uninterested in receiving reading
advice. Once Bok ascended to the editorship, he presumably no longer
had time to devote to his literary musings, but he still harbored serious
literary ambitions for his magazine. In 1896, he made a significant step
towards realizing them when he hired Robert Bridges, who was then the
editor at Bok's previous employer, *Scribner's Magazine*, to pen a regular
advice column under the pseudonym of "Droch." This choice signals the
publications Bok thought of as his competition, as well as evidencing his
willingness to poach from them. In his autobiography, Bok explains that
hiring Bridges was a part of his "idea of making the American public
more conversant with books," but his ambiguous phrasing leaves open

the question of whether this task should be accomplished by making the "literary" more popular or by elevating the popular to "literary" status.[21] When Bridges took the latter approach, his columns were short-lived; as we shall see, when Hamilton Wright Mabie decided to take the former approach, he became a longtime contributor.

From December 1896 through November 1897, Droch's Literary Talks appeared every month, a full-page, four-column article with a thematic organization. Separate columns covered the reading of "old favorites" and "contemporary favorites," British and American fiction, historical fiction, humor writing, heroines, heroes, "outdoor books," and vacation reading, among other subjects. The columns are, as Bok put it, "conversational," with a permissive tone that frequently veers into the condescending.[22] Though Bridges was the editor of a magazine that frequently published works of high literary realism and muckraking pieces like Jacob Riis's *How the Other Half Lives* (1892), "Droch" took the position that readers wanted to enjoy their reading, that they wanted to be reassured and comforted by their reading. Consequently, he rejects any works that would call into question the comforts of the hearth, the embrace of the family, and the idealism of romance. He discourages his readers from taking their reading too seriously and does not want them to read to the exclusion of other activities, like cycling or fishing. In his first column, Droch explains that there is plenty of information out there for people who read to gain knowledge; he is interested in offering guidance for "the pursuit of pleasure in reading."[23] Such privileging of pleasure over any moral or intellectual goal may have been reassuring to some of Droch's readers, but in other ways it comes across as patronizing. He tells his readers in his closing column that "I have tried to advocate a natural, sensible attitude of mind on the reader's part toward the books that may be the amusement of her leisure hours. There are many things more worth while for the average person than 'being literary.' That, also, like the game of wealth, is a game in itself—and there are many called, but few chosen" (November 1897, 15). In other words, true "literariness" is something most of his readers should not even bother striving for—it's not worth it, and it's not something in the reach of the "average" reader.

The insinuation that literature is "supposed to be light" is symptomatic of the Droch approach throughout his year of columns: literature should be pleasurable, recreational, and beautiful. Droch adopts the stance and righteously indignant tone of the consumer advocate, protecting his readers from authors who would offer unsavory fare to an unwitting and defenseless public. In direct address to his audience, Droch insists that "you have a right to demand of a book that you read for simple pleasure, that it shall fill your mind with something of beauty that was not there before—whether it is beauty of thought, of imagery, or of character." Authors who persist in representing "ugly thoughts and images" are "bad company," Droch claims; their unpleasant aesthetic choices are unmannerly, antisocial (December 1896, 23). For Droch, the easiest solution is to embrace classic literature and romances, and he gives his readers this advice in his first two columns. He encourages his readers to return to Shakespeare, Tennyson, and Keats, and suggests substituting Scott, Dickens, and Thackeray for contemporary fiction. "If you are really fond of what you call 'sensation novels,' and it is often a perfectly healthy appetite (a part of the hunger of youth for life), you can find all you want of it in Scott, Hugo, Dumas (excellent translations of the Frenchmen can be easily had)" (January 1897, 15). This kind of reading need not be expensive, either; cloth-bound editions of the classics can be purchased "for less money per volume than the current sensational novel in paper covers. And when you have invested in them you have something that is worth keeping." Inexpensive reprint editions have even managed to flatten the distinctions between Dickens and Thackeray (the fans of the latter having once suffered from superiority complexes "something like the attitude assumed by George Meredith's admirers of the present day"). Reading the classics can even be a part of one's patriotic duty, as Droch insists in a brief postscript to his column "Some Old Favorites": "As an American girl you ought to find one of your keenest pleasures in reading Hawthorne, Irving, Poe and Cooper. These novelists have stood the test of time, both as writers of marvelous English and as the preservers of the heart and core of some phases of American life and tradition" (January 1897, 15). These American romantics are historical, their works have stood the test of time, and they are patriotic—what better reading for the striving young American woman?

Outside the occasional comment about the reading habits and preferences of professional men ("light" reading to rest overtaxed minds), Bridges directed his columns almost exclusively towards a younger female audience, recommending stories and characters that will "appeal to your womanly nature" (January 1897, 15). As this phrasing suggests, these recommendations were not particularly flattering to the feminine intellect. He makes all sorts of blanket generalizations about the kinds of fiction women like, as in his column "Heroines in Fiction" in which he asserts that "the truth probably is that a novel is not worth the name to a woman reader unless it is a love story" (September 1897, 15). When

Droch speaks of older readers, he does so in tones that imply that they would not be reading his column directly—he takes this approach despite Bok's constant insistence that people of all ages read the *Journal*. In his inaugural column, Droch refers to his readers' presumed task of finding a perfect Christmas book for "the dear old lady who preserves in her warm heart the traditions and good will of at least half a hundred Christmases." The portrait progresses in tone from sentiment to condescension, in ways that would probably be odd, if not uncomfortable, for that "dear old lady" were she in fact Droch's primary audience. Though her body is aging, Droch muses that "there is one thing about her that is perpetually young, and that is her dear old romantic heart. So that if you want to please her, give her a real good romance to read. She has no sympathy with modern realism and pessimism. She knows better, for she has lived her life deeply, truly, honestly, and she will tell you that it was *good to have lived it*" (December 1896, 23).

One might imagine that romance thus promoted runs the risk of being classed by a youthful readership as the genre of the grandmother, and therefore of being shunned by a younger audience. Droch's subsequent championing of the mode balances things out, but it is nevertheless true that he has some serious tonal difficulties when it comes to addressing his audience. He patronizes his readers continuously during his year at the *Journal*, and while Bok himself frequently adopted this tone in his editorials, condescension was apparently not a successful approach in the books column. Droch's feature lasted only one year in the *Journal*. This short term was perhaps by design, but one imagines Bok, who took great pride in his responsiveness to his audience, would have figured out a way to prolong the column if his readership had demanded it. As Droch, Bridges sought to minimize his readers' ambitions for literariness and played into a preference for the romance without offering a way for his readers to access works with greater cultural capital. He wrote of financial ambition but did not acknowledge his readers' cultural ambitions or the interconnectedness of the two. Furthermore, Bridges treated all his readers like adolescent girls and young women, and neglected to offer reading advice for the much broader *Journal* audience. Ultimately, Bridges did not read his readers properly, and he thereby could never have acquired the kind of active following that would sustain Hamilton Wright Mabie through a ten-year relationship with the magazine.

Mr. Mabie's Secret Shame

As I mentioned at the beginning of this chapter, if one read only Hamilton Wright Mabie's authorized biography, written with his wife's blessing in the years just following his death, one might not know that he spent ten years as the books columnist for the largest-circulation periodical of the time.[24] The period between 1902 and 1912, when Mabie was occupied with the *Journal*, is actually deemphasized in the biography as "the middle period in Mabie's life—the period following the culmination of his purely literary career . . . and preceding the crowning event of his public activities, his mission to Japan as the representative of the Carnegie Endowment for International Peace" in 1912.[25] The precise coincidence of this supposed "fallow" period with Mabie's tenure at the *Journal* seems to signal at the very least a reluctance to associate Mabie with a popular periodical, and it almost certainly signals the writer's dis-ease with the popularizing approach Mabie took in many of his *Journal* columns. The erasure of such a significant body of work cannot have been accidental or unintentional, and was probably a part of the image rehabilitation project Mabie's widow envisioned for the biography. Jeanette Mabie apparently had some difficulty finding someone willing to write a proper biography of her husband, perhaps because his reputation at his death had been greatly diminished by the post–World War I revolt against the "genteel critics" of the 1890s and 1900s. After contacting a number of his surviving colleagues to request letters to include in an exemplary biography, and searching unsuccessfully for someone who "might truly record and represent his life and the influence of his rare spirit," she settled on Edwin W. Morse, who was essentially a pen-for-hire.[26] She clearly had the right of refusal on details mentioned in the biography, and she did not want the *Journal* to figure in Mabie's lasting legacy.

Read in light of the biography's revisionist project, the letter mentioning the *Journal* actually offers significant insight into Mabie's attitudes about his *Journal* work, revealing his ambivalence about his audience and his strategic approach to the assignment. Morse cites this letter in full, with little commentary; it has no discernable relationship to the surrounding anecdotes, and while it might be going too far to suggest that Morse included it for the sake of its *Journal* reference, it does function a bit like the "return of the repressed." The letter, which is only "about" the Adirondacks insofar as Mabie describes them in a graceful rhetorical opening, was apparently written in response to an acquaintance's commentary on a *Journal* column and actually signals a complex pragmatism on Mabie's part with regard to his writings in the *Journal*:

> It was good of you to read my screed and send your comments on it. Of course character is the root of every virtue and strength. I was, however, dealing specifically with the question of the kind of books young people ought to read; and I have found that the only way to help the Journal readers is to be specific and point out the exact steps to be taken in any field of education or life.[27]

Without the opening salvo in this exchange, it is difficult to gauge precisely why Mrs. E. D. North criticized Mabie's column, and on what grounds she disagreed with him. But there is a suggestion in Mabie's response that she faulted him for an insufficient emphasis on the ideal of reading as a "character building" exercise. We may then read Mabie's justification two ways: if we take him at his word, his answer comes across as an indictment, from the perspective of six years in the books columnist's seat, of the typical *Journal* reader as either, at best, overly dependent and insecure or, at worst, unimaginative or obtuse. This reading is particularly available to us if we adopt the biographer's apparent embarrassment about Mabie's association with the *Journal* as reflective of Mabie's own attitudes. It is more intriguing, and perhaps also more likely given Mabie's continuing tenure at the *Journal*, to read this response as a moonlighting popularizer's attempts to preserve his credibility with the more genteel audiences to whom he owes his reputation by representing the absence of "character" talk in his columns not as an accommodation to popular tastes but as a pragmatic concession to the shortcomings of the general reader.

In addition to barely mentioning the *Journal*, Mabie's biography further downplays that association by obliquely misrepresenting the columns as advice primarily targeted to the youngest readers: "Through his articles on books and authors and literary matters generally he reached an enormous audience of young people, who were entirely distinct from those with whom, through the *Outlook*, his books and his lectures, he had been in touch."[28] While some of the columns do address the reading habits of children and young men and women, most of them have a more general focus, and most, as we shall see, directly address adults pursuing "self-culture." Unlike Droch, Mabie clearly envisioned an expansive audience for his columns, and he rarely addresses any one group to the exclusion of others. Even more remarkably, and unexpectedly, Mabie's recommendations are largely gender-neutral. When a reader's query requires it, he does claim to tailor his recommendations for particular ages and genders, but there is little discernable difference between these targeted lists and the general recommendations that he offers to every reader. This openness apparently vexed a number of his readers, who perhaps joined Mrs. E. D. North in expressing their distress that he gave his readers too much latitude. By the fourth year of his tenure, in his October 1906 column, Mabie felt it necessary to address questions about his approach more explicitly, emphasizing that the conditions of his assignment require that he cast a wide net with his recommendations. After diplomatically observing that "[q]uestions which have been asked and occasional good-natured criticisms show that some readers do not quite understand the point of view from which current books are discussed on this page," he continues, "it is the purpose of the reviewer to keep in mind the needs of a very large and widely-scattered body of readers, of all creeds and conditions, in all stages of education, and to select from the mass of books of the day those which are likely to interest, to educate or to refresh the greatest number."[29] Most important, Mabie does not dissuade certain groups from reading particular books. This position is a part of his larger philosophy of approval rather than condemnation; he simply does not have time to pass negative judgments, but must focus on books "which are, in the judgment of the writer, wholesome and worth reading, and they are described rather than criticized; there is room only for the briefest comment." Mabie chooses to offer a large number of possible books rather than discuss titles in great detail; this approach offers his large audience considerable latitude of choice, and keeps him from the didacticism of Ramsey, Bok, and Droch.

And yet, Mabie does not refrain entirely from evaluative comment; the principle of selection is itself critical comment. If we look closely at the rhetorics of Mabie's advice over his ten years of writing for the *Journal*, tracing in some respects their evolution towards pragmatism and in others a growing conservatism, we can see how he both accommodates popular tastes and works to steer his readers towards accessible "high" cultural products. We can also understand the apparent contradictions in Mabie's literary recommendations and piece together a portrait of upwardly mobile middle-class readers at the beginning of the twentieth century concerned with "profits" both intellectual and pecuniary. Ultimately, we will see how Mabie's columns in the *Ladies' Home Journal* both reflected the larger American culture of "reading up" and worked to produce and validate it through their persistent elision of the languages of aesthetics and economics.

"Read What You Like"

As with all long-running features, it took some time for Mabie's columns to settle into a regular format. In 1902, the columns were all Mabie generated, copiously illustrated with photographs of the authors discussed, and focused on brief reviews appearing after longer discursive sections about burning issues in reading practices. In 1903, authors' houses replaced authors' photographs as the accompanying images, and each column was laid out around the perimeter of a larger-font inset list of recommended directed readings, suitable for book clubs. By 1904, the titles of Mabie's columns begin to change, from Mr. Mabie's Literary Talks to the more explicit Mr. Mabie Tells What to Read, or, with increasing frequency, Mr. Mabie Answers Some Questions. This last format of columns becomes a regular part of the mix from 1904 onward, as reader queries are reproduced, identified only with anonymous initials and sometimes a gendered honorific, to be answered by Mabie. A significant number of these reader queries ask for lists of books, and the lists become more numerous in the body of Mabie's column as a result. Readers apparently wanted to be given specifics, and after 1905, Mabie was increasingly willing to oblige. By 1907, we find entire spreads dedicated to lists of various sorts, of novels suitable for young readers (September and October 1907); "Courses for Private Reading" (November 1908); "Study Programs for Clubs" (October 1910); or "Courses of Novel-Reading" (September 1909). By the end of Mabie's tenure, the columns devoted to answering readers' questions become scarce as Mabie dedicates more of his time to thematic columns, discussing recently published works in dedicated issues and offering longer meditations on subjects both academic ("Our Use of English," February 1909) and practical ("How to Live on 24 Hours a Day," November 1910).

While the internal structure of Mabie's columns changed over the years, the overall philosophy remained remarkably consistent. His ideals are, for the most part, those of the genteel tradition of criticism, which celebrated fineness of sentiment, the mind and originality of the author, and the transformative qualities of the text. According to Mabie, reading could have a profound impact on the reader, and it was therefore his duty to ensure that the reader read the right kinds of books—ennobling and significant books—and to steer them away from the wrong types. At the same time, he repeatedly validates the "refreshing" qualities of literature, and even legitimates reading the book that is "not enduring" but also "not harmful." This task is a delicate balancing act, in which one can discern the pressures of the marketplace: Mabie has a preference for the elite book, but he is writing to an audience both attracted to this book's cultural capital and daunted by its perceived difficulty. His readers already read "recreationally"; rather than rail against that trend, Mabie attempts to refine his readers within this comfort zone, to encourage them to read better books recreationally, and to celebrate their impulses to read at all. This accommodation is key to the working of "reading up" and is foundational to the reproduction of literary standards. Mabie and his readers all acknowledge the hierarchies of literary taste; "reading up" allows for the consumption of serious fiction in a recreational fashion.

An early column about the value of magazines could be read as a précis of the Mabiean mind-set. Mabie is, of course, writing in the circulation leader of all monthly magazines, so his position is awkward to say the least: it is a foregone conclusion that he should validate the reading of magazines against the magazine's critics, but how is he to do so when the criticisms are lodged in the name of literary excellence? He opens with the counterargument: "It is often said that the magazines are the enemies of books; that they divert attention from literature, and that they absorb readers who might more profitably find their mental food in the libraries" (July 1902, 19). But, Mabie contends, the magazine was from its inception a medium of literary fineness, with Dr. Samuel Johnson one of the first contributors to one of the first magazines. "It is not uncommon," he observes,

> to hear people who constitute themselves the custodians of litera-
> ture dismiss the magazines with one sweeping condemnation as
> commercial enterprises which are steadily lowering the intellectual
> tone of the English-speaking peoples. It is a curious fact, in the face
> of these oft-repeated predictions, that since magazines began to ap-
> pear the reading public has steadily expanded, the sale of books
> increased, and the distribution of the classics grown to immense
> proportions.

Without claiming causation, Mabie is either suggesting a correlation between the two phenomena or, at the least, defending the magazine against accusations that it is destroying the "intellectual tone" of soci-ety—albeit in terms of production and distribution, more than in terms of reception, the latter being much more difficult to ascertain with any certainty.

If he were sure that the reading public, his public, had a "proper" rela-tion to magazines, and if he were entirely comfortable with the literary content of magazines, the next portion of his commentary would, of course, be unnecessary. He couches it as "common-sense" but asks, "[A]re magazines the only things which are abused in their use?" What follows sounds a pragmatist's defense of the periodical in which he writes:

> The magazines present every month a good many articles which would best be left unread, not because they lack substance or form, but because other and better things can be read in their place. The same magazines present every month contributions to literature and to knowledge which one who wishes to know his own time, as well as other times, cannot afford to miss. In the tables of contents are found the names of nearly all the men and women who are making literature; in their pages are found the most intelligent and authoritative accounts of recent achievements in art, discoveries in science, experiments in sociology and economics.

Magazines are, it seems, necessary adjuncts to books; they are vehicles for other kinds of information, more "current" literature and nonfiction. At the same time, Mabie cannot countenance everything in all magazines—tellingly, he does not mention the kind of domestic information that makes up the bulk of the *Journal*'s back-of-the-book. This omission is again a marker of the uneasy peace that Mabie has made with his current publication and a sign of why he might have chosen to agree to publish in this venue. He hopes to steer his readers towards the good, away from the bad, in the hopes of making the good the popular. His closing comments about magazines sum up nicely his overall approach to all of the literature he will review and recommend over ten years in the *Journal*: "The end of the whole matter is that there are good and bad magazines, that magazines must be read with intelligence, not with omnivorous appetite, that they have their own place and work in the modern order of things, and that no wise reader will ignore them" (July 1902, 19). That there are few absolute pronouncements but an abundance of strategic suggestions in Mabie's articles no doubt is the key to his enduring success both with the *Journal* readers and with his opinionated editor, Edward Bok.

Mabie's columns are frequently broken up with editorial headings, the authorship of which is uncertain. It seems unlikely that Mabie wrote, or even approved of, some of them, as they often misinterpret the upshot of the discussion that follows. In the July 1902 column on magazine reading, for example, a paragraph that concludes that readers need not like all genres of literature but should "select the best of the kind to which we are attracted" is given the much more permissive heading "Read What

You Like" (July 1902, 19). Mabie does not mean that one should really read whatever one likes; he instead wants to steer his readers away from reading history, for example, simply because they think they *should* read history. Rather than suffer miserably through Edward Gibbon's histories, his readers should choose a quality novel or a quality biography. The heading, though, is either reassuringly permissive to the skimmer (who would be unlikely to follow any of Mabie's other advice anyway) or suggestive and intriguing to the casual reader, intended to draw that reader in. This paratextual material also conditions response to Mabie's advice and renders it more palatable, renders the definitions of "the best" a bit looser.

Even after following Mabie closely for months or years, the *Journal* reader might have only a fuzzy notion of what "the best" is in any given situation. Mabie gives specific recommendations, of course, but his meditations about "enduring" books versus "books of the moment" are frustratingly inchoate. Take, for example, the following discussion from his column "Mr. Mabie Comments on Books of the Season":

> In every season a few novels of real importance appear; many more
> wholesome and readable stories are published which are not to be
> numbered with the books of permanent value, but which, in mod-
> erate numbers and as recreation, are worth reading; and beyond
> these, in the outer circles of the vast field of book-making, are to
> be found an immense number of stories, made up, so to speak, for
> the market; untrue to life, full of sham sentiment, of false views
> of human relations, of distorted pictures of society, and as devoid
> of any kind of beauty as many contemporary houses are devoid of
> any truth or beauty of architecture. The cheap, trashy, vulgar story
> ought to be left untouched on the newsstands; it lies in the power of
> the public to put an end to its prolific life; when such stories cease
> to be read they will cease to be written. (January 1906, 30)

We can see here the idiosyncratic nature of Mabie's writings in the *Journal*. His reviews are primarily concerned with managing the book-selection process and, ultimately, the reading experience. He early on takes the tack that "reading is preeminently an individual matter, to be determined solely by what we *need* and by what we *like* [italics mine]," insisting that "[i]t is better to be honest and ignorant of the classics than to profess a liking for them because it is good intellectual form to know them" (July 1902, 19). Such advice tells us a good deal both about Mabie's readers and about the dual nature of his mission in the *Journal*—to reassure readers who find themselves lost when it comes to the classics and to prod them to try and read whatever of the "classics" falls within their comfort zone. Striving for excellence is not only a good idea; it is imperative: "Duty to our highest growth does not compel us to like all great books or any one class of great books; it demands of us that we se-lect the best of the kind toward which we are attracted." Still, the *Journal* reader is Mabie's client, and Mabie must therefore liberally sprinkle his recommendations with support for stories "which cannot be regarded as literature, but which are well worth reading," like *The Hound of the Baskervilles*. But in the same column, Mabie can become a firmer guid-ing hand, as when he tells his readers that "[n]o one has any right to allow children to grow up in a bookless home" (July 1902, 19). Mabie is inflex-ible when it comes to the idea that people should read; he is more ecu-menical when it comes to what they should read, and how. In October 1906, he explains that "cheap, vulgar, morbid books, however widely cir-culated, are intentionally ignored. Many books of great value are passed over in silence because they appeal to small groups of people." At the same time, "books of no permanent value are often mentioned [in this column] because they are diverting and restful; and people need diver-sion quite as much as they need education." The promotion of "divert-ing" qualities in literature, particularly fiction, is ultimately not distress-ing to Mabie because he "contents himself with a simple warning that the book is for the hour and not for all time" (October 1906, 22). He is, in other words, allowing his occasionally philistine readers the "refresh-ment" of light fiction, without any apparent anxiety about the possibility that such literature might crowd out more "serious" volumes for space on publishers' lists. We might recall here that this was precisely Edith Wharton's concern in "The Vice of Reading," published in the *North American Review* just three years before Mabie's statement of reviewing philosophy. Unlike Wharton, whose chief concern was for the authors of serious fiction, Mabie is primarily concerned in his *Journal* writings with the needs of his readers, and the "greatest number" of them at that.

The most striking comment in this passage, however, may be his con-tention that any critical work in the column happens between the lines, in the exclusion of a book from consideration if it does not meet his stan-dards of "value" and "wholesomeness": "The element of criticism on this page is to be found chiefly in the selection of books" (October 1906, 22). Mabie is utterly comfortable recommending books that may have "no element of permanency"; such is his stance, for example, towards Kath-erine Cecil Thurston's *Max* in March 1911. Thurston's previous offering,

The Masquerader, had been a frequent recommendation of Mabie's over the previous years, despite his admission that the novel was merely "a very clever piece of fiction, written simply to help readers pass away the time. It was entirely devoid of reality, but it was distinctly entertaining, an audacious invention" (March 1911, 30). While *Max* is in the same vein and, moreover, "is overcharged with sentiment," Mabie is willing to list it in the "New Novels of Incident" section of a column titled "New Books Worth Reading" because "it will interest a good many people." These are hardly stringent criteria for inclusion. Overall, while Mabie's process of selection is also a process of deselection, the criteria for both are ultimately profoundly subjective, and frequently contradictory—or, more generously, ecumenical. This attitude allows Mabie considerable latitude to navigate the critical debates of the day and allows Mabie's readers a generous measure of freedom in their reception of the literature to which Mabie directs them. And it enables Mabie to continue his mandate to talk about "which among the books of to-day are really worth reading, and something of their authors."[30] While he recommends particular books of the "enduring" sort more frequently and consistently than the books "of the moment," the latter ultimately make up the bulk of his recommendations in the aggregate. These recommendations, while fascinating, are scattershot, and are rarely repeated; we can tell more about Mabie's aesthetic goals for his audience by looking at his repeat recommendations and at his occasional essays on the processes of self-culture, the importance of the "reading habit," and the aesthetic goals of the novel. These reveal the underlying philosophy that Mabie's readers would absorb from their reading of his columns, and it is here that we can see the competing and interdependent motivations that sustain the practice of "reading up."

A Taste for Feeling

In Robert Bridges's "Droch" columns, the old-fashioned romance was preferable on many levels to realism because it was comfortable, comforting, and spiritually elevating. Even though Bridges was editor of a competing periodical that would publish muckraking journalism and cutting-edge realist fiction, as "Droch," speaking to a presumably less intellectual audience in the *Journal*, he took the path of least resistance by playing into what he perceived as his readers' preexisting inclinations. Hamilton Wright Mabie took a different tack, and the popularity of his column indicates that it served him well. While continuing to privilege the romance at all turns, and to hold up particular romance novels as the pinnacle of literary achievement, he refused to demonize realism, and even recommended certain works of realism as important books. Key to this accommodation was Mabie's imprecision when it came to generic classifications; he terms texts, or elements of texts, "realist," or "romantic," or even "sentimental" and "sensational," without rigorously defining these categories or analyzing the aesthetic and political implications of each category. In other words, he speaks in buzzwords that are all but evacuated of their meaning and allows his readers to fill in the blanks with their own conceptions—whether accurate or inaccurate—of what those terms mean. This terminological imprecision, as we shall see, also allows Mabie and his readers to creatively recategorize some texts or to read texts in ways unintended by their authors—to identify with particular characters who might resemble romantic heroes or heroines, for example, despite the fact that they appear in a realist text that undermines their "heroic" qualities. In other words, such ambiguity was not just sloppiness on Mabie's part; in his writings in the *Outlook* he was an outspoken and intellectually precise critic; it was, rather, strategic, because it enabled Mabie to encourage particular texts without having to worry about their aesthetic alignments. Mabie recognized the cultural importance of realism, even if he could not condone all of the principles behind realism, and this strategic positioning offered his readers the chance to add realist texts to their personal libraries while retaining a fondness for romance.

Mabie pursued this strategy from his very first *Journal* column, and his very first recommendations. After an opening that complimented the reading public for its progress towards elevated tastes, he directs his readers to the works of "Miss Wilkins and Miss Jewett," whose stories "have been talked about and read most widely during the past four or five months" (March 1902, 17).[31] He introduces Wilkins, pictured in the act of taking tea, as having "a field which is not wide but which she thoroughly understands . . . the abnormal types produced by excess of individuality and bearing fruit in what is called 'crankyism,'; with occasional experiments in the portraiture of the half-nun-like simplicity and monotony of spinsterhood." After this oblique reference to Wilkins's already famous short story, "A New England Nun," Mabie turns to her new novel, *The Portion of Labor*, in which

> she describes factory life in a small town with a first-hand knowledge which makes her readers feel the terrible weight of the

significant title of her story resting on their hearts before they are half through the book. The family of the young girl who is the central figure is characterized so vividly that every member of it stands out with perfect distinctness. The girl is a beautiful creation; a new figure in American fiction; a kind of woman who is growing up in all parts of the country, but who has never before had a biographer. This is a story to read for information quite as much as for pleasure. (March 1902, 17)

Mabie's opening comments about Wilkins classify her work by region and by focus—she is a character-driven author, and one whose "definite pictures of American life and sharply defined types of American character" are, above all, accurate. At the same time, he guarantees a dramatic, emotional reading experience, which he describes in slippery terms—readers will "feel" the importance of Wilkins's title and will find it has a "terrible weight"—that suggest either sentimental identification, or romantic escapism, or both. Mabie specifies that the book focuses on a young woman, thereby ensuring the interest of young women who look for characters like themselves in their fiction, and he entices the sociologically inclined reader with the claim that the novel works as a "biography" for a new American type. He finally synthesizes these somewhat scattered and polarized observations by describing the novel as one that will, in fact, satisfy those at both extremes of the realism-romance reader expectation continuum—those pursuing "information" as well as those pursuing "pleasure."

I am here interested not so much in determining whether Wilkins and Jewett were "really" sentimental authors, or "really" romantic, or "really" realists, as I am in mapping Mabie's categorization of their work as simultaneously realistic (with "accurate" portrayals of factory town life); romantic (offering "pleasurable" reading experiences); and sentimental (with sympathetic protagonists and affecting plots). In many ways, this conundrum is endemic to regionalist writing, and Mabie is hardly doing something revolutionary by signaling the way Wilkins's novel responds to several readerly positions.[32] Not coincidentally, *The Portion of Labor* in its negotiation of the demands of realism and the popular interest in romance and sentiment is even more ambivalent than much of Wilkins's work. The novel, published in 1901, was widely anticipated after her comments on it in a *Harper's Bazar* interview published in January of the previous year: "The new novel at which she is hard at work is a strictly modern one, the scene laid in the shoe-factory of a large city. Miss Wilkins says of it: 'I do not try to solve the labor problem. I simply present it. The story seems to me to promise well. I like it myself. It is rather realistic, but not grimly so, its pathos being cheerful rather than tragic.'"[33] There are two plotlines in *The Portion of Labor*, both centered on the protagonist Ellen Brewster. Ellen, a prototypical young girl from the provinces, has a working-class background and comes to work at her town's shoe factory through a series of misfortunes. She leads the workers on a strike against pay cuts, but then leads them back to work after she sees their suffering during a harsh winter. Ellen is also romantically involved with, and finally marries, the factory-owner's nephew. As Dorothy Berkson contends, "The first plot emphasizes class solidarity and the dignity of labor; the second, the aspiration of the working class to attain the leisure, education, and taste of the upper classes."[34] Given the *Ladies' Home Journal's* audience and the task with which Mabie was charged, this combination is for him ideal, and he will repeatedly assure his audience that "reading is preeminently an individual matter, to be determined solely by what we *need* and by what we *like*" (July 1902, 19).

While Mabie offers the book as relevant to a number of reading practices—those associated with "feeling," "pleasure," and "information"—he also de-emphasizes important aspects of the novel. The only details he touches on are the protagonist's age and gender, the fact that her family is an object of focus in the novel, and the general subject, factory life in a small New England town. Mabie does not discuss the labor element of the novel, except to note that the "full significance" of the title, *The Portion of Labor*, becomes clear to the sympathetic reader. While he gives little indication that the novel is deeply concerned with the parameters of labor-management conflict, he likewise gives no signal of the romance plot. The element that receives the most attention is Wilkins's reputation for accurate representations of quirky regional characters, and the novel's fulfilling of that reputation. When we wed this to the rhetoric of "pleasure" and "feeling" in the review, we can see that Mabie is mingling genres and readerly expectations in a particular way: he champions a realistic writing practice but validates romantic and sentimental responses to that realism. Such promotion of realist literature through an emphasis on its romantic and sentimental qualities becomes a hallmark of Mabie's columns throughout his tenure at the *Journal*, and only intensifies in the later columns.

In Jewett's case, with *The Tory Lover*, Mabie is confronted with a novel that departs radically from the author's previous work. He also clearly does not think it a wholly successful book, but he takes the opportunity of its relatively recent publication to recommend her canon as a whole. Noting that the novel "carries her reader overseas, but . . . begins in one of the finest old homes near Portsmouth, and a good deal of New England is found in cabin and forecastle in the little bark in which Paul Jones sails to try his fortunes and win fame on the other side of the world," Mabie strains to make Jewett's romance consistent with her earlier works. "The story of adventure is new in Miss Jewett's hands," he explains, and he admits that "she is not as much at home with it as with the other tales of character in which she has long excelled," but he can still see his way clear to recommending it because of something that goes beyond subject matter—the *style* of the writing, and the spirit behind it: "[I]t is not so successful as some of her earlier books, but it is written with characteristic refinement" (March 1902, 17). The *Journal* reader cannot go wrong by reading Jewett, because she is always refined, always able to evoke the "delicate sympathy" of her readers.

It is worth noting that Mabie is hardly a fan of "sentimentality" widely construed, and he displays his disdain for many of the works typically associated with that rubric in a particularly vituperative portion of his column "Are the Best-Sellers Worth Reading?" While he gives credit to *Uncle Tom's Cabin* by noting that there are "'best-sellers' not in the first rank of literary excellence which are not unworthy, by reason of intellectual integrity and seriousness of purpose, to find permanent place in the libraries," he reassures people who lament the apparent "degeneracy" of contemporaneous fiction with a reminder that "[e]arly in the last century 'Charlotte Temple' was wept over by a host of people who did not see how pretentious and hollow was its pathos and how deadly dull its sentimentality." If that were not consolation enough, he continues, "[s]till later, about the middle of the last century, tears fell in showers over 'Queechy,' 'The Wide, Wide World,' and 'The Lamplighter.'" Though for the most part these novels were "all moral as far as sex relations were concerned," as opposed to many of the current batch, they were still not as good or wholesome for "vitality, simplicity, and interest" as the "second class" of novels of the 1910s (November 1911, 30). Mabie's explicit concern here with sexual morality is much shriller than in his earlier columns, even when discussing naturalists like Émile Zola—he typically reserves his caution about "morals" per se for columns directly addressing juvenile reading, while here he seems to concern himself implicitly, through reference to so much sentimental fiction, to woman readers.[35] The problem seems to lie not in sentiment itself, however, but with a "maudlin," or "inartistic," evocation of tears. Weeping over Harriet Beecher Stowe's work is acceptable and, as it turns out, "feeling" for any number of characters in "realist" novels is both acceptable and desirable. Mabie is determined to retain elements of each genre that he still finds useful, and he does some intricate work decoupling terms from their previous associations—and giving them new ones—throughout his *Journal* columns.

In his *Journal* pieces, Mabie is frustratingly vague about the distinction between "romance" and "realism." I want to suggest that this vagueness was entirely intentional on Mabie's part, as it afforded him an opportunity to claim the best of each category for whichever texts he chose to champion, allowing him to avoid positive assessments of any genre as a whole. His list of "novels of realism," for example, is presented as a genre lesson, set beside a list of "romantic novels," among which appear Nathaniel Hawthorne's *Marble Faun* and Sir Walter Scott's *Quentin Durward*. Mabie's explanatory heading barely touches on the possibility that there is a difference between "realism" and "romanticism," but it is largely up to the reader to discern what that difference might be: "Realism and romanticism are terms constantly used in the discussion of fiction and extremely difficult of definition. The reader of novels who wishes to get a clear and definite impression of these two forms of writing, and the diverse attitude toward the material used and the characters which appear, will do well to study groups of novels which may be distributed under these two heads" (September 1909, 28). In other columns, though, Mabie begins to blur, or even obliterate, the line between fanciful fiction and realism, as in his 1912 pronouncement about Frank Norris: "Norris, a man of powerful imagination though of imperfect artistic development, saw the human relations of business; and wherever there is a human relation there is material for romance" (April 1912, 42). Granted, Norris himself in "A Plea for Romantic Fiction" was careful to separate the romance from "sentimentalism" and preserved a special place in the literary pantheon for romance properly executed. He also elevated romance above the "stultifying," "harsh, loveless, colorless, blunt tool called realism," claiming Zola as a writer of "romance" and, backhandedly, assuring realism's critics that realism could be "respectable as a church and proper as a deacon—as, for instance, the novels of Mr. Howells."[36] But Mabie's placement of Norris in the canon of romance seems tied less to a complicated relationship with Norris's own critical gymnastics than to a move to render Norris palatable to the *Journal* audience. Mabie's approach to Norris is always tentative—in the 1911 column "Are the American Novelists Deteriorating?" he gives his imprimatur to several fictions about the "Central West" without once mentioning Norris—but as early as May 1903 he opened the floor for discussion of Norris's position in contemporary literature with a mixed review of *The Pit*. First, he calls Norris's *The Octopus* a "very defective but powerful story," because it "was too long; it was overweighted with detail, and its manner was too suggestive of Zola; but it was first-hand work; written, that is to say, by a man who had studied the life he described with the utmost care and conscientiousness." Mabie finds in Norris a unique "insight" into the "dramatic possibilities" of industrial America, which tempers some of his realistic and naturalistic impulses (May 1903, 15). Norris seems in this sense a threshold artist, paving the way for others who do not have such affinities with Zola to enter the territory.

While literary taxonomies seem to have lost some of their critical traction in the *Atlantic* group, they do still seem to have some purchase for Mabie—even if applied haphazardly.[37] This makes sense given his didactic project—literary syllabi need separations, after all, and the classification of works renders something about them "learnable." Despite the attention he pays to works aligned in the early twentieth century with "realism," Mabie's readerly sympathies, and, it seems, the assumed preferences of his audience, clearly lie with the idealism of romance. In his advice regarding children's literature, he recommends the romantics, particularly American romantics, to the near exclusion of everyone else. His September 1904 column "Mr. Mabie on Sunday-School Books" lists a number of specific works that would pertain to religious learning and morals, but he also generally advises that "[i]t is a religious duty to give young readers a taste for the best literature by placing in their hands the best books. [. . .] American children . . . ought to read Irving, Cooper, Hawthorne, Emerson" (September 1904, 18). He insists that children of both genders should read Scott. He answers without qualm a request for "ten romances, stirring, full of adventure and wholesome, for a girl of fifteen" (May 1905, 18). Interestingly enough, Mabie here adopts the means of Howells as he supports choices Howells explicitly condemned; as Nancy Glazener notes, Howells thought Scott inappropriate reading for young Americans because of its attention to "Old World political systems." As Glazener puts it, "[S]uch literature would not produce democratic citizens, according to the very crude model of internalization and imitation that was sometimes generated by realism's supporters."[38] Mabie clearly had affinities with this "crude" model of reception; while he does not generally differentiate the types of books that should be read by men as opposed to women, he does work diligently to classify books by the maturity of the reader, and recommends different books for boys and girls. Primary among books that one should take care to keep away from younger readers are, of course, "books of disease . . . which make one feel as if one had been in a hospital or madhouse" (November 1907, 28). Even adults should not overload on such books, which in the descriptions Mabie offers sound like works we now consider "naturalist" and which he generally designates, as in the Norris review cited above, with a general reference to "Zola."

But even when it comes to naturalism, Mabie equivocates. In 1905, in response to a reader's query about why Zola would be considered a "radical realist," Mabie offers the following meditation:

> Zola was a realist in method because he attempted to portray, and in many places did portray, the facts of life with uncompromising accuracy. He was essentially, however, a romanticist because he selected his facts instead of taking them as they are presented in life. The realists have always charged the romanticists with presenting a false picture of human experience by the method of taking what was attractive, poetic and happy in that experience and excluding what was unpoetic, undramatic, and commonplace. Zola reversed the practice of the romanticists; he took in many cases the most revolting, gross, and repulsive aspects of life and pictured them with very little shading; so that his view of life is as untrue in one way as the view of George Sand is untrue in another. Both present a great deal of truth; neither tells the whole truth. Realism as practiced by some of its more ardent advocates is as untrue as the most radical romanticism. (September 1905, 18)

If Mabie was evasive in his introduction to "Courses of Novel-Reading," he here utterly undermines the notion that there is any substance to realism's claims of "truth" or romance's claims of ideality outside of the experience of the reader. He is explicit about separating method and intent from result—Zola is as much a "romanticist" as any other writer is, he just selects the unsavory aspects of life to portray. Indeed, Mabie contends that realists' attention to "method" is nothing more than an assessment of subject matter; because of their reflexive rejection of a supposed "idealism" in romanticism, they are susceptible to overcompensation by exclusive attention to the negative. In the next month's column, Mabie revisits these terms to clarify them, after asserting that "the really good novel must be interesting, but it must also be sound, sane, well constructed and well written. To say that a novel must be sane does not mean that it must deal with the normal phases of life only; it means that its point of view and its treatment must be healthful and sound." The "sane" story is "both sincere and true to life," and the "truthfulness" of the story inheres not just in "truth to the best in the writer," but also "truthfulness to the fact of observation, of experience, of divination of character." What is the representative text for this kind of truthfulness? *The Rise of Silas Lapham*—though Mabie is quick to add that "this emphasis on truthfulness does not mean that a novel must belong to the class called realistic" (October 1905, 20). This stance is a far cry from Mabie's 1885 review, which finds *Lapham* symptomatic of realism's tendency to thrust dull and degenerate characters into the hands of the gentle reader. I discuss Mabie's engagement with Howells and *Lapham* at greater length in chapter 2, as an entrée into Mabie and the *Journal*'s vexed relationship with Howellsian realism.

Confronted with the question, "What do you consider three tests of a good novel?" Mabie answers with a number of examples that span genres, with language plucked directly from Henry James's "The Art of Fiction" (1884), but in ways that adapt these texts to tastes James would be reluctant to validate:

> 1. That it shall be interesting. No matter how able it may be, a dull novel is a dreary failure. 2. That it shall either tell a story so well as to compel the attention as in "The Masquerader," or describe a character with such insight and feeling as to create genuine dramatic interest, as in "The Conquest of Canaan," "The Debtor," "The Divine Fire," "The House of Mirth." 3. That it shall be, in point of style, clear, strong, picturesque, or stirring. (March 1906, 20)

When James contends that "the only obligation to which in advance we may hold a novel without incurring the accusation of being arbitrary, is that it be interesting," he does so in the service of validating his own authorial practice, and ultimately to the end of claiming primacy for authorial intention as against critical assessment (at least, negative critical assessment of his own works).[39] Mabie invokes this famous Jamesian dictum in this case to argue against the "dull novel," where "dullness" clearly is in the eyes of the beholder, not the author. In his second contention, he gives primacy of place to the "story" that "compel[s] attention," and he references a historical romance he has already termed "a fairy-story in contemporary dress" (September 1905, 18). When he addresses characterization, specifying that the character description must have both "insight and feeling," he uses a buzzword of both romance and sentimental literature, and offers as examples works by Booth Tarkington,

Mary E. Wilkins [Freeman], May Sinclair, and Edith Wharton—novelists traditionally considered marginally realist, regionalist, proto-modernist, and realist or naturalist, respectively. When it comes to style, Mabie again uses terminology that resonates with realism alongside those tell-tale keywords from romance and sentimentality, "picturesque" and "stirring." By mixing his references, Mabie is in some ways flattening the hierarchy between romance and realism, but he is also eliding the differences between the genres and, therefore, making a romantic reading of a realist text possible, even likely, from his readers. This lays the groundwork for misidentifications with characters who might have been romantic heroes or heroines but who, in realist texts, are supposed to be atavistic holdovers, often insupportably romantic and frequently doomed to failure in the realist world. Mabie's ecumenicalism blurs the boundaries between the genres, even renders them arbitrary, and releases readers from the responsibility for reading any text according to a set of generic rules.

Self-Culture, Profits, and Pleasure

It would be fair to say that Mabie can play fast and loose with literary critical terminology because in the pages of the *Journal* he is not writing for the literati. The presumption that his readers come from a position of relative ignorance but harbor a driving self-culture agenda is explicitly referenced throughout Mabie's ten years of columns in the *Journal*. As I mention above, he periodically devotes entire columns to readers' letters, and at least one letter in each such column asks some variation of the question, "[H]ow can I get self-culture?" Though the connection of "self-education" with "self-making," with the latter's pecuniary implications, is the raison d'être for Mabie's columns, at the beginning of his tenure at the *Journal* he took pains to distinguish the two, as in one (possibly fictitious) exchange published in November 1904 under the encouraging heading "Self-Culture Is Possible through Books":

CONWELL: Is self-culture possible through the reading of books where one's boyhood surroundings were hard and no education could be secured?

MABIE: Yes; self-educated men are found everywhere. They are less numerous than so-called self-made men, but they are quite as much in evidence if one looks for them. Education is largely a matter of books, of observation and of time; he who knows how to use books, how to study men and how to make the most of such time as he can command may become an educated man. Such men have learned languages, arts, literature and the sciences. There are some kinds of training which a man cannot secure without schools and teaching, but any man who has half an hour a day at his command and who has access to books may gain the intelligence, the ripeness, the judgment and the sound taste to go a long way toward what is called culture. To become cultivated one must be willing to be self-denying, patient and invincibly industrious; he who is willing to pay the price may compass the great end of self-development. (November 1904, 20)

By distinguishing the "self-educated" man from the "self-made" man, Mabie is drawing a distinction between success culture and self-culture, defining the latter in the tradition of William Ellery Channing. Channing "rejected any idea that [self-culture] would contribute to material advancement" and emphasized the process of self-education over the end result.[40] Even so, Mabie is hardly a stern taskmaster. He cannot be, and keep his audience. His closing contention that one must be "self-denying" is slightly ameliorated by his previous statement that one needs only a spare half hour per day (he will shorten this time span periodically during his *Journal* tenure). Only two years later, in encouraging readers to educate themselves so that they will achieve some form of personal advancement, Mabie is less coy, assuring his readers that "if we know how to educate ourselves so as to be and enjoy and achieve, on the largest possible scale, we should solve the problem of living, so far as it can be solved in this present stage of existence" (November 1906, 22). The separation between cultural and economic capital was impossible to sustain in the pages of the *Journal*; his audience was, after all, reading his columns because of the underlying assumption that in fact reading literature could somehow "pay."

Connecting cultural and economic capital was the key to enshrining "quality" literature and to making it popular, best-selling literature—literally making it "pay" for him and for the authors who wrote it. This instrumentality lies at the heart of Mabie's columns, driving both his writing and the queries of his readers. Mabie's suggestions for what his readers are supposed to "get out of" these novels range from the oblique to the explicit. He embraces the need for his readers to "depend on the current novel for mental rest and diversion" (July 1906, 18), at the same time that he insists that "[n]o one ought to be content with reading only the books that attract at the moment, or doing only the things that one enjoys doing; strength, training and growth come largely from reading books and doing work which at the time are [sic] hard and often repellant" (November 1907, 28). Mabie is pulled in both directions during his time at the *Journal*, but he cannot decouple the languages of profits and aesthetics even when he seems to be most strongly resisting their interdependence; while he insists that "no man is so shockingly cheated as he who barters inward wealth for outward riches" (January 1908, 28), he had noted four years earlier that "the home in which good books are read cannot be vulgar, for vulgar people do not care for good things" (December 1904, 19), connecting the outward appearance of a home with the mental furniture of its inhabitants. While Mabie's statement relies on the logic of correlation rather than causality, his whole *column* relies on a logic of causality. One might therefore expect that readers of Mabie's column, who are after all finding in the rest of the magazine advice about what kinds of "good things" they might accumulate for their home, could read this passage as an implicit promise that people who read good things will thereby be able to own good things—will thereby have the ability to pay for good things.

The conflation of "good books" and "good things" appears at the end of a lengthy meditation titled "The Relation of Books and Wealth" that opened Mabie's annual holiday books column in December 1904. Lamenting that "many of the most depressing conditions of the time are created by the ignorant rich," Mabie explains that "there is nothing which needs greater intelligence than the spending of money, and the wealth that comes suddenly to some people throws their unfitness to possess and use it into high light." He then tells of one of these nouveaux riches, in a story, presumably "true," that sounds like nothing so much as the story of Silas Lapham's house-building adventures. This wealthy man, building a monstrous home that "promises to be a lasting source of grief to his neighbors and the whole community," forgets to include a library in the well-appointed excrescence until an acquaintance asks about it, at which point he blithely decides to "ask the architect to put one in." Mabie goes no further in explaining the grotesqueness of this moment (it is up to the reader to understand, presumably, that the problem is either the wealthy man's lack of concern about the books that should go there or his apparent lack of book ownership), but he does expound at some length on the moral of this vignette:

The country is full of people who are self-educated socially as well
as intellectually, and who are a credit to American society and
among its best products; but there are many who become rich without suspecting the relationship between wealth and education, and
who furnish material for the comic journals and bring grief to their
more intelligent countrymen. No disgrace attaches to ignorance
if it is unavoidable, but to flaunt ignorance against a background
of wealth is to invite and justify the severest criticism. (December
1904, 19)

In this formulation, it is difficult to tell whether "education" is necessary
for wealth or a by-product of it. Mabie wants to have it both ways here—
presumably to sell reading both to the person who has already "made
it" and wants to have a chance to be legitimate and to the person who
wants to "make it" but does not have any options aside from reading.
Both readers will ultimately do the right thing by reading books, as long
as they do not think too much about whether Mabie's logics are consistent or try to determine the connection between "education" and "intelligence." It is very clear, regardless, that "ignorance" is to be avoided at all
costs, and no reader of Mabie's columns, having been shown the folly of
a lack of education, can continue on this course, lest he or she becomes a
"flaunter" of ignorance. Mabie turns directly from this parable and lesson to deal with some novels that address striving for success themati-
cally, such as Robert Herrick's *The Common Lot*, thereby reinforcing the
interconnection of culture and wealth.

In fact, Mabie might be, albeit perhaps somewhat unwittingly, one
of the earlier adapters, if not the coiner, of the phrase "intellectual capital." He first uses the phrase to describe the writings of Ralph Waldo
Emerson—"This generation does not remember much of what Emerson
wrote, but Emerson's thought has become part of the intellectual capital
of the country" (September 1903, 15)—and he clearly enjoys the phrase,
using it again on several occasions. He discusses the "unused educational capital in the possession of men and women of culture and some
leisure," which needs to be tapped by intrepid organizers of local reading clubs (September 1909, 28). These terms give his readers license to
think of literature in economic terms, while simultaneously feeding off
the fact that his readers are already thinking this way. Mabie is a books
columnist who understands, and even embraces, this elision and who
acknowledges that his column's existence is predicated on an instrumental attitude towards reading and literature. Taste must work within the

economic systems that support it; Mabie cannot insist that his readers stop feeling sympathy for characters, any more than he can allow them to read only "classic" works of literary romanticism. Both approaches would be untenable, as Robert Bridges's "Droch" columns prove. Mabie's tacit agreement with the attitudes of his readers, both in validating their readerly desires and in pressing them to read the things they knew were "good for them," is what made him such a successful contributor to the *Journal* where his predecessors failed.

There is throughout the columns a sense that the Mabie reader is profoundly concerned with the connection between financial and social success and the acquisition of cultural capital. The opening of one of Mabie's columns acknowledges the ongoing conundrum of the would-be reader who is also striving for financial wealth: "If making a living were the whole of life there would be good ground for the question which many people are asking: 'Why should I spend my time reading books when there are so many real things I can do for myself and for others?'" (March 1909, 42). Coming as it does in the later part of Mabie's tenure at the *Journal*, this apparently perennial question shows that the course he had sporadically pursued, that of emphasizing the inner rewards of a course of good reading, was not satisfying many of his readers. Mabie follows the above with the remark that "[f]ortunately those who are eager for books far outnumber those who are skeptical to their uses," but when he attempts to circumvent the skeptics' desires for material benefits from reading, he slips into the language of materialism: "[True readers] not only escape from themselves, but they also come into possession of themselves." In an era of possessive individualism, the claim for self-possession would certainly resonate at the very least as a claim for social advancement with an upwardly mobile reader of the *Journal*. This is another way of framing the idea of cultural capital, and of finding it even in "escapist" literary practice, and it is predicated on a rhetoric that understands the American self as, at base, something to be possessed.

Indeed, Mabie is a consummate modern rhetorician, adopting the language of Taylorism in his frequent discussions of the time his reader should devote to the "reading habit." One column, titled "How to Live on 24 Hours a Day," connects economic and cultural capital even more explicitly by positing that the time outside of the working day, in which his readers could be reading the best literature has to offer, "furnishes the by-products out of which fortunes may be made" (November 1910, 36). There is a compelling push-and-pull in this column between the language of wealth, thrift, fortunes, and profits and Mabie's occasional insistence that "[a] man's inward wealth is his real fortune"; this tension is best exemplified in his attempts to liken the unread mind to the untilled soil of the American West:

> In individual as in National life there has been an enormous waste of energy and material; as there have been wide tracts of country which have produced nothing because they have lacked water and soil, so there have been many lives which have been largely unproductive because they have not had intelligent direction. A vast force remains unused in society because a host of men and women do not study their resources as the resources of the Nation are now being studied. There was a great section of the Far West which was once described in the old atlases as "The Great American Desert," and regarded as so much useless land. This arid country now bears many kinds of grain because irrigation has supplied the one thing it needed. And what is called intensive farming has multiplied manyfold the bearing capacity of fields that were formerly almost sterile. The capacity of the earth to make men rich is only beginning to be understood, and we are yet far from the mastery of its forces which will make it a magical servant of men in days to come. There are hosts of men and women who are not putting half their power at work, and are failing to get out of life half the interest and happiness that are within their reach.

Putting aside for a moment the hindsight that reminds us of the agricultural disaster intensive farming proved to be in the American West, we can see that Mabie has evoked one of the more potent get-rich schemes of his time in his drive to promote reading as a profitable enterprise. And, though he mutes the materialism that might be implied by "the interest" one could get out of life through reading, he connects reading so closely to "the capacity of the earth to make men rich" that it is difficult to disentangle the material undertones from "interest." Indeed, Mabie's language of "productivity" implies a workplace benefit to the study of literature, and he ambiguously hopes that his words will "open the eyes of any young man or woman, or any old person, to the possible wealth that lies in turning the by-products of life to account": life should be regulated like a business, and more wealth is accumulated when nothing is wasted.

Mabie's compulsive use of the language of business, wealth, profit, and accumulation, along with his repeated acknowledgment that his readers clamor to be convinced of concrete benefits from reading, and the results-oriented language of his columns, is a marked departure from earlier self-culture advocates like Chandler, for whom character work was an unquestioned, and sole, goal for reading the right type of literature. We can see that in his letter to Mrs. E. D. North, which I cited above, Mabie indeed felt the pressure to maintain this focus on character. Mindful of his audience in the *Journal*, though, Mabie always validates the book which will give pleasure; he cautions that "it is a mistake to make reading a task, because much of the benefit which flows from coming in contact with another's thought or writing is received only when the whole mind can be surrendered to another" (January 1904, 17). Such support of a reader's thrall to the text comes in marked contrast to the earlier reading manuals, where, particularly in the case of female readers, the idea that the text could enthrall one, or take one out of oneself, or offer an attractive alternative to one's reality, was a primary danger of reading.[41] Warnings against the dangers of the wrong type of novel reading were still common at the time that Mabie was advising his readers to give in to such pleasures, especially in the pages of the more elite magazines. In 1898, in the pages of *Arena*, George Clarke (whose Ph.D. is prominently displayed in his byline) warns that "the power which we have of sympathizing with others in their ambitions, joys, and sorrows—that gift of the imagination by which we are enabled to contemplate the careers of others with a personal interest by identifying ourselves for the moment with them—supplies us with a means of obtaining a sort of happiness by proxy, while our own attitude is entirely passive."[42] Recall though that Mabie also asserted that through reading "[true readers] not only escape from themselves, but they also come into possession of themselves." Apparently, "the whole mind surrendered to another" meant not a loss of the self but a potential profit to the self—a paradox that answers his audience's simultaneous clamoring for profit and escapism and marks the influence of mass desires on the reading adviser. Rather than attempt to swim against the current of his readers' desires, Mabie embraced the idea of sympathetic surrender and worked to redirect it towards a different type of book. While William Dean Howells, the "Dean of American Letters," in 1899 condemned "[b]y far the greatest number of people in the world, even the civilized world," as "people of weak and childish imagination, pleased with gross fables, fond of prodigies, heroes, heroines, portents and impracticalities, without self-knowledge, and without the wish for it,"[43] Mabie would applaud the reading public in 1904 for having begun to select better books, noting that "[t]he novels which have attained to very wide popularity, and the sales of which have been sensationally advertised during the last few years, have been for the most part well worth reading" (March 1904, 16). There was a lot at stake for Mabie in congratulating and accommodating his large upwardly mobile audience, because this group paid for his cultural labor and, ultimately, kept the literary world relevant and solvent. A portion of a 1905 column, appearing under the repeatedly used generic catchall title "Mr. Mabie Tells about the Books," places the several motivations driving Mabie and his readers in close communication:

> Every one who becomes a true reader of books becomes a buyer of books as well, for it is impossible to love books without desiring to possess them. . . . There is a truer romance, however, than that of collecting books because they are rare or have personal associa-tions: the romance of collecting books because they are loved, and collecting them as a result of rigid economy and self-denial. . . . The family which is slowly accumulating a little library is always a ris-ing family. (January 1905, 20)

The "true" reader, also a romantic, falls under an utterly valid if not-yet-nuanced consumerist longing. With enlightenment, this possessiveness becomes anticonsumerist self-denial, and all of this works in the service of ineffable upward mobility. Is it any surprise that the members of a "rising family," or a family that wants to be such, should read this pas-sage and others like it as road maps for mobility, drawn in by identifica-tion with the discussion of "romance" that preceded it? Or then that the library, while it may consist of realist works purchased under Mabie's tutelage, would be read regardless of authorial intent as an extension of the romantic project? We must consider this as a distinct possibility, since much of the impetus to read such books—even if they were not to be "read for realism"[44]—came from popularizers like Mabie who cannily adapted a new reading list to their audience's older, and persistent, read-ing practices.

2 / The Compromise of *Silas Lapham*

The limitations of his work are also the limitations of his insight and his imagination, and this fact, fully understood in all its bearings, makes any effort to point out those limitations ungracious in appearance and distasteful in performance; if personal feeling were to control such matters, one would content himself with an expression of hearty admiration for work so full of character, and of sincere gratitude for a delicate intellectual pleasure so varied and so sustained.
—HAMILTON WRIGHT MABIE, "A TYPICAL NOVEL" (1885)

Hamilton Wright Mabie's 1885 review of *The Rise of Silas Lapham* could be used as a primer for the art of the patronizing backhanded compliment. Writing in the genteel *Andover Review*, Mabie praises William Dean Howells faintly for his "evident fidelity to a constantly advancing ideal of workmanship," for his "earnestness," and for his "exacting conscientiousness," then goes on to suggest that writing a truly substantial book may simply be beyond Howells's reach. "If he has failed to touch the deepest issues, and to lay bare the more obscure and subtle movements of passion and purpose, it has been through no intellectual willfulness or lassitude; he has patiently and unweariedly followed such clews as he has been able to discover, and he has resolutely held himself open to the claims of new themes and the revelations of fresh contacts with life." Howells holds himself back in one essential particular, and this, Mabie diagnoses, is the cause of his novel's "failure": "Mr. Howells never identifies himself with his characters, never becomes one with them in the vital fellowship and communion of the imagination; he constructs them with infinite patience and skill, but he never, for a moment, loses consciousness of his own individuality." Howells has not been closed-minded, writes Mabie, but he lacks the ability to capitalize on his efforts because he remains too personally distanced from his characters. Bemoaning the waste of literary effort and potential on "commonplace" and un-Ideal subjects, Mabie finally argues that Howells's failings are endemic to realist literary projects and indicts the entire mode for "its hardness, its lack of vitality, its paralysis of the finer feelings and higher aspirations, its fundamental defect on the side of the imagination."[1]

Mabie's review has become a frequently cited episode of literary history, with Mabie cast as the standard-bearer for exhausted romantics waging a futile war against the newer, more vigorous realism.[2] But Frank Norris was already terming Howells's novels "respectable as a church and proper as a deacon" in 1901, and Howells's reputation would get closer to Mabie's during the ascendance of literary "modernism" in the 1920s and 1930s. In these decades, Mabie and Howells were most frequently classed together as "genteel critics," in George Santayana's resonant phrase; for example, in his 1930 Nobel Prize lecture, Sinclair Lewis ridiculed Howells as "a pious old maid whose greatest delight was to have tea at the vicarage."[3] By 1937, Malcolm Cowley was sure enough of Howells's gentility to register ironic surprise that a reference to dynamite in the manuscript of *Lapham* had been censored by the *Century* magazine, a bastion of gentility: "Even William Dean Howells sometimes failed to meet [*Century* editor Richard Watson Gilder's] schoolmistressly standards."[4] Howells and Mabie could even be mentioned in the same dismissive breath, as in Burton Rascoe's summation that "the literature controlled, acknowledged and accepted by the Gilders, Henry Mills Aldens, the Hamilton Wright Mabies and the Howellses was prim, desiccated, proper and puritanical."[5]

In short, the classification of Mabie and Howells as either diametric opposites or brothers under the skin depends more on literary-political maneuvering than on clearly delineated ideological differences. The result is in part a function of the workings of literary history, and the ways that the writers of such histories are themselves jockeying for aesthetic positions. But it is also because Mabie and Howells are slippery targets, both of them astonishingly prolific and culturally ubiquitous over the course of lengthy careers. Both were canny businessmen of letters, appearing in highbrow and mass-market media as the need arose, and both were willing to accommodate the requirements of their various audiences. This perspective is lost when we look just at their writings in the pages of literary magazines like the *Atlantic Monthly* or the *Outlook*, or when we focus on novels and critical pieces published in book form without considering their initial appearance as serials in magazines like the *Ladies' Home Journal*. When we investigate the Howells-Mabie relationship through the lens of both men's involvement with the *Journal*, we can see that the requirements of the mass audience trumped any previously staked ideological claims. In the pages of the *Journal*, a periodical that both constructed and reflected a popular aesthetic zeitgeist, realism became a literary brand, and desirable cultural capital. Particular texts and authors acquired status by their association with the realist label. But this supposed "realism" actually looked a lot like "sentiment" or "romance"—categories which, like "realism," became evacuated of any ideological underpinnings and became labels used primarily to signal literature that was comfortable, moral, or reassuring. And in the pages of the *Journal*, both Mabie and Howells came to validate the aesthetics and reading practices of the traditions they had repudiated in other venues.

Howells was not a victim of this compromise but was a willing participant whose appearance in the *Journal* in the 1890s solidified his status as an author and critic of note, bolstered the magazine's literary credentials, and gave *Journal* readers the chance to say they had read their Howells. Ten years later, Howells's *The Rise of Silas Lapham* would be second only to Thackeray's *Vanity Fair* in the number of recommendations in Mabie's *Journal* columns. After establishing the ways that Howells was branded as cultural capital in the pages of the *Journal*, and identifying the openings he himself left for "reading up" readers, we can see how easy it is for Mabie's favorite Howells novels—*Lapham, The Lady of the Aroostook,* and *A Hazard of New Fortunes*—to serve as the accidental conduits for a host of unintended messages.

The *Journal* and the Dean I: *The Coast of Bohemia*

Edward Bok, the editor of the *Ladies' Home Journal*, was not generally inclined towards humility; his plans for the *Journal* were grandiose, and by the 1890s he had the means to pursue them. Though he was the editor of a magazine that appeared to be solely focused on homemaking and fashion, his goal, as he describes it in his autobiography, was that of "putting into the field of American magazines a periodical that should become such a clearinghouse as virtually to make it an institution."[6] Once he felt satisfied that his advice columnists had done this work in the domestic departments, it was time to "give . . . his magazine the literary quality it needed" and to do so by usurping the rights of more-established literary periodicals to big-name authors. "The two authors of that day who commanded more attention than any others were William Dean Howells and Rudyard Kipling," Bok contends, so naturally he pursued their works for his magazine. Writing in the third person, Bok describes the acquisitional legerdemain—or perhaps more accurately, espionage—he employed in securing back-to-back Howells serials:

[Bok] bought Mr. Howells's new novel, "The Coast of Bohemia," and arranged that Kipling's new novelette upon which he was working should come to the magazine. Neither the public nor the magazine editors had expected Bok to break out along these more permanent lines, and magazine publishers began to realize a new competitor had sprung up in Philadelphia. Bok knew they would feel this; so before he announced Mr. Howells's new novel, he contracted with the novelist to follow this with his autobiography. This surprised the editors of the older magazines, for they realized that the Philadelphia editor had completely tied up the leading novelist of the day for his next two years' output.[7]

It was a publishing ambush and, at least in Bok's retrospective version of events, an important moment in the *Journal*'s quest for literary respectability, even if the signing of the contracts mattered more than the actual content of Howells's pieces. Bok notes that Howells's ability to confer legitimacy on the *Journal* made his large advances worthwhile in the mind of the magazine's publisher, Cyrus Curtis, whose chief concern was advertising opportunity and revenue. "[Bok] paid Mr. Howells $10,000 for his autobiography, and Mr. Curtis spent $50,000 in advertising it. 'It is not an expense,' he would explain to Bok, 'it is an investment. We are investing in a trade-mark. It will all come back in time.'"[8] In combination with the $5,000 payment for *Coast*, the *Journal* was paying dearly for the chance to attract big-money advertisers; Curtis began using Howells's name while courting advertisers as soon as the ink was dry on these contracts.[9] The *Atlantic* and its ilk rarely committed such sums, nor could they command such an audience for Howells; in the pages of the *Journal*, he would be able to reach nearly a million subscribers.[10] For a man committed to "raising the tone of American life through literature," the opportunity to offer a literary autobiography to this audience would have been attractive in and of itself; the size of the advances also, doubtless, contributed their blandishments.[11]

Thus it was that, from December 1892 through March 1895, the *Ladies' Home Journal* would be able to deliver to its readers and advertisers the work of William Dean Howells. While the *Journal* serialized material representing both arenas of Howells's literary production—his literary critical work and his fictional work—it is important to note that Bok's interest in Howells did not extend to an embrace of either Howellsian realism or Howellsian notions of "proper" reading. Howells is a brand for Bok, and for Curtis; he helps burnish the *Journal*'s "trade-mark."

The Howells texts' substance is, in the final analysis, less important than their sheer presence, and this relative lack of concern about substance can go far to explain any of the apparent contradictions we see between the *Journal*'s editorial stances and the things that appear in Howells. As we have already seen in chapter 1, the *Journal* was more eclectic than monolithic, a posture guided by the necessity of appealing to a broad swath of the American population. Howells's texts are part of that eclecticism, though the paratextual presentation of the two serials also works to control the reception of both, acknowledging and ensuring that the reader of Howells remains first and foremost a reader of the *Journal*.

The three years of Howellsian homage began with fiction, in the form of the serialization of *The Coast of Bohemia*, whose rather conventional romance plot was set against a gentle critique of the contemporaneous New York art scene. While there is a good deal of subtle criticism of the position of women in the art world in *Coast*, the romance plot, bolstered by insistent accompanying illustrations, no doubt took precedence for the *Journal* readership. Cornelia and Ludlow "meet-cute" amid artistic atrocities at a midwestern county fair; she is a provincial girl with cosmopolitan potential, he an aesthete-in-training newly returned from a pilgrimage to France. We know Ludlow and Cornelia are meant for each other by the way he praises her talent faintly ("Nothing is commoner than the talent and beauty of American girls. But they'd better trust to their beauty") and the way she determines to correct his misperceptions ("It would be fun to show him, some day, that even so low down a creature as a girl could be something").[12] Cornelia's spunkiness and Ludlow's offhand recommendation land her in New York at an artists' academy, where she becomes friends with the novel's comic relief, the wealthy art-dabbler Charmian Maybough. Cornelia has more raw talent than Ludlow, who is stymied by overthinking both his technique and his choice of subject, and this conflict nearly renders their relationship untenable. But despite a misunderstanding over the reemergence of an erstwhile suitor of Cornelia's in the penultimate installment, we open the October 1893 issue relieved to see a huge illustration of Cornelia and Ludlow in wedding garb, exiting a church, over the caption "They were married at Pymantoning." In the two-column denouement, we learn that while Ludlow tries halfheartedly to support Cornelia's artistic career after the wedding, he is no more successful than he was before. He outwardly claims that "she had the rarer gift," but Cornelia is not convinced of his performance. Little wonder, since he spends much of his time inserting himself into her work:

He painted passages and incidents in her pictures, sometimes illustratively, and sometimes for the pleasure of having their lives blended in their work, and he tried to see how nearly he could lose his work in hers. He pretended that he learned more than he taught in the process, and that he felt in her efforts a determining force, a clear sense of what she wanted to do that gave positive form and direction to what was vague and speculative in himself.[13]

Cornelia's voice, which has been dominant throughout the novella, essentially disappears in the denouement, just as her image disappears into a clump of hollyhocks in Ludlow's new, critically panned painting. "It was probably intended to express a moment of electric passion; but there was something so forced, and at the same time so ineffectual in the execution of the feebly fantastic design, that it became the duty of impartial criticism to advise Mr. Ludlow, if he must continue to paint at all, to paint either girls or flowers, but not both at once, nor both together, nor convertibly."[14] Cornelia, whose aesthetic sensibilities are impeccable, had not wanted Ludlow to show the painting, but "here, as often elsewhere, she found him helpless to yield to her, even though he confessed that she was right." By the last paragraphs of the story, he is answering for her at a dinner, and Cornelia has been effectively subsumed into marriage. The final words of the piece are Charmian's, as she laments that "now, I'm afraid [Cornelia's] going to be perfectly respectable."[15] Like Henrietta Stackpole's final assessment of Isabel Archer at the end of *The Portrait of a Lady*, Charmian's evaluation is an imperfect attempt to cinch the ending of the novel, to allay the distresses of any readers who mourn the suppression of certain aspects of a sympathetic heroine's character. And as we shall see in the case of *Portrait*, this benediction can serve a compensatory function for that dissatisfied reader; Charmian remains single, vocal, and artistically productive, and if the moments of the text in which Howells undermines her as a potential heroine may be overlooked, she can serve as an alternative heroine. Indeed, in *William Dean Howells: A Critical Study* (1922), Delmar Gross Cooke contends that Charmian is "the one fundamentally well-balanced and clear-sighted character in the novel," this at the same time that he cites the way she "cleverly arranges her studio . . . with a low-hung canvas ceiling to simulate poverty." Focusing on Charmian's "innate common sense, which Howells conceals from the reader as artfully as she conceals it from herself," Cooke is able to salvage the novel from a critique that would find it a plebian, or philistine, failure because of the "foolish tragedy of Cornelia." Charmian,

Cooke asserts, "is constantly saving the aberrant natures surrounding her from lapsing into vapidity"—the novel is therefore not about the triumph of the marriage plot but about the salvation of Charmian from such a quotidian fate.[16]

The novel's availability for alternate readings renders *The Coast of Bohemia* in many ways a perfect *Ladies' Home Journal* fiction piece. There may have been some readers who, with Cooke, recentered their readings on Charmian after the conventional marriage ending, but it is more likely that the marriage would have been embraced by the *Journal* audience. The illustrations that accompany each installment work to reinforce the romance plot as the central concern of the text; even scenes that are written as triptychs, such as a scene in which Cornelia, Charmian, and Ludlow have a snack in Charmian's studio, are illustrated as tête-à-têtes between Ludlow and Cornelia, Charmian receding into the shadows on the side of the image.[17] The reader who is guided by such images would probably find the novel's ultimate reinscription of the normative middle-class marriage with its standard gender roles reassuring. While our heroine, Cornelia, is spunky and talented, she is also an active participant in the marriage market throughout the novel and is focused on her social life as much as she is on her artistic career. As such, she is a prototypical *Journal* heroine, offering some vicarious rebellion to the middle-class reader, but ultimately validating her own position in a stable, standard marriage plot.

The novel's domestication of an ostensibly exotic segment of society is likewise a customary *Journal* move. While the characters are artists, they are genteel artists, with sufficient financial resources, who embrace bohemia as an aesthetic pose rather than a true lifestyle. Howells plays this for laughs, as in an extended passage where Charmian struggles against her mother's dictum that, while it need not be tidied, her studio should be dusted every morning ("But don't you see, mamma, that if you have it regularly dusted, it can never have any sentiment, any atmosphere?"); chokes on a cigar which she decides to smoke though its previous purpose had been purely decorative (Ludlow subsequently compliments her on her "perfect pallor"); and attempts to find the perfectly bohemian snack to accompany afternoon tea prepared over a spirit lamp (the winner: popcorn served in an overturned Japanese shield).[18] The potential edgy artistic threat of bohemia is thoroughly undercut by these silly scenes, in which even the more "legitimized" artist, Ludlow, emerges as ridiculous. And while Howells will occasionally suggest that there is a "true" bohemia whose artistic lifestyle is genuinely felt, not a pose, the

Journal audience may certainly leave Howells's text with the sense that all bohemian gestures are, indeed, ridiculous, that all "bohemians" are just playing at aesthetic superiority and edginess. This notion would no doubt be comforting for the *Journal* reader, particularly one removed from even the "coast" of bohemia, whose interests in the precincts of culture were sincere but unalloyed with a sense of either security or authority, as evidenced by the tone of numerous *Journal* articles explaining the significance of various works of art.

Alongside Jonathan R. Eller, we may contend, then, that "*The Coast of Bohemia* . . . proved that Howells could write fiction for and about genteel American women."[19] For any *Journal* reader still hesitant about Howells because of his reputation as a hard-line realist, it would have been reassuring, perhaps even functioning as a gateway novel to the more canonical of Howells's productions. And for any *Journal* reader unclear as to what titles would belong in this category, the first issue after the conclusion of *The Coast of Bohemia* would obligingly include a list in the introduction to *My Literary Passions*.

The *Journal* and the Dean II: *My Literary Passions*

In November 1893, the *Journal* prefaced the serialization of *My Literary Passions* with a brief biography by Howells's close friend and realist coreligionist Hjalmar Hjorth Boyeson. As a project in branding, the essay is exemplary; it works to reconstruct Howells, elite proponent of realism, as Howells, family man and avuncular guide to the kind of reading that can make one a success in life. The piece takes up two four-column pages and is generously illustrated with a large portrait of Howells (the "most recent" one, "considered by him to be the most satisfactory one extant"), a photograph of the man at work, and a rough sketch of the humble exterior of his midwestern birthplace.[20] These pictures are not only visual markers of the important components of Howells's life—humble birth to lavish success—but the captions also lay claim to Howells's time, and render him a product to be consumed exclusively by the *Journal* audience. Howells sat in his study, on a particular day and at a particular time, to have his portrait "taken specially for the *Journal* while writing his autobiographical papers for this magazine." The *Journal* audience would not, then, be a group of outsiders accidentally encountering a work that was literarily out of their range; Howells, the man of letters, had indeed written *My Literary Passions* expressly for them. It is a flattering notion, for the reader, and a self-congratulatory move on the part of the *Journal*, and yet another component of the branding of Howells taking place in the biography that accompanies the pictures.

Boyeson's biography covers primarily the period of Howells's life before he became editor of the *Atlantic Monthly*, tracing his humble origins and his rise, by dint of hard work and self-sacrifice, through the journalistic ranks. Once it arrives at Howells's East Coast career, the sketch treats his literary production only briefly, with a hasty chronological catalog of his literary output to date. This haste results in some unusual spot assessments of Howells's fiction—*The Rise of Silas Lapham* is "unquestionably the most American novel which an American has ever produced"[21]—but it also signals the fact that Howells was well known to the readers of the *Journal* as one of the most significant authors of the day. Indeed, it was his notoriety that made *My Literary Passions* such a publishing event for the *Journal*, particularly since it was a series explicitly produced for, and in extensive consultation with, the *Journal*'s editor, Edward Bok. In the preface to a 1909 book version of the series, Howells recollects that "the name was thought by the friendly editor of the popular publication where [the chapters] were serialized a main part of such inspiration as they might be conjectured to have, and was, as seldom happens with editor and author, cordially agreed upon before they were begun."[22] Howells had originally proposed to Bok a memoir, titled "My Book Friends," in 1892. Bok offered $4,200 in payment, a sum considerably less than the $5,000 he had recently promised for the publication of *Coast of Bohemia*. When Howells countered with a request for $5,000, Bok agreed, pending the expansion of the text and a reconsideration of the approach.[23] In a letter dated 24 September 1892, Bok gently suggested to Howells,

> I think your idea of the series "My Book Friends" is an excellent one in the main, but, and it is a big "but": I fear that the interest, so far as the public is concerned, would centre & end—that is, practically—, with your reading in the English. It might, in a measure, extend to the French, but when it came to your German, Spanish and Italian reading I am afraid the interest would lag. I know only too well from a close association with the importing department of the Scribners how little interest there is in foreign literature outside the French & the German. . . . In short, the great, popular interest which is so essential to a large success now-a-days—& that is the only kind of success I want to make with anything from your pen— would be, I fear, lacking for the series as a whole.[24]

Bok's focus on the "practical" in this note is telling—his readers were practical people, as he was, with his emphasis on the "large success" he wished for Howells's piece.

Success became the keyword for Bok's approach in the negotiations, in fact; he was doubtlessly already thinking about the way he would brand Howells for his magazine. He continued his letter with a countersuggestion that Howells reframe the series as "My Literary Life" or "My Literary Autobiography," explicitly evoking the popular genre of exemplary biography in his description of the result. "In this you might, of course, tell of your reading, but it would give a wider scope of interest to thousands of the public who are ever absorbed in the course of a successful man's life from its beginning."[25] Bok wanted Howells to present himself as a model of the successful man; the reading was somewhat secondary to Bok's considerations, really a concession to the predilections of his subject. Reading thereby also becomes somewhat antithetical to the "practical" interests of the *Journal* readership, an adjunct to the progress of Howells's career. It will fall to the editorial apparatus, to the Boyeson introduction and the marketing of the series, to reframe reading as the *means* of Howells's success, and therefore in itself a practical activity.

The final discussion of the title seems to have taken place in person, in a meeting proposed by Bok in a letter to Howells dated 1 October 1892. After mentioning two letters he had received from Howells (neither of which has survived), Bok writes, "[I] would like to have a personal talk with you upon this general subject, and I think it will be much easier for us to reach a conclusion than through any quantity of letters . . . in a personal conversation I am sure we can arrange the general scope of the series." Though there is no documentary evidence that the meeting ever took place, Howells's acknowledgment of Bok's role in the selection of the title suggests that Bok was able to carry his point somehow, even before Howells began writing the memoir. As we will see, Howells in his writing did not stick faithfully to Bok's preferences—obscure foreign literature in the original constitutes a good deal of his reminiscence—but the framework of a rags-to-riches story does organize the series and is legible underneath the bildungsroman sensibility of the piece as a whole. In the serialized publication, Howells mentions nearly ninety authors and devotes considerable time to assessing literary movements in general.[26] While there is no explicit charge in the piece to present Howells's reading as a "program" of reading to be followed by others, the avuncular tone of the piece, and its hagiographic framing, makes this implication clear: Howells's reading produced a Howells, so it may presumably behoove any ambitious individual to follow his lead. Lest this portrait look exclusively masculine, Howells also becomes a paragon of domestic virtue in the Boyeson introduction; the female audience of the *Journal* can thereby look to Howells as an exemplar not only for her husband and sons but for herself and her daughters as well.

Boyeson's profile reinforces the notion that *My Literary Passions* belongs in the genre of exemplary autobiography, and even goes so far as to extend this functionality to realist literature as a whole. Its operating assumption is that Howells, from humble and non-eastern origins, had managed to become "the foremost man of letters in the United States who is yet in the active exercise of his talents," occupying this position, at least, "since the death of James Russell Lowell."[27] Howells was therefore, in theory, an ideal literary guide for *Journal* readers, who were likewise not members of the New England literati, and whose families likely resembled Howells's more than Lowell's. The Boyeson piece functions, moreover, to predispose the readers of the *Journal* towards Howells, and perhaps to ameliorate some of the more prickly and self-aggrandizing moments which are in the offing in *My Literary Passions*. Readers are introduced to Howells's stance on realism, for example, via the contention that "mature and cultivated readers" should prefer "a narrative dealing in a vigorous and luminous style with the problems of life which they are themselves daily encountering, and with characters which they recognize as being flesh of their flesh and bone of their bone."[28] Rather than be frightened by the prospect of bleakness in realism, readers might now think of realism as a potential guide to coping with the realities of daily modern life. Realism, in other words, could function like an advice manual, as an exemplary narrative about people like oneself or people one might wish to be like. By suggesting this instrumental reading for realism, Boyeson takes the first step towards the kind of instrumentalism Mabie would fully embrace in his *Journal* columns ten years later.

Boyeson could not make a case for realism in the pages of the mass-market *Journal* without addressing romanticism. Romanticism was, in the 1890s, still more popular than realism, even if realism was generally acknowledged to be the more highbrow literary mode. It is because of his reputation for "hurting the feelings of the admirers of Walter Scott, and bringing down upon his head the wrath of the worshipers of Dickens" that Howells needed such a careful introduction to the readership of the *Journal*. For Boyeson to attack romance directly would be to invite the same kind of counterproductive hostile reaction; he therefore chooses instead a time-honored indirect approach: the appeal to the concerned parental mind. He offers that "the romantic novel, with its hairbreadth escapes and unwholesome excitement" has a deleterious effect on young minds, "distorting their views of life and by so much incapacitating them for the battle with actuality."[29] As we shall see, in *My Literary Passions* Howells will repeatedly discuss his own "passion" for romances, a youthful predilection which apparently did not render him unfit to live in the world. Boyeson's piece, however, is concerned more with preparing the reader to read Howells sympathetically, even at the risk of cognitive dissonance.

The appeal to parents, particularly mothers, continues with a determinedly heartwarming portrait of the Howells family at home. We see Howells's children as young children no older than eleven, wide-eyed, precociously literary, with charmingly childish nicknames. Howells himself appears a doting father, generous with his time, performing the bedtime ritual nightly, and dispensing gentle solace when his children are sad. One can hardly find fault with the man who is the patriarch of this adorable family, in which "the tender and considerate conduct of each toward all made domestic life beautiful, and love found its expression in caresses as naturally as mirth seeks vent in laughter and grief in tears."[30] This description of course might have been excerpted from any number of the sentimental domestic novels or short stories that Howells had delegitimized in his *Harper's* Editor's Study columns, where he rejected sentimentality out of hand and insisted on realism as a corrective to a romanticism grown "effete," "exhausted," and ultimately, overrefined.[31] But again, Boyeson has a clear goal in mind: winning over the *Journal* audience. Given the rest of the magazine's editorial and fictional content, its readers are likely to be more receptive to his subject if his home can be shown as a model of domestic tranquility. And so, Boyeson packages Howells as the angel of the hearth: "I have never seen a more beautiful instance of the spontaneity, the inevitability with which a rich and lovable personality radiates its own genial warmth and light through all relations, the closer as well as the more remote."[32] What better animating spirit to offer literary advice in these pages? And what better model, given the obvious influence of Howells's lifetime of reading clearly on his domestic circle? The Howells family circa 1872 is the closing image of Boyeson's piece; the anachronism of the portrait might not register with the *Journal* reader, an oversight that ultimately works to garner more sympathetic identification with Howells.[33] His daunting authority and gatekeeping function vis-à-vis high-culture literary realism, for the purposes of the *Journal* audience, become secondary to his identity as a family man, even though it is his literary reputation that presumably lends *My Literary Passions* its authority.

Howells begins his series in the spirit of Boyeson's introduction, by effacing his intellectual reputation and instead insisting on the affective quality of his literary experience. He insists in the opening of the first installment that he "shall try not to use authority," touting not the full extent of his reading (which one imagines has been considerable and would therefore be daunting) but rather writing "only of those books, or of those authors that I have felt a genuine passion for."[34] But it does not take long for Howells to turn critical; while he admits to reading, in his boyhood, serialized adventure stories from the newspaper, he cannot resist noting that the name of the author of these stories, Emerson Bennett, "will be strange to polite ears," nor can he resist a parting shot that simultaneously indicts the literature of his youth and promotes his current preferences for literary realism:

> [The stories] must have been bad stuff for the most part, and yet there was something in the author's wish to deal with the annals and legends of his own region that I still respect. They could have taught me nothing of the art which has since employed so great a part of my life but what I should have been the wiser for instantly forgetting, and, in fact, I did forget it all and very thoroughly; but I cannot help smiling to think that these wildly romantic historical novels were the first fiction I willingly read or greatly enjoyed. They were not imaginably the training of a realist, but at that time I should probably have despised realism as hotly as the grown-up children despise it now.[35]

Granted, readers unsympathetic to realism may have avoided Howells's piece in the first place, but Howells is hardly performing outreach by branding any *Journal* reader with ambivalent feelings towards realism a "grown-up child." It is worth noting, too, that *Gulliver's Travels*, initially mentioned as a lead-in to the Bennett stories, has fallen away in Howells's rush to excuse, and then to fairly condemn, his boyhood reading of historical, romantic genre fiction. It is worth noting, by way of comparison, that Mabie will later explain to his *Journal* audience that he comes not to condemn, but to praise, and promises that he will rigorously avoid mentioning any book or author for the purposes of rejecting it. Howells, on the other hand, allows indictment to enter into a work whose title insists on a positive stance, because he has disavowed so many of the "passions" he describes. By the parameters Howells sets for himself—he will discuss the literature for which he has a "passion"—he is required to mention Bennett, but he does so only to suggest that youthful indiscretion can ultimately be overcome and that even an inclination that has found the wrong outlet (like his inclination for regional fidelity) may eventually find the proper channels, to good effect. These rhetorical gymnastics, which are repeated throughout the serial, are the condition of possibility, it seems, for Howells to appear in the pages of the *Journal*.

Howells also seems to have made concessions to the *Journal* audience in his selection of texts to discuss. Of the texts and authors mentioned in *My Literary Passions*, the majority would in fact be considered "romantic" as opposed to "realist." Rather than validate the romance, however, Howells evokes these texts ultimately to criticize their romantic content. He spends considerable time excusing his youthful reading that seems inconsistent with his eventual preference for realist literature, finding in even the most avowedly romantic texts the roots of his realist inclinations and taking every opportunity to make pointed asides about realism's critics. When discussing Shakespeare, he states: "In those early days I had no philosophical preference for reality in literature, and I dare say if I had been asked, I should have said that the plays of Shakespeare where reality is the least felt were the more imaginative; that is the belief of the puerile critics still; but I suppose it was my instinctive liking for reality that made the great Histories so delightful to me, and that rendered Macbeth and Hamlet vital in their very ghosts and witches."[36] Of Thackeray, he notes: "I reveled in the romanticism of Henry Esmond, with its pseudo-eighteenth-century sentiment, and its appeals to an overwrought ideal of gentlemanhood and honor."[37] Regarding Ik Marvel, on the other hand, Howells is surprisingly unapologetic, describing a very romantic scene of reading to go along with a sentimental text: "The book is associated especially in my mind with one golden day of Indian summer, when I carried it into the woods with me, and abandoned myself to a welter of emotion over its page. I lay under a crimson maple, and I remember how the light striking through it flushed the print with the guiles of the foliage."[38] Unlike the newspaper adventure story, this Thoreauvian sylvan idyll is never even remotely repudiated by Howells, who seems unembarrassed in joining at least a million other nineteenth-century readers who entered into the "detached intimacy" offered by Marvel.[39] When Howells narrates his revelatory reading of Heinrich Heine, he takes another swipe at his critical opponents, "a great many children supposed to be grown-up," who have remained partisans of the romance into their adulthood.[40]

Howells spends a good deal of his time detailing his youthful attraction to Spanish literature, an interest initially spurred by his love of *Don Quixote*. In the August 1894 installment, for example, he describes writing away to specialty booksellers in New York to purchase more Spanish literature: "I dare say that my letters were sufficiently pedantic, and filled with a simulated acquaintance with all Spanish literature. Heaven knows what they must have thought, if they thought anything, of their queer customer in that obscure little Ohio village; but he could not have been queerer to them than to his fellow-villagers, I am sure."[41] Howells then describes, with purple prose that seems at once ironic, and then perhaps not so much so, the fervid scenes of reading that ensued once his books arrived from New York: "The paper and ink had a certain odor which was sweeter to me than the perfumes of Araby. The look of the type took me more than the glance of a girl, and I had a fever of longing to know the heart of the book, which was like a lover's passion." Howells offers equally torrid descriptions of his work translating and reading the poetry of Heine: "It seemed to me the make of a highly intellectual orgy, and I should be glad if I could enjoy anything as much now."[42] Howells takes the charge to write about his "passions" seriously, and perhaps a bit literally, and the result tends towards the hermetic and, indeed, the onanistic. The text is sometimes uncomfortably confessional, and certainly tests the limits of the *Journal*'s customary propriety. Howells indulges even as he contends forcefully for the expurgation of some literary texts, hoping "that what is lewd and ribald in the great poets shall be left out of such editions as are meant for general reading, and that the pedant-pride which now perpetuates it as an essential part of those poets will no longer have its way."[43] He can be even blunter, in fact: "The filthy thought lives with the filthy rhyme in the ear, even when it does not corrupt the heart or make it seem a light thing for the reader's tongue and pen to sin in kind."[44]

Howells does resist some of the requirements of the *Journal* readership by promoting serendipitous and leisured reading. Such casualness is the antithesis of the reading plans that will later form a part of Mabie's columns and that even accompanied *My Literary Passions* in the pages of the *Journal*. This cavalier attitude ultimately works to preserve a degree of Howellsian mystique; his reading practices should not be too accessible, or anyone could become a cultural arbiter for him- or herself. In the February 1894 installment, for example, Howells adamantly tells readers: "The book which you read from a sense of duty, or because for any reason you must, does not make friends with you."[45] He admits that, while such a book may "yield you an unexpected delight," it is only because the book is too strong not to impress even the most unworthy of minds. Even more deadly to Howells's reading experience has been the reading of books for review, because this was self-interested reading:

> I have usually been aware that the book was subtly withholding from me the best a book can give, since I was not reading it for its own sake and because I loved it, but for selfish ends of my own, and because I wished to possess myself of it for business purposes, as it were. The reading that does one good, and lasting good, is the reading that one does for pleasure, and simply and unselfishly, as children do. Art will still withhold herself from thrift, and she does well, for nothing but love has any right to her.[4]

Though Howells cannot expect that his *Journal* audience will ever read books for formal review, he likens such reading to the systematic reading programs of clubs or of reading manuals. The "profit" motive, construed both literally and figuratively here (one presumes he was being paid for those reviews) taints the reading experience and prevents the full realization of reading's benefits. Choosing instead to talk of the "lasting good" that can come of reading, Howells disingenuously suggests that his readers could avoid "tainted" reading by approaching books innocently—but of course no reader of his would be able to do so, having read the great man's opinion of those books. This insistence is not only out of touch with his audience's position as readers of *his* text; it is also out of touch with the likely position of his audience with respect to both finances and leisure time. Howells is not quite a literary popularizer, though he has been placed in that position by the framing of his serial in the *Journal*; this role would not be filled until Mabie joined the magazine in 1902.

One imagines, for example, that Howells would have had mixed feelings about the programs of study that had just been promoted by J. Macdonald Oxley's "Literary Improvement Clubs" in the *Journal* for January 1894. In this article, Oxley offers for reading groups four possible formats that will be "both interesting and profitable," all of which run directly counter to Howells's cautions against dutiful and self-interested reading. In one of Oxley's models, for example, the organizer of the society would assign each member a different representative work by one author for presentation to the whole circle. This is an efficient way, Oxley notes, of helping each member determine "whether or not [the author under investigation] is an author to be cultivated," one tailor-made for busy modern readers.

To busy men and women many of the most promising authors of
the day are little more than names met with from time to time
in the papers or magazines. They know nothing of their relative
worth, and think they have not time to find out for themselves.
Now if they would join a reading circle, and, taking for granted that
the standard authors, the Hawthornes, Scotts, Thackerays, Coo-
pers, Tennysons and Poes, are already sufficiently known, would
confine their attention to living authors, they would inevitably
find their range of literary vision wonderfully widened, and would
soon be able to step surely where otherwise they would not dare to
venture.[47]

There would need to be strict guidelines for the club, Oxley notes, particularly with regard to time; the members should arrive at each meeting
promptly, and each work should be discussed in no more than twenty
minutes. The presentations should be completed by ten o'clock to allow
ample time for discussion. If the twenty-minute rule is not followed, Oxley warns, "non-adherence thereto may shipwreck the circle"; to avoid
such disaster, a timekeeper should be appointed. Finally, Oxley genteelly
suggests, "no member should feel bound to point out flaws when really
there is not sufficient time to indicate all the excellences." Interestingly
enough, and probably not coincidentally, given the *Journal*'s preoccupation with Howells in 1894, Oxley suggests that Howells be one possible
subject for such a club, provided that all of the genres in which he has
worked are adequately covered by the readers. Oxley's officious tone runs
directly counter to Howells's asserted objections to reading programs,
but the format of *My Literary Passions* has already undercut Howells's
ideal of leisured, peripatetic reading. The very presence of Howells's literary autobiography, likewise, belies his stated objections to self-interested
reading, or reading for "profit." The cautions against dutiful reading
need not, then, pose an insurmountable contradiction for the *Journal*
reader; indeed, the genteel, disinterested ideal could easily be preserved
in the midst of "dutiful" practice.

Howells's text contains other genteel remnants, which are likewise
maintained side by side with their opposing practices. The idea of a
"friendship" with books seems to have been at the center of Howells's
thoughts from his initial conception of the project, which he had originally proposed to Bok as "My Book Friends."[48] It is somewhat surprising
coming from Howells, who, in his fiction, worked towards the elision
of the authorial voice in the text, as did other realist novelists. Barbara

Hochman has shown that the desire to "get at the author" was persistent with late-nineteenth and early twentieth-century audiences despite realist authors' attempts to flee such scrutiny, and, as we shall see, Mabie validated his readers' desires to think of their reading as a "conversation" with the author.[49] But it would be a mistake to see Howells's references to friendly reading as a capitulation to his *Journal* audiences' perceived desires; he is, rather, setting up such reading as a complement to his more explicit rejections of romanticism. In his discussion of Shakespeare, for example, Howells draws an interesting distinction between befriending a character within the pages of a book and thinking one might be friends with a real-life manifestation of that character. Howells fancies his sixteen-year-old self uniquely appreciative of Falstaff, contending that he "fully conceived of Falstaff's character, and entered into the author's wonderfully humorous conception of him." At the same time, he is compelled to note that "[a]s to Falstaff personally, or his like, I was rather fastidious, and would not have made friends with him in the flesh, much or little."[50] It seems a little unusual to need to contend that one would not be friends with Falstaffian figures in "real life," but one might begin to understand this as an adjunct to Howells's gradual decoupling of the personal author from the text. So, for example, while Howells had held a "fancied converse" with many of the authors he mentions, he does not do so with Hawthorne, in part because "Hawthorne himself seemed a remote and impalpable agency, rather than a person whom one might actually meet," though Howells did in fact end up meeting him in person.[51]

The first twelve installments of the series proceed in this vein, leaving the impression more of a literary cautionary tale than of an exemplary literary biography. It turns out that most of these "passions," while important to Howells in his youth, remain significant largely insofar as he has grown through and then beyond them. Little wonder, then, that in the December 1894 display advertisement of coming attractions for the following year (an annual feature in the *Journal*), readers are promised that "Mr. Howells' Literary Autobiography will continue through a portion of the year and increase in charm and interest as he reaches the reading of contemporary authors whose books are now in everyone's hands."[52] Had *Journal* readers expressed to the editors that they were neither charmed by Howells's attacks on his critics nor interested in the vagaries of obtaining Spanish literature in the original? The marketing department must have at least discerned these reactions as distinct possibilities. This difficulty was of course anticipated by Bok in his negotiations with Howells for the series. Bok did not win this editorial battle, but one imagines that he knew his audience well and that there was indeed waning interest in Howells's "passions" for obscure literature in the original language.

While the *Journal's* circulation continued to increase during the serialization of *My Literary Passions*, it would be difficult to attribute causality to Howells's memoir as opposed to, for example, the ongoing series "Wives of Famous Pastors." And while Howells does wax more contemporary in the final three installments of *My Literary Passions*, the overall tone of the piece remains the same. In the penultimate installment, for example, Howells offers what he confesses are embarrassing admissions about great works of literature he has not read or did not read until quite late in his career:

> Long after I had thought never to read it—in fact when I was *nel mezzo del commin di nostra vita*—I read Milton's Paradise Lost, and found in it a splendor and majestic beauty that justified the fame it wears, and eclipsed the worth of those lesser poems which I had always stupidly and ignorantly accounted his worthiest. In fact it was one of the literary passions of the time I speak of, and it shared my devotion for the novels of Tourguénief and (shall I own it?) the romances of Cherbuliez. After all, it is best to be honest, and if it is not best, it is at least easiest; it involves the fewest embarrassing consequences; and if I confess the spell that the Revenge of Joseph Noirel cast upon me for a time, perhaps I shall be able to whisper to the reader behind my hand that I have never yet read the Aeneid of Virgil; the Georgics, yes; but the Aeneid, no.[53]

This oddly fastidious and embarrassed confession about having read and enjoyed a French dime novel functions as an entrée to the even greater admission that he has never read Virgil's epic. It is as if Howells is trying to gain credibility with his less-sophisticated readers, as just another one of the many who enjoys trashy novels and who has not read Virgil's masterpiece, but he cannot stomach the result. Not only does he introduce the move with an unattributed citation in Italian (easily recognizable to his *Atlantic* audiences, but perhaps less so to *Journal* readers), he quickly and almost compulsively identifies himself as an elite reader again by telling his audience that he has read Virgil's didactic *Georgics*—the more "realistic" poems, as opposed to his more romantic eclogues. The end result is hardly the portrait of a man of the people. As an adviser his moves are equally clunky; he elevates *Paradise Lost* only at the expense of other Milton poetry such as, perhaps, "Il Penseroso" or the "Ode on Christ's

Nativity," the only two Milton works that would be recommended by Mabie. Ultimately, Howells is tone-deaf when it comes to his *Journal* audience, even when he is trying to assert his camaraderie with them.

There are finally two problems with Howells as a reading advisor: his reading is far too exclusive, too narrowly literary and intellectual, for the broad audience of the *Journal*, and his tone is too smug, prescriptive even when it means to be descriptive. He is less like the benevolent Tom Corey of *The Rise of Silas Lapham*, moderating his advice to fit the needs of his striving audience, than he is like Tom's father, Bromfield Corey, obsessed with arcane foreign literature and self-congratulatory when it comes to his disapproving reconsiderations of texts that he had enjoyed once in his youth. He discusses frequently literature that he considers "unmeet for ladies," hardly a useful strategy when writing for an audience primarily (though not entirely) female.[54] Bok reminisces that Howells once asked him "how he classified his audience"—perhaps in preparation for *My Literary Passions*, but the context is unspecified—and that Bok replied, "We appeal to the intelligent American woman rather than to the intellectual type."[55] Presumably Howells then knew to whom he was speaking, but he chose to pursue the "passion" side of the title, producing an inwardly focused bildungsroman rather than Bok's preferred model of the exemplary biography.

One wonders, then, what the *Journal* audience was supposed to have gotten from the serial as Howells finally constructed it; why would a famous author's youthful reading be of any interest unless it was somehow considered a reputable counsel for themselves or, at the very least, for their sons. There is some indication that the series may have been reaching a receptive audience, for at the close of the October 1894 installment a notice is appended that readers sending $1.00 will be sent all of the *Journal*'s back issues containing *My Literary Passions*. But this may well have been "nudge" marketing; the prompt to readers in December suggests audience disaffection equally strongly. While Howells was a paragon, he was not a workable model, and his advice far exceeded the *Journal* audience's capacity to follow it. Hamilton Wright Mabie's advice, on the other hand, would be distinctly anti-exemplary; he would offer suggestions, and opinions, but never prescriptions, and as we shall see, this approach seems to have been one of the keys to his success in the pages of the *Journal*. Mabie never recommends that his readers locate *My Literary Passions*, nor does he ever mention *The Coast of Bohemia*. These two Howells texts were not "must reads" for *Journal* audiences after all— the novel neither significant enough nor entertaining enough, and the literary memoir too critical. Instead, Mabie would come to embrace the novel he is now so famous for maligning—*The Rise of Silas Lapham*—and two other Howells novels, from different ends of the Howells spectrum: *The Lady of the Aroostook* and *A Hazard of New Fortunes*. His embrace of these titles is a function of their capacity to be read either as diverting romances or as cautionary tales for the upwardly mobile, as guides, like Mabie's columns, to the cultural milieu of the successful. And they, more than Howells's literary autobiography, would be "practically" interesting to the *Journal* readership.

Lapham Revisited

In his 1885 review of *The Rise of Silas Lapham* in the *Andover Review*, Mabie finally found that the novel, along with James's *Bostonians*, had "no throb of life . . . the pulse of feeling, if it beats at all, is imperceptible; and of the free and joyous play of that supreme force which we call genius there is absolutely not one gleam."[56] And yet by the time he was offering advice in the *Journal*, Mabie would contend that "[i]t may be taken for granted that anything which Mr. Cable, Mr. Howells, Mr. Allen, Mr. Page, Miss Jewett or Miss Wilkins is willing to put before the public will be worth serious attention, though even the best writers sometimes nod" (June 1902, 17). Mabie did not just embrace Howells in a general sense; he seems, by 1902, to have reconsidered his hesitations about *Lapham* in particular. *Lapham* appears in a 1903 list of "all the earlier [American] novelists or short-story writers whose work has permanent value . . . [and] the foremost later writers," along with Howells's *The Lady of the Aroostock* and *A Hazard of New Fortunes* (March 1903, 17). It is also among the selections in the American literature list in his "Courses of Reading for Summer Moods" (July 1903); in "A Short Course in Fiction," alongside *The House of the Seven Gables*, Thomas Nelson Page's *Red Rock*, *David Copperfield*, and *The Portrait of a Lady* (October 1908); in "Novels Descriptive of American Life," as one of thirty-eight titles (November 1908); and in both the "Novels of Character Study" list and, with *The Bostonians* and Wharton's *The House of Mirth*, in the "Novels of Realism" list (September 1909). In November 1911, Mabie classes *Lapham* with *Treasure Island*, *Old Creole Days*, and *Barchester Towers* as a novel that will probably join *Vanity Fair* and *Ivanhoe*, among others, as perennial popular favorites in libraries. In all, Mabie recommends *Lapham* more than any other single novel besides Thackeray's *Vanity Fair* over the ten-year span of his columns for the *Journal* (see appendix

A). While it is impossible to know with any certainty the reasons for Mabie's changing opinions, it is clear that, even if Mabie had not revised his aesthetic assessment of *Lapham* and other realist offerings, he now felt they were novels that belonged on lists directed towards the reader longing for self-culture, as groups of novels that are worth reading. It is likely that he included them because they are novels his readers expected to be told to read.

Mabie writes at length about Howells on a number of occasions, all of which support the idea that he recommended Howells because he thought reading Howells was to be expected or would be "good for" his readers. Early in his tenure, Mabie has the opportunity to introduce Howells on the occasion of the publication of *The Kentons*. Though the discussion appears at the very end of the column—after a contemplation on the haste of modern life; a quick assessment of Jane Austen as, in contrast, "a novelist of the quiet life"; some thoughts on the value of poetry; and brief reviews of works by the popular novelists F. Hopkinson Smith and Mary Tappan Wright—the page layout flags the Howells discussion as a marquee attraction through images. There is a small picture of Smith at the opening of the column next to the drop cap, but the only other image appears in the center of the page: a stacked diptych subtitled "Mr. William Dean Howells in His Study." The top picture shows an unoccupied, but sumptuously arrayed, book-lined room; the bottom picture, presumably a reverse shot, is the same picture that accompanied the November 1893 Boyeson sketch of Howells (thrift being a virtue even in wildly popular mass-market publications). As was his habit with established authors whose work he has not previously discussed, Mabie traces the arc of Howells's career before reviewing the newest contribution; he praises him first as "not only one of our most distinguished writers but . . . also one of our most representative men of letters—one who lives in, for and by literature," and he goes on to a thumbnail assessment of Howells's strengths: "He has trained himself for his work by long and intimate familiarity with the most characteristic modern literature, and has become an accomplished craftsman; he understands thoroughly how to construct a story and put it into limpid English." The latter assessment might be construed as faint praise, but it seems that for the most part, it is Howells's "lightness" that recommends him to the *Journal* reader. His novels are "full of delicate characterization, light humor, close observation." While he has turned at times to more serious subjects, "his touch is still light and deft, and he remains a painter of manners on comparatively small canvases. Two or three times he has handled a larger subject strongly and successfully, and in 'Silas Lapham' and 'A Modern Instance' he has contributed to our literature novels of an insight and power which will give them great value to later generations" (October 1902, 17). *Lapham* will become the most-recommended Howells novel in Mabie's columns, with fourteen mentions, but *A Modern Instance* will not appear again, supplanted by *A Hazard of New Fortunes* and *The Lady of the Aroostook* as Mabie's other Howells favorites, each mentioned six times.

Despite this nod to "larger" novels, Mabie seems more inclined to spend time with some of Howells's "lighter" pieces, like the current novel under consideration, *The Kentons*. In Mabie's treatment, in fact, *The Kentons* looks a bit like a fitting *Journal* piece, at least, until he introduces his oblique critique. It is a portrait of "an average American family," Mabie contends, "full of natural refinement, of unselfish devotion, but thoroughly unsophisticated; a group of unworldly people, of intense domesticity of habit, excessively self-conscious and endowed with the nervous American temperament." Are these people with whom one would be interested in spending time? Or is the novel a diagnosis of contemporaneous American social ills? It finally seems the latter—*The Kentons* is "devoid of striking incidents, and there are pages which drag, not because the novelist fails to do his work well, but because his people are not always interesting." In the novel, Mabie contends, Howells has captured a range of both positive and negative attributes in the family, and these are mixed together both in the Howellsian representation and in Mabie's review: "The cleanness of the average American family, its lack of knowledge of the world, the deference of the husband to the wife and the subordination of the parents to the children, the ease with which the American girl becomes slangy without becoming vulgar, the tendency to excessive introspection, and the sharp nervous reactions within the family are deftly suggested" (October 1902, 17). *The Kentons*, in other words, presents a family that may well resemble the quotidian reality of the *Journal* reader's family, but by no means does it resemble the ideals promulgated in the magazine's pages. As a deviation from that ideal, it is open to the same kinds of critique that Mabie leveled against *Lapham* in the *Andover Review*, where he sees it as representative of a realism that

is crowding the world of fiction with commonplace people; people whom one would positively avoid coming in contact with in real life; people without native sweetness or strength, without acquired culture or accomplishment, without the touch of the ideal which makes the commonplace significant and worthy of study. To the large, typical characters of the older novels has succeeded a generation of feeble, irresolute, unimportant men and women whose careers are of no moment to themselves, and wholly destitute of interest to us.[57]

While its lightness is a potential positive attribute, it extends to the moral realm as well, and *The Kentons* in the final analysis looks like "a typical [realist] novel." As a parting shot, Mabie acknowledges the critical stance that could make Howells persona non grata with some *Journal* readers—his disdain for the romance: "In the young brother, who falls in love with Queen Wilhelmina, Mr. Howells has humorously and good-naturedly made his point about the romantic and semi-historical novel" (October 1902, 17). Even this briefest of allusions would probably remind Mabie's readers of the central incident of the previous year's best-selling, romantic, semi-historical novel, George Barr McCutcheon's *Graustark*, and would signal the fact that Howells was satirizing that text in his own. Given that the *Journal* would be offering *Beverly of Graustark*, the second novel in the series, as a subscriber premium as late as 1906, this allusion might well turn a number of Mabie's readers against Howells's text—though it might also attract either those who wanted to follow a literary feud or those who hoped to refine their reading beyond the best-seller list.

If the same qualities come in for the same critique in Howells's 1902 columns, then, what has changed with regard to *Lapham* that makes it no longer a typical novel or, at last, renders it a "lasting" novel, whereas, in June 1903, *The Kentons* is relegated to a more recreational reading list, "Novels for Summer Reading"? While the titles included in the latter are acceptable because of "interest, good workmanship, variety, and wholesome sentiment" (June 1903, 15), and the list makes strange bedfellows of such titles as *Just-So Stories* and *Mrs. Wiggs of the Cabbage Patch*, *Lapham* is repeatedly considered on a continuum with *The Scarlet Letter* and *The Last of the Mohicans*. Perhaps it is the fact that *Lapham* treats a "larger subject" and does so with "strength," "insight," and "power." These are all code words Mabie uses when describing literature he sees as having canonical potential, in lists "made in response to numerous requests" directed towards "readers who would like to make or renew their acquaintance with English fiction at successive periods in its representative works" (July 1903, 14). Mabie simply needed to address realism in lists that aspired to canonicity, and *Lapham* had already achieved that canonicity by 1902. By the time Mabie was penning his advice columns for the *Journal*, he was writing into a set of expectations that included Howells, and *Lapham*, because Howells had by this time fully assumed the mantle of Dean of American Letters.

Of course, the situation of upwardly striving readers is an abiding concern in *Lapham*, and Howells is by no means complimentary to the "non-cultivated" reader (*SL*, 116). A Mabie reader encountering *Lapham*, directed by lists like the July 1903 "Courses of Reading for Summer Moods," or by a list of novels up for the designation of "three best American novels" in March 1904, or by the September 1909 list "Novels of Realism," would no doubt have a complex relationship with the novel's multiple representations of the upwardly mobile Laphams' literary pursuits, and to the Coreys' running commentary on the Laphams' missteps. Mabie's readers, encountering Howells, would have found moments that both affirmed and destabilized their sense of their own command of culture; by affirming that his audiences could and should read *Lapham*, Mabie rendered them more savvy than Penelope Lapham and, ultimately, more likely to identify with many of the Coreys' intellectual pronouncements. That the desire of the upwardly mobile to acquire reading is so skewered in *Lapham* would thus become the very impulse that led many readers to *Lapham* and that gave Tom Corey's lists of good books for a library an even wider audience. Tom's suggestions carry an even greater weight by virtue of Silas Lapham's insistence that he is a "natural-born business man" (*SL*, 109), a hard worker and a modest one, not despite his Brahmin ancestry but because of it. While the second generation of Coreys—Tom's father, Bromfield—is dissipated, the family patriarch, Philips Corey, was a businessman like Silas, whose hard work created the financial basis for the later generations' literary and intellectual sophistication. Indeed, it seems the heroes of the "success" story in *Lapham* are the eldest and youngest of the Corey family—Philips and Tom—and Bromfield Corey joins Silas Lapham as the cautionary tales against abstracted, impractical literary pursuits and unethical business practices, respectively.

Howells's own ambiguity towards the Coreys complicates the identificatory positions in scenes like the interview between Tom and Bromfield after Tom has offered a Mabiean list of recommended books for the new Lapham library. Tom wonders aloud to his father about "the average literature of non-cultivated people" (*SL*, 116), a speculation that, while it comes from the mind of the most generally admirable character in the novel, and the one readers would most naturally identify with Howells himself, would certainly cause some discomfort to readers who were themselves "non-cultivated" but who were trying their best by reading *Lapham*. Over the course of the conversation, though, there is considerable opportunity for identificatory rearrangement. Bromfield answers Tom's superior tone with the observation that "the average is pretty low even with cultivated people" and that conciliatory decoupling of literary taste from educational opportunity opens the door for readers to agree with, or to learn from, Tom's subsequent description of his own reading practice. "I think I read with some sense of literature and the difference between authors. I don't suppose that people generally do that; I have met people who had read books without troubling themselves to find out even the author's name, much less trying to decide upon his quality. I suppose that's the way the vast majority of people read" (*SL*, 116). The Mabie reader can at this point, secure in the knowledge that he or she is in fact well aware of both Howells's name and his quality, return to a comfortable and even self-congratulatory camaraderie with the Coreys. Bromfield's lament that "I don't suppose that we who have the habit of reading, and at least a nodding acquaintance with literature, can imagine the bestial darkness of the great mass of people—even people whose bonuses are rich, and whose linen is purple and fine" (*SL*, 117), can be met with a knowing nod by the Mabie devotee who has taken to heart Mabie's endorsement of the "habit of reading," a campaign begun in the first line of his inaugural column in 1902 and echoing precisely Bromfield's phrase. As an added benefit, readers may join Bromfield in his disdain of the owner of "fine linen" whose mental life languishes in darkness, thereby asserting their intellectual superiority over those with pecuniary superiority.

This comfort does not last long, though, because Bromfield quickly identifies the Laphams as the wealthy philistines of his critique, and the Laphams, like the Kentons, look a little like the typical reader of the *Journal*. Though Bromfield seems skeptical that the Laphams have "knowledge enough to be ashamed of their ignorance," and we as readers know that Penelope certainly does, Tom concedes only that they do "in certain ways—to a certain degree." While he defends them as "quick," and "shrewd and sensible," Bromfield insists that this designation in itself does nothing to raise them to the state of "civilization": "All civilization comes through literature now, especially in our country. A Greek got his civilization by talking and looking, and in some measure a Parisian may still do it. But we, who live remote from history and monuments, we must read or we must barbarize" (*SL*, 118). While all of Bromfield's pronouncements must be considered as potentially satirical, this one certainly seems to adhere to the underlying principles of the Mabie columns. Reading must go beyond the information-gathering mode of the newspaper and the lecture; it is essential to moving beyond a "primitive" state.

But Bromfield is an ambivalent mouthpiece for this seemingly sage advice; his dilettantish literary and artistic pursuits have bankrupted the once-proud Corey family, and he is reliant on his more practical son to save the family either through his own labor or through marriage to the daughter of a rich captain of industry. Bromfield has lived his life as a romantic, fighting not in the American Civil War, for example, but with Giuseppe Garibaldi's Red Shirts. He serves as the mouthpiece for a romantic sensibility that the whole novel is metafictionally positioned against: "You can paint a man dying for his country, but you can't express on canvas a man fulfilling the duties of a good citizen" (*SL*, 202). Another practical Corey relative, the worldly and industrious Charles Bellingham, repudiates this proclamation from Bromfield, voicing Howells's realist manifesto: "The commonplace is just that light, impalpable, aërial essence which they've never got into their confounded books yet. The novelist who could interpret the common feelings of commonplace people would have the answer to 'the riddle of the painful earth' on his tongue" (*SL*, 202). Turning a Tennyson phrase against the romantics, Howells proposes a subject for literature which will allow a proper relation to literature, and locates its champions firmly in the cosmopolitan world of business.

How, though, might a Mabie reader who comes to *Lapham* straight from Ik Marvel situate him- or herself with regard to *Tears, Idle Tears*? Since part of Howells's literary project was to engender a realist aesthetic sensibility in his reader, it is not entirely unlikely that a Mabie reader would have seen the error of his or her sentimental ways after reading of Penelope Lapham's odd susceptibility to the excesses of a sentimental novel. Pen is sensible enough to recognize the absurdity of *Tears, Idle Tears* when she is commenting on it as a novel, but she is unable to resist its ideology when she is presented with the same dilemma in her own life. Countering Tom's attempts to disinterestedly examine the book's logics of self-sacrifice, Penelope offers a wholesale condemnation:

> But it *wasn't* self-sacrifice—or not self-sacrifice alone. She was sacrificing him, too; and for some one who couldn't appreciate him half as much as she could. I'm provoked with myself when I think

how I cried over that book—for I did cry. It's silly—it's wicked for anyone to do what that girl did. Why can't they let people have a chance to behave reasonably in stories? (*SL*, 217)

One of the pleasures of the text for some *Lapham* readers is, of course, the ability to recognize that Penelope is recapitulating the mistakes of the *Tears, Idle Tears* heroine, and to applaud their own condemnation of the false ideal of self-sacrifice. While an easy juxtaposition of the Penelope-Tom plot and the plot of *Tears, Idle Tears* might seem sufficient to make this connection, and thus evoke such a critique, Howells somehow feels it necessary to draw the connection with a very heavy hand. It hardly seems realistic that Penelope should so quickly revert from discussing the absurdity of "renunciation" in the dime romance to enacting precisely the same renunciation in her own drawing room, particularly since she has been portrayed up to this point as a character with more than her share of common sense. One might go far in explaining this apparent clumsiness on Howells's part by noting the importance of immediate juxtaposition at this moment: the reader must not be allowed to miss the equation of the *Tears, Idle Tears* romance and the *Lapham* romance. To allow any space between the two would be to allow space for the reader to imaginatively differentiate the two—*Tears Idle Tears* might then be seen to represent false renunciation, but Penelope's act in *Lapham* might be redeemable by simple virtue of the widely acknowledged "quality" of Howells's novel, among other possibilities.

This is not to say that Howells anticipated the canonization of his novel, or would even have anticipated its being recommended to a large mass audience in the pages of a magazine such as the *Ladies' Home Journal*; rather, it is to suggest that readerly eccentricities, and the desire to get something in particular out of a text, may well have led Howells to didactic moves like the rather clumsy drawing-room scene between Penelope and Tom. Howells, in other words, could not be certain that his reader would read like Tom, and indeed may have been more reasonably certain that he or she would read like Penelope. It can be no mistake that, after this scene, there is very little discussion of literacy, or of taste in literature, for the remainder of the novel. The education of the reader in the ways of proper reading, and the construction of a mental "bookshelf" to frame the novel, is finished for now, and the reader is to use that knowledge in the assessment of the quasi-romantic plot points that remain in *Lapham*. Whether the reader would do so is, of course, utterly outside the control of the author, and the embrace of *Lapham* by a Mabie reader may well have rested on the fact that ultimately, like Cornelia and Ludlow, Penelope and Tom do make a love match.

While Penelope and Tom's marriage does technically fit the definition of a "happy ending," it is not an entirely comfortable pairing; the two must live together in a self-imposed Mexican exile, which we are told lasts only three years, though their return remains unrepresented in the novel. Howells expends considerable energy describing the Corey family's uneasy acceptance of the marriage, and their relief that they will not really need to have any social contact with Penelope ("I'm glad she's going to Mexico. At that distance we can—correspond" [*SL*, 360]) or with their in-laws. Penelope's opinions about the estrangement go markedly unremarked: "Whether Penelope, on her side, found it more difficult to harmonize, I cannot say. She had much more of the harmonizing to do, since they were four to one; but then she had gone through so much greater trials before" (*SL*, 360). Trumping Penelope's true feelings about her uncomfortable relationship with the Coreys is her ability to retreat into "manners and customs," insists the Howellsian narrator, who returns forcefully in this penultimate scene. When, on their departure for Mexico, Penelope offers Tom an explanation for a sigh that has no relation to his family or their awkward parting, the narrator explains that

> there is no proof that she meant more, but it is certain that our manners and customs go for more in life than our qualities. The price we pay for civilization is the fine yet impossible differentiation of these. Perhaps we pay too much; but it will not be possible to persuade those who have the difference in their favor that this is so. They may be right; and at any rate the blank misgiving, the recurring sense of disappointment to which the young people's departure left the Coreys is to be considered. That was the end of their son and brother for them; they felt that; and they were not mean or unamiable people. (*SL*, 361)

The passage shifts very quickly from a consideration of Penelope's meaning, which is indecipherable even to our omniscient narrator, to an ambivalent acceptance of the superiority of "civilized" manners, and an implicit rejection of the romantic performance of emotion.

This same kind of ambiguity attended the marriage resolution of *The Coast of Bohemia*, and Howells changes the subject in a similar fashion, by returning his readers to the "moral spectacle" of Silas himself, now happily returned to his homestead in Lapham, Vermont. Minister Sewall and his wife take the role of Charmian Maybough, offering a third-party reading of the Lapham situation that could distance some readers from identification with any of the central characters. Sewall polices reader response for Howells, first by chastising his wife, and any recalcitrant readers, for the residual sentimentality that would make one resentful of Penelope's triumph with Tom: "That is wrong, cruelly wrong. I'm sure that's out of your novel-reading, my dear, and not out of your heart. Come! It grieves me to hear you say such a thing as that!" Mrs. Sewell then voices her consolation, which should be the reader's own: "Oh, I dare say this pretty thing [Irene Lapham] has got over it—how much character she has got!—and I suppose she'll see someone else" (*SL*, 363). Though Howells does assure us that Irene has not seen anyone else, Mrs. Sewell's concession, inaccurate as it may be, remains the cold comfort that exists for the reader who would still adhere to a sentimental economy—and Howells makes certain it is still available for such a reader. The final Lapham-Sewell interview, in which Lapham concludes that he "should have to" do things the same way, is vestigial to the reader focused on the romance plot, but it provides the cautionary note for the reader interested in the novel's frustrated narrative of financial upward mobility: Lapham has achieved ethical success, but the fact remains that he has to sacrifice pecuniary success only because he first dabbled in unethical business practices. Lapham tells Sewell: "[I]t seems to me I done wrong about Rogers in the first place; that the whole trouble came from that. It was just like starting a row of bricks. I tried to catch up, and stop 'em from going, but they all tumbled, one after another. It wa'n't in the nature of things that they could be stopped until the last brick went" (*SL*, 364). And while the text is ambiguous on this point, a reader can interpret Sewell's response, offered with "subtle kindness," as indicating that Silas ultimately deserves his fate because he does not acknowledge that he wronged Rogers in the first place.

> "I should be inclined to think—nothing can be thrown quite away; and it can't be that our sins only weaken us—that your fear of having possibly behaved selfishly toward this man kept you on your guard, and strengthened you when you were brought face to face with a greater"—he was going to say temptation, but he saved Lapham's pride, and said—"emergency." (*SL*, 364)

Sewell hesitates before describing Lapham's final test as "temptation" and substitutes the more value-neutral "emergency"; but "temptation" is still there for the offering, and the reader may still couch the analysis in those terms. Whether Lapham was immoral or simply unwise, the lesson for the striving Mabie reader is the same: things need not have gone this way. Lapham's financial fall precipitates his moral rise only because he was not ethical in the first place, but ethics and wealth are not mutually exclusive. Financial success need not be predicated on immorality. Be on the lookout for men like Rogers, treat all your business partners fairly, don't buy on margin, and read your Howells.

Of Labor Riots and Marriage Plots

The other Howells texts that receive consistent mention in Mabie's columns are *The Lady of the Aroostook* (1879) and *A Hazard of New Fortunes* (1890), with six mentions each. Mabie tended to recommend pairs of novels by authors, particularly when composing lists, and these two novels accompanied *Lapham* on lists of "novels of realism" and in short courses of fiction. *Aroostook* appears frequently in the first half of Mabie's tenure at the *Journal*; he begins to replace it with *Hazard* in 1906. Why the shift? *Hazard* is a far murkier novel than *Aroostook*, and a novel focused primarily on business, whereas *Aroostook* rarely strays from the courtship rituals of young, relatively well-heeled New Englanders. *Aroostook* is an easier novel to read with an eye to learning social mores; the story of an ingénue, it provides a reader with representations of inappropriate behavior in a number of circumstances, and offers internal commentary on that behavior from knowledgeable, moral, and trustworthy characters. *Hazard*, on the other hand, is a much more ambiguous novel, whose moral center lies somewhere to the side of the frequently too-cavalier protagonist, Basil March. *Hazard*'s pro-labor conclusion threatens to derail the only engagement in the novel, and the other courtship plot, which follows a couple identical to *The Coast of Bohemia*'s Ludlow and Cornelia, ends grotesquely. But there is a happy ending to *Hazard*, in which the proprietorship of a literary magazine is handed over to the pair who knows the most about the venture, the editor and the publicist. *Hazard* is, in short, the romance of business that Mabie champions in the later period of his *Journal* columns, and as such becomes the ideal companion to *Lapham*.

Before Mabie articulates the notion of the romance of business, he readily recommends *The Lady of the Aroostook* to his *Journal* audience. *Aroostook* truly is a comedy of manners that chronicles the unconventional shipboard courtship of a young woman from western Massachusetts, Lydia Blood, by James Staniford, a young man of Boston Brahmin stock. The courtship is unconventional not simply because of the difference in the social standing of the hero and heroine but also because the ship, the *Aroostook*, is not a passenger steamer but a cargo sailing ship, and the unworldly and unsuspecting Lydia is the only female on board. There are three other passengers aside from the ship's crew, all three young gentlemen, only one of them engaged to be married. The two single men, of course, fall in love with Lydia, but one is an unreformed alcoholic who was sent aboard for a forced drying-out period and who relapses after the ship's first port of call. It is through the point of view of Staniford that the reader experiences the Atlantic crossing, and he begins the journey in cynical examination of Lydia, whom he dubs "Lurella" when in confidential conversation with his companion, the affianced Dunham. But Staniford slowly recognizes the native morality and wisdom of Lydia, and finds himself in love just as they are about to disembark in Italy. Staniford determines to tell Lydia of his affections in the conventional order of things, once she is no longer an unaccompanied woman, but the final third of the novel sees Staniford kept, by mishap, from meeting Lydia in Venice to declare his affection and intentions. During this period Howells offers a critique of a hypocritical expatriate Venice through Lydia's eyes, noting well the contradiction between the city's fastidious public prudery and its private decadence. When Lydia and Staniford are finally reunited, he shuttles his concerns about the propriety of declaring his attentions to an unaccompanied woman, and the relative freedom afforded to the American girl is finally upheld as superior to the sham protections of the European chaperone.

Aroostook has been read as a companion piece to James's *Daisy Miller*, albeit one that diverges from James's text by affording the innocent American girl some measure of romantic satisfaction.[58] Lydia and Staniford settle in California on their marriage, a conclusion which, even if one does not go as far as William Wasserstrom in deeming this an "exile . . . to the antipodes," does seem to signal Howells's inability, as John W. Crowley puts it, to "give . . . imaginative form" to the possibility of feminine social freedom in America.[59] Even acknowledging that a move to California is a "return" for Lydia, who was after all born there, and taking account of the fact that her worldly aunt, Mrs. Erwin, leaves Venice with her Americanophile husband for the more salutary climate of Santa Barbara, we must concur with Crowley's assessment of the end of *Aroostook* as "sketchy," at best, and therefore just barely offering the desired "happy ending" to his heroine. Even so, we may assume that the gesture that sufficed for the wish fulfillment of many of Mabie's readers pointed to *Aroostook* as one of the "best American novels" (June 1905,

28); as the other Howells novel to read in a course providing a "beginning in the best fiction" (October 1905, 20); as a representative novel of American fiction, alongside *Lapham* and *Hazard* (March 1903, 17); or as a suitable novel "for older girls" (June 1903, 15). In the review of *The Kentons*, Mabie evokes *Aroostook* as the high-water mark for Howellsian "lightness," praising the way Howells "draw[s] with an affectionate hand an American type of unsophisticated purity and loveliness," suggesting an ideality in *Aroostook* that Mabie would find lacking in *The Kentons* (October 1902, 17). In the recommendation for "older girls," Mabie lists *Aroostook* with two other early Howells novels, *Their Wedding Journey* (1872) and *A Chance Acquaintance* (1873), both of which are also centrally concerned with the marriage prospects and the "native decency" of young American girls. Crowley notes that *A Chance Acquaintance* was particularly frustrating for its contemporaneous readers because of its refusal to realize their romantic desires: "Despite the enormity of the mismatch between Kitty and Arbuton, which Howells stressed from first to last, readers of romantic taste chose to overlook Howells' realistic intentions and to hope against hope that he would find a way to marry the lovers. When he did not, some complained of their frustration and demanded at least a more satisfactorily connubial sequel."[60] Presumably, with the connubial prequel and sequel in hand, Mabie's "older girl" would be able to sustain her interest through the frustrating conclusion of *A Chance Acquaintance*; it is telling that this is the only mention of that novel in all of Mabie's columns. As with *Lapham*, the more uncomfortable marital resolution of *Aroostook* was preferable, it seems, to an ending that thwarted the marriage plot.

During the second half of his decade at the *Journal*, Mabie came to mention *Hazard* more frequently to his audience as the Howells novel to read after they read *Lapham*. *Hazard* has considerable potential interest to the informed reader of the *Journal*, as it is intimately concerned with the question that drove Edwin Bok as he tried to make the *Journal* a legitimate literary magazine—what kind of literature would appeal to female readers, the *Ewig-Weibliche* which Basil March's partner, Fulkerson, continuously evokes. The observant, and long-term, *Journal* reader might also notice that Alma Leighton and Angus Beaton are precursors to Cornelia and Ludlow in *The Coast of Bohemia*. Like Cornelia, Alma has come to New York on the recommendation of a young artist who visited her rural hometown on vacation; like Cornelia, Alma takes art lessons and initially holds out hope that her young artist will recommence his courtship. But, unlike Cornelia, Alma is recognized publicly for her skill, and she has illustrations commissioned for the pages of *Every Other Week*. And unlike Cornelia, Alma decides to focus on her career and to stop paying any attention to the self-absorbed Beaton. When he suggests that they might be able to work together as a married couple, Alma counters with the argument that she would not be able to work with him as an equal: "Second fiddle. Do you suppose I shouldn't be woman enough to wish my work always less and lower than yours?"[61] Alma is not destined to be subsumed by hollyhocks.

Alma feels like a revision of Cornelia, but in fact she was Cornelia's predecessor. Just three years after the publication of *Hazard*, Howells enables a marriage between Cornelia and Ludlow that suffers from precisely the kind of dysfunction to which Alma refused to subject herself. Is the resolution different because Howells knew he would be publishing *Coast* in the *Journal*? There is no documentary evidence that speaks to this question, but it is an intriguing possibility. *Hazard* was a successful novel in its time, selling twenty-three thousand copies in its first year.[62] Howells did not face ravening crowds who resented his inability to successfully pair Alma, as Edith Wharton would after killing off Lily Bart at the end of *The House of Mirth*. But Howells did have considerable prejudices against the intellectual capacity of audiences like the one he would have expected from the *Journal*, and it is not at all surprising that he ended *Coast* more conventionally than *Hazard*. Bowing to market pressures was of course something that Howells disdained; indeed, just after the publication of *Hazard*, a frustrated Howells could hardly keep his language in check after encountering the dreck produced for the holiday market. "There seems," he observes, "a demand for inferior quality in all of the arts," primarily because there are people who will never be able to appreciate good work:

> Certain sorts of intelligences, which famish upon excellence, pasture with delight upon what is less than excellent. The appetite of youth, indiscriminating and uncultivated, remains the taste through life of a vast multitude of people who never mature aesthetically. These cannot get the good of what is wholly good; they can only get the good of what is partly good; and no doubt it is their need that accounts for the existence of mediocre artists and mediocre works in every kind.[63]

Literary hierarchies are inevitable, because there is a natural hierarchy of taste that cannot be corrected—the bovine masses will never "pasture" on things that are "wholly good"; they are constitutionally unable to process and benefit from quality art. Though he closes his column with a halfhearted call for "true criticism" to "endeavor patiently to convert [primitive appetites] to a taste for better things," the prognosis is poor.

Was Mabie attempting to convert the appetites of his readers away from romance, away from sentiment, and away from the expectation of a happy ending, as he recommended they read *Hazard*? We should not forget, of course, that the novel chronicles a relatively stable mature marriage and that while Beaton is never domesticated, and Conrad Dryfoos is murdered before he can reach an understanding with Miss Vance, one of the young couples does successfully wed. The courtship of Fulkerson and Miss Woodburn is hardly compensatory for all the frustrated romances in the novel, though; it begins late, and the reader is given little satisfaction in the abbreviated development of the relationship. But the final nail in the coffin of the marriage plot is Basil March's unequivocal speech against the conventional notion of a happy ending, in which he blames novel-reading for people's unrealistic expectations of marriage. "We get to thinking that there is no other happiness or good fortune in life except marriage; and it's offered in fiction as the highest premium for virtue, courage, beauty, learning, and saving human life. We all know it isn't." March goes even further to propose that a novel should be written "from the anti-marriage point of view . . . begin with an engaged couple, and devote [the] novel to *dis*engaging them, and rendering them separately happy ever after in the dénoûment" (*HNF*, 479). Seekers after matrimonial happy endings need not apply to *Hazard*, a novel that imagines an author would "make his fortune" from the demolition of a potential union.

The sentimental is rejected as roundly as the romantic in *Hazard*. Conrad Dryfoos's murder is perhaps the apotheosis of the novel's anti-sentimentality; just before his death, Conrad has a fight with his management-sympathizing father. Wandering the streets in a daze, Conrad then encounters Miss Vance, whose passionate yet delicate sympathies for the working men are in conflict with her fear of "what people would say" (*HNF*, 420) if she were to talk to the strikers. Miss Vance's pleas both confirm Conrad's romantic attraction to her and inspire him to go to the scene of the strike, initially because he hopes to "do something," to help the strikers in some way, but ultimately because he gets wrapped up in an imagined scenario in which Miss Vance appreciates his ability to understand her desires. "Thinking of her pleasure in what he was going to do, he forgot almost what it was" (*HNF*, 421). Conrad's sympathetic impulses spring not from a feeling for the workers but from a feeling for Miss Vance. When he does finally awaken from this reverie it is too late; he cannot prevent a policeman from beating the elderly socialist war veteran Lindau because he himself has already been shot.

The sympathetic impulse, which was motivated more by self-interest than by true feeling for others, is ineffectual. Conrad's murder does not end the strike, and it does not make his father sympathetic to the strikers. Likewise, Miss Vance's sympathies are wrongheaded and inadequate; she tries to recompense Conrad's death by serving the poor as a Sister of Charity, but her motivations in so doing actually come into question from both Basil and Isabel March. Mrs. March "was not sure but that the girl was something of a *poseuse*, and enjoyed the picturesqueness, as well as the pain; and she wished to be convinced that it was not so" (*HNF*, 452). Basil, on the other hand, dismisses Miss Vance's self-sacrifice as an unworkable posture, given that one needs to actually live in the world: "Oh, Christ came into the world to teach us how to live rightly in it, too. If we were all to spend our time in hospitals, it would be rather dismal for the homes" (*HNF*, 452). Whether self-sacrificial charity is hypocritical or just ill conceived, it is not finally an option in the world of *Hazard*, and any reader inclined towards sentimentality would find it difficult to stomach this cynical critique.

There is a residuum of both sentiment and romance in *Hazard*, though, and it can be found in the *business* plot of the novel. The story of the launch and success of March and Fulkerson's literary periodical *Every Other Week*, considered in isolation, gives us the happy ending that the characters' relationships lack. The plot contains a conventional complication, with the interloping but materially necessary philistine investor Jacob Dryfoos. This complication is resolved by Dryfoos ceding the field, and the magazine, to the rightful pair, and we end with a marriage between March and Fulkerson, and a happily-ever-after denouement in which we see the business partners and friends living and working together in perpetuity. The rhetorics of the novel, particularly near the end, frequently elide the languages of business and romance; after Dryfoos offers to give the magazine to March and Fulkerson, for example, Fulkerson celebrates: "It's just throwing the thing into our mouths ... The wedding will be this day week. No cards!" (*HNF*, 484). It is not immediately apparent that Fulkerson is actually referring to his wedding with Miss Woodburn; it initially sounds like a metaphoric description of the business transaction. His marriage is an adjunct to his business success; the business plot is the real romance.

Mabie tries on numerous occasions to convince his readers of the romantic possibilities of the workplace, and his most rousing argument is offered in a column in which he lists *Hazard* as one of the best works of fiction published in the previous ten years. "The romance of the workshop," he argues, "is as pure in quality and is perhaps greater in mass than the romance of the castle and the palace" (March 1904, 16). Though the "workshop" Mabie has in mind sounds a bit more blue-collar than the offices of *Every Other Week*, the general principles are the same: this romance can be located in the lives of everyday men and women, and its happy ending comes from the protagonist's elevation through work to a state of psychic and financial felicity. *Hazard* works this way if we think of March and Fulkerson triumphing over a patronage system to finally control their own business destinies. They are no longer working for someone else, someone who is utterly disinterested in their product, but are working for themselves. If one reads *Hazard* in this light, several things can fall by the wayside; Lindau and his socialist ideals, for example, become collateral damage, all the more so because they have been marginalized throughout the text by the dialect in which they are proffered. The success of *Every Other Week* inheres finally not in its aesthetic superiority, and not in its glancing likeness to a shop that is now owned by the workers, but in its sales profile. Despite the desires of many critics to see *Hazard* as Howells's attempt to pay tribute to the victims of the Haymarket and New York streetcar-strike riots, in this reading *Hazard* quite firmly asserts the potential rightness of a capitalist model. March and Fulkerson's ultimate control over those profits is capitalist, not socialist, or even quasi-socialist.[64] If one reads *Hazard* hoping to achieve someday the measure of success that finds the Marches living comfortably, if not ostentatiously, in a flat over the *Every Other Day* offices, one need not spend much time contemplating the futility of the labor movement or remembering the heavily accented political views of Lindau.

* * *

Though Howells worked to differentiate himself and the realist aesthetic from romance and sentimentality, the echoes of these modes are present enough in his texts to facilitate readers who still want to perform sentimental or romantic readings. By the time Howells was appearing in the *Ladies' Home Journal*, he was known as the preeminent American man of letters; the *Journal* turned this identity into a brand and rendered him accessible cultural capital for its readers. By recommending Howells so frequently to his readers, Hamilton Wright Mabie likewise turned

Howells into a line item on a checklist of cultural acquisition. Whatever Howells's aesthetic project was, to the reader in pursuit of cultural capital it became secondary to the instrumentality of *having read* Howells. The Dean of American Letters was ultimately one of the more obliging of the American realists when it came to the mass market, offering himself willingly in the pages of its greatest mouthpiece, *The Ladies' Home Journal*, and profiting magnificently from the transaction.

3 / James for the General Reader

*The point upon which people differ is the artistic one, and the fact that
such differences of opinion exist makes it possible that two writers
as widely separated as Mr. Henry James and Mr. Rider Haggard,
for instance, find appreciative readers in the same year of the same
century—a fact which the literary history of the future will find it hard to
explain.*

—F. MARION CRAWFORD, THE NOVEL: WHAT IT IS (1893)

By the time he was writing his "major phase" masterpieces in the early
1900s, Henry James had perfected his pose of nonchalance about the
mass audience's rejection of his work. His much-cited 1890 letter to his
brother, William, after the failure of *The Tragic Muse* epitomizes this attitude as it bravely resolves to embrace self-reliance:

> One must go one's way and know what one's about and have a gen-
> eral plan and a private religion—in short have made up one's mind
> as to *ce qui en est* with a public the draggling after which simply
> leads one in the gutter. One has always a 'public' enough if one has
> an audible vibration—even if it should only come from one's self.
> I shall never make my fortune—nor anything like it; but—I know
> what I shall do, and it won't be bad.[1]

By now, it has become a critical commonplace to note that this stance
was "mere bravado" and that this was the same Henry James who, in
pursuit of literary fame and fortune, was willing to publish his works
widely in periodicals considerably less burnished than the *Atlantic*.[2] Despite his self-fashioning as the indifferent "Master," James had an intense
and very human interest in the popularity of his works—not least because he depended on his royalties for his sustenance.

James was actually quite active in pursuing more popular venues for
his work, venues whose payments would keep the wolves away from the
door, but he was equally interested in reaching a mass audience, even
when the remuneration was less than lucrative. While discussing James's

little-acknowledged but significant involvement with syndication, Charles Johanningsmeier cites a telling letter James wrote to William Dean Howells after publication of *The Turn of the Screw*. James called the novella an "abject, down-on-all-fours potboiler," but confessed that he would "do it again & again, too, even for the same scant fee."[3] Johanningsmeier estimates that James "published over 600 pieces of fiction and nonfiction in periodicals during his lifetime" and notes that he chose to publish a number of his works in newspapers before any other medium.[4] Such a significant exposure in the most mass-accessible periodicals of the day means James was very much a known quantity for the larger mass of the reading public. These publications presented him as a "celebrated author" and a "famous" and "noted novelist," promoting his notoriety more than his aesthetics when advertising his stories.[5]

James was, in short, well known for being well known; he was a "name" in the literary world and would have been recognized as such by even the least-literary of audiences. His name would surely have been missed if he were left off any lists purporting to recommend the "best books" to novice or aspirational readers. The readers of Hamilton Wright Mabie's reading advice columns in the *Ladies' Home Journal* would certainly have expected to be told to read James, and Mabie would have known that they were waiting for James. Herein lay a dilemma: Mabie liked to recommend the most "current" books by living literary legends, but the Master was at the time writing works in his experimental, highly wrought, late-phase style. He was generally considered a "difficult" writer to read. If James, the least accessible of all authors at the time for general readership, was nevertheless necessary for cultural capital, what then were the imperatives for creating a readable James? Though Mabie's mission was ostensibly to direct his readers towards the best books of the day, he could hardly recommend James's contemporaneous works to an audience that was still inclined towards more "popular" fiction like Kate Douglas Wiggin's. The solution for Mabie when it came to James, even more so than in the case of Howells, was to direct his readership towards the books of yesterday—most frequently *Roderick Hudson*, *The Princess Casamassima*, and *The Portrait of a Lady*. Mabie's readers could thereby tick James off their list of "important authors to read" without having to bully their way through *The Golden Bowl*.

Having spent nine years contributing ninety-seven columns to the *Journal*, Mabie penned three final columns that were published in February, March, and April 1912. This triptych functions as a closing argument, the final thoughts with which he wishes to leave his readers as he moves on to his career as cultural attaché. The titles—"Living Novelists Best Worth Reading" (February); "Are the Later Poets Worth Reading?" (March); and "Which Way Is Literature Going?" (April)—signal his intent to end his time at the *Journal* with a commencement address of sorts, consisting of predictions that will serve his readers after he no longer appears monthly at their doorstep. By 1912, James's career was also nearing its close; after the unsuccessful publication of the New York Edition in 1907–9, he completed only one more novel, *The Outcry*, in 1911, and he had become the recipient of honorary degrees from Harvard and Oxford—the sure sign of an aging lion. The declining James did not fare poorly in the parting columns of the departing Mabie—he was generally acknowledged as important, but primarily as a relic of the past, certainly not as a harbinger of the future. James is the first author Mabie mentions in his column "Living Novelists Best Worth Reading," and he comes in for considerable praise as "one of the very small group of living writers to whom the word 'distinction' can be applied" (February 1912, 42). Mabie follows this immediately with a caveat, articulated first seriously and then with a suggestion of ridicule, about James's late works: "There are many readers who find his later stories fatiguing in their demands on attention, and this is a serious fault in a work of literature, just as the failure to explain itself is a serious defect in a painting. There was a substantial grain of truth in the statement of a witty woman that 'The Wings of the Dove' got its title because it has neither head nor tail." This said, Mabie does hold out hope for the reader who does not want to trudge through Milly Theale's career—"one has to go back only a few years to find Mr. James writing stories of the rare quality of observation and style of 'The American' and 'Portrait of a Lady.'"

James clearly posed a problem for the reading advisor who like Mabie needed to steer his readership towards some sophisticated literature, but who found *The Golden Bowl* "a subtle study of American and Italian temperaments" saddled nonetheless with a "very disagreeable plot" (March 1905, 21). Mabie's compromise, to praise the later James's "technical skill" but to downplay the "interest" of James's late works, allowed his readers to self-select; the highbrow benefits of James would accrue just as readily to the reader of *Portrait* as to the reader of *The Ambassadors*. One important step was to decouple James from a continental realist, or naturalist, lineage that might associate him with Émile Zola, who Mabie says "took in many cases the most revolting, gross and repulsive aspects of life and pictured them with very little shading" (September 1905, 18). Instead, Mabie associated James with a more genteel notion of literariness. On numerous occasions, Mabie responds to reader requests for "a course of fiction reading" with lists that present early James (*Portrait, Roderick Hudson*) on a continuum with Dickens, Thackeray, Eliot, Scott, and Austen (October 1908; October 1905; September 1909). In his March 1904 column, Mabie answers a question about the "three best American novels" by asserting that *The Scarlet Letter* is certainly one of them, but that the other two spaces could be filled by a number of novels: *The Deerslayer, The Last of the Mohicans, Uncle Tom's Cabin, The Marble Faun, The Portrait of a Lady, The Rise of Silas Lapham, The Choir Invisible, Pembroke, The Grandissimes, Deephaven, The Prophet of the Great Smoky Mountains,* and *The Adventures of Huckleberry Finn.* While Howells, and certainly James, might have felt themselves outliers in this group (and Mark Twain certainly would have taken umbrage at his inclusion on a list with James Fenimore Cooper), the texts Mabie chooses are apparently easy to conceptualize in a continuum with transcendentalist romance, with regionalism, and with Harriet Beecher Stowe. Mabie consistently overlooked the aesthetic and methodological distinctions made by James and Howells at their most critical, allowing his readers to blur the line between James and James Lane Allen.

This elision was the key strategy by which Mabie rendered James "general reading." By representing James's fiction as of a piece with more genteel works, Mabie in fact makes it possible for his readership to approach James with a wholly different set of expectations, and he facilitates a range of possible reader responses that might seem unintuitive, even philistine, to orthodox James readers. This is of course not to say that such reactions were entirely inconsistent with James's novels even without the critical intervention of a Mabie, and Mabie is hardly forthcoming in his interpretations of James—much of our work here is speculative, based on contextual cues and the general scope of Mabie's recommendations and his stated preferences by way of plots and themes. Mabie is, in fact, atypically reticent when it comes to James—he lists him frequently as someone to read but does not offer protracted meditations on the significance of individual works. However, in recommending only certain early James novels, and through the company they keep in his columns, he renders more likely a number of strong misreadings that emphasize James's continuity with romance and popular literature, and de-emphasize his innovations in form. This is why, nearly twenty years after the initial appearance of *Portrait*, Isabel Archer's story regularly came to Mabie's aid as he attempted to prescribe James to the general reader.

Portrait and Mabie's other favored James novels, *Roderick Hudson* and *The Princess Casamassima*, lent themselves fairly easily to readings more in line with a romantic sensibility. The central figure of each of these novels is someone striving for upward mobility, be it financial, social, or both. While the protagonist in each fails in some profound sense, there is always a more conventional foil, someone whose flame does not burn as brightly as the protagonist's, but who is the last character standing at the end, and who renders commentary on the destroyed protagonist. These are the figures who James, in his New York Edition preface to *Portrait*, dismissed as the "fishwives who helped to bring back to Paris from Versailles, on that most ominous day of the first half of the French Revolution, the carriage of the royal family."[6] James's protestations aside, it is these figures with whom a Mabie reader was most likely to connect. Indeed, such protest evinces James's uneasiness about too many people paying too much of the wrong kind of attention—identificatory attention—to these characters. In his New York Edition prefaces, James bemoaned the misreadings wrought on all these novels by critics and nonprofessional readers alike, particularly their attraction to these "diligent" minor characters, who were mediocre counterpoints to the striking, if tragic, protagonists of the novels. Tellingly, Mabie paid no attention to the New York Edition, though he was writing his columns, and recommending James, concurrently with the Edition's publication. In his November 1904 column, there is no question that the *Portrait* Mabie recommends is James's 1881 edition, not the heavily revised New York Edition. But which *Portrait* was he commending in 1912, or in 1909, for that matter, when he recommends his readers study *Portrait* as part of a program of reading that contrasts "novels of character study" to "novels of incident"? James's revisions of *Portrait* were, of course, extensive and, he hoped, would "have hugely *improved* the book—& I mean not only for myself, but for the public."[7] But the adviser who reached one of the most extensive mass audiences of the time, Mabie, never mentioned James's edition, though he mentions the publication of "editions de luxe," of other authors, such as Edgar Allan Poe (January 1909, 30), and even suggests giving such editions as gifts (December 1902, 19). Though Charles Scribner's Sons did not advertise the New York Edition widely, Mabie would surely have known about it from the substantial literary gossip surrounding the project; at the very least, he would have seen notices of its publication and early reviews. We may assume, therefore, that the radio silence on the substantial revisions of two of Mabie's most favored James works, *Portrait* and *Roderick Hudson*, is intentional, signaling Mabie's own attachment to the original pieces, and even more, his presumption that his audience would neither care about nor care for the changes.[8]

An early column goes a long way towards substantiating this suspicion about Mabie's rejection of the New York Edition. In November 1904, Mabie reproduces a reader query regarding James's reputation as "the psychologist in fiction."[9] Asking whether "there [is] not an element of psychology in all fiction," the reader goes on to ask, "which do you regard as Mr. James's more important stories?" The reader's query suggests that James was a familiar name, recognized as an important author, but perhaps a daunting one—all this talk of the "psychologist" made his work sound obscure. Yet if James's "psychologizing" could be brought into relation with any other fiction ("is there not an element of psychology in all fiction?"), he might be recuperated as an accessible author, perhaps even on a par with other perennial favorites of Mabie's columns and readers, like F. Marion Crawford and George Washington Cable. Mabie's response essentially reiterates the critical stance against which James was struggling in "The Art of Fiction." He explains that "there is an element of psychology in all fiction which deals with character. In novels of adventure this element is very slight because the interest turns almost wholly on incident. There is very little psychology in novels of action; in such stories character is disclosed by what men do, not what is said about them." Juxtaposing Thackeray to James, Mabie finally comes around to his point: "[James's] later work has shown an excess of the analytical over the dramatic or narrative interest, and while much of his work has high value as an intellectual feat or achievement it has comparatively slight value as fiction, and therefore, as literature." There is little subtlety to unpack here—Mabie is clearly marking the "intellectual feats" of James's late phase as violations of the rules of readerliness, and therefore unworthy of the designations "fiction" or "literature." He goes on further to say that the people who appreciate *The Wings of the Dove* and *The Ambassadors* do so because they are "most deeply interested in James as a type of mind"—reading these books is apparently akin to reading psychological case studies of the author—and he recommends that his readers "who are most deeply interested in him as a writer of novels" spend time with *The Passionate Pilgrim*, *Roderick Hudson*, *The American*, and *Portrait*, and even lists some short fiction, "Lesson of the Master" and "The Real Thing" (November 1904, 20).

It is therefore little wonder that Mabie never recommends the New York Edition. James's revisions for the Edition rendered these earlier, more amenable, novels more like other late-phase James, and thereby rendered them less "literary," in the Mabiean definition, and therefore necessarily unattractive to the Mabie audience. The failure of the New York Edition, despite James's reputation and his desirability as cultural capital, can be understood as at least in part a function of the following: by altering his original texts, James made it more difficult to identify hopeful alternatives to his failed romantic protagonists and thereby made his fiction less accessible to a general reader. Mabie's silent treatment was of a piece with, and perhaps in some way even an instrument of, the Edition's eventual failure. But whatever his opinion of the James of the 1900s, Mabie persisted in recommending the James of the 1870s and 1880s to his self-improving audience.

Sympathy for Whom? *Roderick Hudson*

Mabie mentions *Roderick Hudson* more frequently than he does any James work aside from *The Portrait of a Lady*, and he typically does so when he wants to suggest an entry-level James novel. *Hudson* is the representative James novel in Mabie's "Best American Novels" list (June 1905) and in "A Beginning in the Best Fiction" (October 1905); it is listed in "Some Standard Novels," a column directed towards young readers (September 1907); in addition, it is listed as a positive alternative to "psychological James" in the November 1904 column—in all cases, Mabie's target is a beginning reader, a reader for whom *Hudson* may be the very first James novel ever attempted. *Roderick Hudson* works well as a beginner's James novel, as it turns out, because it lends itself to a variety of identification practices; in recommending it, Mabie casts a wide net for the multiply motivated *Ladies' Home Journal* reader.

Roderick Hudson originally appeared serially in the *Atlantic Monthly* from January through December 1875 and was published in book form in America before the end of the serial run by J. R. Osgood in November of that year. James revised the text significantly in preparation for the first publication in book form in England by Macmillan in 1879, and the next American edition of the novel, bound under the Houghton Mifflin imprint in 1882, consisted of sheets imported from this 1879 edition. The American reader of Mabie's columns thus would have had access to two different editions of the novel; the purchaser would most likely buy the 1882 Houghton edition, and the library patron might encounter either. The temptation is great to speculate about the edition Mabie most likely had in mind, as James's primary concern in the 1879 revision was to tone down the sentimentally inflected prose stylings of 1875, and a Mabie preference in either direction would therefore mark his predilections more precisely. In the absence of any evidence in this realm, however, we must content ourselves with knowing that he was drawn to one of the earlier texts of the novel, while he was apparently not driven to recommend the revision (if he even read it) when it appeared in 1907.[10]

Contemporary reviewers in 1875 hailed the novel as the first offering of a promising young novelist, though they did not hesitate to find fault with the characterizations: the reviewer for the *Chicago Tribune* found Mary Garland and Rowland Mallet "uninteresting in their undeviating goodness," and the *New York Herald* contended that "Mrs. Hudson is the only real person in this last book of Mr. James', and consequently she is the least interesting."[11] There were problems with the ending, too; though the *Herald* writer initially contends that this matter is just a tic of James's—"none of his books end in a conventional way"—he or she is not able to sustain that philosophical tone, complaining by the end of the review that Roderick "behaved like a lunatic. In fact, he was little better than insane at the best of times"; in short, he "is the most exasperating character.[12] The *Tribune*'s reviewer imagines a more satisfying alternate ending in which "Rowland should have recognized the exacted worth of Christina's native character, and by marrying and lifting her out of an evil atmosphere give her the opportunity that she helplessly strove for, of salvation." This coupling, the reviewer contends, would be "far more artistic" because it would be in line with the "law of counterparts," but it is a suggestion strikingly at odds with all of James's depictions of their interactions.[13]

The element of the earlier text that James found most lacking is in fact the condition for *Roderick Hudson*'s suitability to the Mabie audience. James's preface to the significantly revised 1907 text, the first offering of the New York Edition, sees the author distressed that he had failed in the earlier iteration to make his eponymous protagonist more "sympathetic": "My mistake on Roderick's behalf—and not in the least of conception, but of composition and expression—is that, at the rate at which he falls to pieces, he seems to place himself beyond our understanding and our sympathy."[14] But it is not at all apparent from Mabie's recommendations that Roderick was unsympathetic, or even that he was the character with whom the audience might be supposed to sympathize. While Roderick is the "genius" of the piece, his hardworking doppelganger, Sam Singleton, might be said to more closely resemble the diligent, dutiful reader Mabie worked to cultivate in his advisory columns, and Roderick's fiancée,

Mary, closely resembles the young women Mabie frequently addresses in his columns.

As we have already seen, Mabie continuously constructs his readers as eager seekers of self-culture and social cultivation. But he does so while frequently cautioning that reading properly is something that must be worked at, not something that can be expected to come naturally: "There is no easy way to that kind of knowledge of the classics which makes them supremely interesting. One must be educated before one can really comprehend a profound or valuable work of art" (November 1902, 17). While Roderick initially travels to Italy to undertake this manner of diligent study, he ultimately relies much more heavily on his innate talents, waiting for the elusive muse to strike rather than pursuing a steady course of work. This cavalier attitude is of course part of his folly, and James's indictment of this approach is perfectly consistent with the attitude Mabie wants to foster in his readers that patient and dutiful application is the only path to real achievement. While cautioning his readers against succumbing to the "pedantic" study of detail typical of some scholarly work—"The end of art is to deepen and intensify the sense of life, and that end is missed when one becomes absorbed in the study of language, form, conditions and circumstances" (April 1902, 17)—encouraging them instead to cultivate "a cooperative imagination," as the only avenue for proper appreciation of art, Mabie always offers a caveat. "Nevertheless," he continues, "there ought to be method in reading, and reading ought to be study in the truest sense" (September 1903, 15). An ideal Mabie reader combines the cooperative imagination with application, and thereby tends to diverge from the increasingly dissolute ways of the mercurial Hudson. Mabie even uses the figure of the diligent painter to underscore his contention that working on reading is the only way to become someone at ease with reading:

> It is folly for a painter to talk about spontaneity until he knows his brushes, his pigments, and his methods. He must undergo a searching education of many years before he can begin to be spontaneous. [. . .] Artists know that to keep themselves prolific and inventive they must keep all the time at work; in other words, in an attitude which keeps all their thoughts and skills together. (May 1905, 18)

This attitude of continual education, of diligent application to craft, is a Sam Singleton attitude. A devoted and sympathetic Mabie reader would, one imagines, be profoundly disinclined to entertain any implications of pedantry or plodding in James's depiction of the dutiful landscape watercolorist. His dedication to work, and his discipline, mark him as one poised for true, sustained success.

Roderick, on the other hand, is a cautionary tale for the Mabie reader who has paid attention to the importance of application and the dangers of relying too much on uncultivated, "innate" talents. In a particularly telling column in this regard, the November 1906 "Mr. Mabie on the Home as a School," Mabie expiates at length on the importance of inculcating discipline and obedience in small children. The alternative seems close to the portrait James paints of his wayward sculptor. "The training of education which makes boys keen and 'smart' makes them superficially successful, and, for the most part, the most lamentable failures in the end. What is needed in America is fewer 'smart' men and more able ones; and the beginning of real ability, like the beginning of real success, lies in the will, not in the intellect." The "smart" student is too frequently left to his own devices, and at best this leads to an incomplete realization of talents, at worse, to dissipation and failure. Discipline is the key to avoiding such bad ends, but an alarming number of young people (boys in particular, though Mabie does apply his precepts to girls as well) have been treated too indulgently: "Through carelessness, easy-going ways, mistaken notions of good-fellowship, too many boys go to school without having learned to obey any one, to deny themselves any pleasure, or to submit to any authority; they do not know how to study, to speak their own language, to meet people with courtesy, or to make themselves and others happy" (November 1906, 22). These are all faults of the Roderick Hudson we meet in the opening chapters of James's novel; when he first meets Rowland Mallet, he has arrived in a peevish mood at the house of their mutual friend, complaining "of the heat, of the dust, of a shoe that hurt him, of having gone on an errand a mile to the other side of town and found the person he was in search of had left Northampton an hour before."[15] He continues by responding rather impertinently to a compliment, turning it into what Mabie would certainly classify as a "smart" rejoinder: "'A connoisseur?' he cried, laughing. 'He is the first I have ever seen! Let me see what they look like'; and he drew Rowland nearer to the light" (*RH*, 63). His talk is less conversation than soliloquy; "Hudson rattled away for an hour with a volubility in which boyish unconsciousness and manly shrewdness were singularly combined. He gave his opinion on twenty topics, he opened up an endless budget of local gossip, he described his repulsive routine at the office of Messrs. Striker and Spooner, counselors at law, and he gave with great felicity and gusto an account of the annual boat-race between Harvard and

Yale, which he had lately witnessed at Worcester" (RH, 65). Hudson is, of course, indulged in his "youthful grandiloquence" by both Mallet and his cousin Cecilia; the latter exclaims that Roderick is "too delicious" and the former excuses Hudson's impertinence as "a sign of the natural self-sufficiency of genius." But these are precisely the kinds of indulgence that Mabie diagnoses as the precursors to pampered failure.

Roderick's early home training comes in for much of the blame at the beginning of the novel; though his hapless and indulgent mother did manage to get him into a position in a law firm, we learn from Cecilia that "he grew up á la grâce de Dieu; he was horribly spoiled" (RH, 67). And indeed, this early permissiveness wrecked havoc with his schoolwork: "Three or four years ago he graduated at a small college in this neighbourhood, where I am afraid he had given a good deal more attention to novels and billiards than to mathematics and Greek. Since then he has been reading law at the rate of a page a day." Roderick never formed the habit of application, and he never feels the urgency of careful study, and yet Cecilia and Rowland read his behavior not as a serious character flaw that will likely reemerge in any context but as a sign that "[g]ood, bad, or indifferent, the boy is an artist—an artist to his finger's ends." To be a "true artist" is apparently to be absentminded, dilettantish, and mercurial. These assumptions lead throughout the novel to characters continually excusing the "genius" for a lack of application; after he reaches young manhood, Roderick's friends simply continue the kind of coddling that his widowed mother began. Even Rowland, who initially takes Roderick to Europe precisely to institute a program of rigorous study, cannot stop himself from indulging his charge because he trusts so much to the primacy of artistic inspiration. As Mabie would have predicted, the absence of discipline leads ultimately to Roderick's dissipation and ruin.

James's Hudson suffers because his artistic impulses are not tempered by discipline, but James certainly does not mean to suggest that discipline should subsume artistic inspiration—and neither does Mabie, either in the case of the artist or in the case of the "average" reader (or his or her children). In fact, when Mabie wants to describe home training that can combine proper discipline with "an atmosphere of poetry," he turns to the example of Goethe, the uber-romanticist, noting that he "spoke of his mother as the inspirer of his poetic life":

> Her love of story-telling, the vivacity of her nature, the freedom of her imagination, a certain generosity and spontaneity which pervaded her, did more, probably, to give the boy a key to the world

than any other power or influence. Every home ought to teach children definitely, and persistently how to obey, how to do their work, how to concentrate their attention; but it ought also to surround them with an atmosphere of poetry. This is a working world, and getting to be a very rich world; but if we are to be taught how to work rather than how to live it is going to be a more unhappy world than it has ever been before. In every home there ought to be the books, and, above all, parents ought to open Nature, art, literature, religion to the children, and make them understand at the start that while the world has many workrooms it is not a workshop. (November 1906, 22)

Following Mabie, then, we can read Hudson's mother as failing on two counts, first by indulging his tendency to dissipation, and then by her attitude towards sculpture, which Cecilia describes as a "holy horror" of "an insidious form of immorality" (RH, 68). Roderick, while pitiable on this score, is not likely to be "sympathetic," strictly speaking, to the Mabie reader—nor does he need to be for the novel to serve well the Mabie reading public. As the protagonist easily becomes a textbook example of the perils of imprudent upbringing and improper adult behavior, James's novel becomes a cautionary tale that offers instead a alternate hero, one whose industry and talent combine to leave him standing—and, while not emotionally unscathed, functioning—at the end of the book. This hero is Sam Singleton, a diligent and quietly inspired American landscape watercolorist who has, like Hudson, come to Italy to perfect his art. Singleton's steadiness at the discovery of Roderick's lifeless body is admirable—he is not unfeeling, exclaiming that "he was a beautiful fellow," but he is also undaunted by the task of returning to face Hudson's mother and fiancée with the news. "'I remember [whom I will have to face],' the excellent fellow answered. 'There was nothing I could ever do for him in life; I will do what I can now'" (RH, 387). Singleton could, of course, have done a good bit for Hudson in life, particularly by way of example; while he had "painted worthless daubs and gave no promise of talent" on initially arriving in Rome, "[i]mprovement had come . . . hand in hand with patient industry, and [Singleton's] talent, though of a slender and delicate order, was now incontestable" (RH, 118). Singleton's comportment throughout the novel is equally admirable, both modest and pleasant, though of course it comes in for ridicule from Hudson on numerous occasions. When they meet after a long separation in the Swiss Alps, just before Roderick's death, we learn that Sam had been using in "economic" industry the period over which Roderick had been dissipating and declining. Even Hudson is now inclined to see the convergence, even the interdependence, of industry and skill that characterizes Singleton. "Roderick had said to Rowland at first that Singleton reminded him of some curious little insect with a remarkable mechanical instinct in its *antennae*; but as the days went by it was apparent that the modest landscapist's unflagging industry grew to have an oppressive meaning for him. It pointed a moral, and Roderick used to sit and con the moral as he saw it figured in Singleton's bent back, on the hot hill-sides, protruding from beneath his white umbrella" (*RH*, 360). While the jaundiced James reader, and indeed James himself, might be expected to share Roderick's cynicism regarding Singleton, whom he likens to "a watch that never runs down," it is impossible to deny that Singleton's method, and his "equability," is infinitely preferable in the end to Roderick's volatility, or even to Rowland's enabling dependence on Roderick. James portrays Singleton as having a "quickened sense of his indebtedness to a Providence that had endowed him with intrinsic facilities," a characterization that belies admiration, or at the very least authorial wistfulness, more than cynicism. A Mabie reader would certainly be more inclined to err on the side of Singleton than on the side of his critic.

Roderick Hudson offers another avenue for identification in the character of Hudson's fiancée, Mary Garland. While few critics, either contemporaneous or modern, focus on Mary, preferring instead to read the central relationship of the novel as that between Rowland and Roderick, Mary is the heroine of the novel's love triangle, and thereby inhabits a standard position for sympathetic identification. Her likeness to a significant subset of the Mabie audience would certainly intensify this tendency. As an eager-to-learn but relatively unschooled young American woman in Europe for the first time, Mary approximates the *Journal* readers who might eagerly follow Mabie's numerous reading suggestions regarding European history and society or who wrote in with frequent requests for "some recent interesting books about Italy, especially books which will give an impression of the character of the people and their artistic sense" (May 1905, 18). When Roderick fails to meet her on arrival, Mary is able to negotiate cabs and charwomen with "the assistance of such acquaintance with the Italian tongue as she had culled from a phrase-book during the calm hours of the [transatlantic] voyage" (*RH*, 257). Roderick's mother, on describing her feeling that she is ill equipped to have entered Italian territory, laments that "[w]e are told that you must know so much, that you must have read so many books. Our taste has not been cultivated. When I was a young lady at school I remember I had a medal with a pink ribbon for 'proficiency in ancient history' . . . but I have forgotten about all the kings" (*RH*, 259). We learn that Mary has worked independently to make up for this lack of "cultivation," following a course of reading not unlike that prescribed by Mabie in some of his columns directed to armchair travelers. While at home, she has read Madame de Staël's *Corinne* aloud to her future mother-in-law in the evenings and spent her mornings working her way through a fifteen-volume history, J.-C.-L. Simonde de Sismondi's *History of Italian Republics*, and "a shorter one—Roscoe's *Leo the Tenth*." While she dutifully studies the drier histories that a rigorous dedication to realism would require, she also selects the uber-romantic *Corinne*, presumably to appeal to Mrs. Hudson's tastes, but surely not without absorbing herself in the tale of the Byronic heroine. This kind of mix is germane to Mabie's readers, whom Mabie has pointed towards both the Byronic canon and historical works such as Sismondi's both in preparation for Italian travels and as a means of vicariously experiencing other lands even when a passage cannot be achieved. "Traveling is one of the most enjoyable and fruitful means of education," Mabie writes, "but in order to travel it is not necessary to go outside the walls of one's home . . . if the opportunity to visit Europe does not come travel by the aid of books" (January 1904, 17). He comforts the homebound that, in fact, "[s]ome of the most graphic descriptions of countries have been written by men who have never crossed their boundaries." To approximate the travel experience, Mabie appends reading lists that will imaginatively locate his readers "on the canals of Venice" through eight titles—including Sismondi's *Italian Republics*—or help them approximate "a few weeks in Rome" via Mrs. Humphry Ward's *Eleanor* and Hawthorne's *Marble Faun*. He likewise insists that the traveler who is in fact making the journey must do some research ahead of time: "Those who travel wisely know that really to see the world one must take the history of the world with him. [. . .] No man can cross the 'Place de la Concorde' in Paris and really see that 'brilliant immensity,' as Mr. James has called it, unless he can recall through his memory and imagination the historic tragedies that have taken place on that magnificent stage" (June 1910, 34). Mrs. Hudson's sense of the pressure to be prepared would surely resonate with a Mabie reader, whom Mabie has urged to be prepared—and Mary's reading program, at which Rowland Mallet "could not help laughing," would hardly seem mockable.

Mary continues to study while in Europe, again, like a good Mabie reader. She approaches her tourism with an industry that both amuses

and charms Mallet, perusing conscientiously the books of "artistic or an-
tiquarian reference" to which he directs her. When he takes her out to see
the artistic sights of Rome, Mallet marvels at her potential for "development": "Her enjoyment was not especially demonstrative, but it was curi-
ously diligent. Rowland felt that it was not amusement and sensation that
she coveted, but knowledge—facts that she might noiselessly lay away
piece by piece in the fragrant darkness of her serious mind. . . . There was
something exquisite in her pious desire to improve herself, and Rowland
encouraged it none the less that its fruits were not for him" (RH, 269).
Mary is both the attentive reader of her Guide to Rome, by John Murray, and an eager student to Mallet; when he tells her that she has "an
insatiable avidity for facts," she responds that she "must lay up a store
of learning against dark days," anticipating the possible return of her
armchair traveler days: "After all, I can't believe that I shall always be in
Rome" (RH, 272). The Murray guide, while it would have been eclipsed in
popularity by Baedeker's by the early twentieth century, was the standard
guidebook for American and British travelers in the nineteenth century,
and it offered its readers a mix of practical and historical information
alongside a generous amount of Byron, selected to "guide the finer feelings of the tourist" through atmospheric prompts.[16] For example, Murray
excerpts act 3, scene 4, of "Manfred," popularly known as "The Coliseum
by Moonlight," at length in the 1875 Handbook entry on the Coliseum,
noting that "the scene from the summit [of a particular staircase] is one
of the most impressive, and there are few travellers who do not visit the
spots by moonlight in order to realize the magnificent description in
'Manfred,' the only description which has ever done justice to the wonders of the Coliseum."[17] As James Buzard notes, Murray's Byronization
of the tourist experience became a commonplace of nineteenth-century
travel literature, and his influence accounts perhaps in part for Mabie's
liberal recommendations of Byron to the traveler about to embark for
Europe in June 1910—recommendations which include, of course, "The
Coliseum at Moonlight."

Mary's guidebook and readings exist on a continuum with Mabie's
reader recommendations, and her attitudes echo the attitudes already
existing in, carefully cultivated by, or aspirationally pursued by the Mabie reader; it would hardly be surprising that such a reader would sympathetically identify with her plight as Roderick's spurned fiancée or would
root for her to transfer her affections to the sympathetic guide, Mallet,
who is always so glad when she pays more attention to his conversation
than to her guidebook.

He had been waiting once while they talked—they were differ-
ing and arguing a little—to see whether she would take her fore-
finger out of her *Murray*, into which she had inserted it to keep her
place. It would have been hard to say why this point had interested
him, for he had not the slightest real apprehension that she was
dry or pedantic. The simple human truth was that the poor fellow
was jealous of science. In preaching science to her he had over-esti-
mated his own powers of self-effacement. Suddenly, sinking science
for a moment, she looked at him very frankly and began to frown.
At the same time she let the *Murray* slide down to the ground, and
he was so charmed with this circumstance that he made no movement to pick it up. (*RH*, 272–73)

To the romantically inclined Mabie reader, Mallet's pleasure is fairly
transparently—and wholly—a symptom of his affection for Mary, rather
than a mixture of the affections and his disdain for prescriptive guidebooks. Indeed, when read with an eye to sympathetic identification with
Mary, *Roderick Hudson* becomes a fairly standard, if not cheerfully resolved, romance plot with a love triangle. Such a reader might even go
further, to uncritically agree with Mary that Mallet should really consider writing a book, "a history; something about art or antiquities" (*RH*,
275), even though this suggestion is presented cynically in the text.

In the Mary-focused reading, the reader sees Hudson's faults not just
as the destruction of an artistic genius but as the ruination of a selfless
love. Mary's final agonized cry at the sight of her fiancé's body resonates
in the reader's mind as it resonates in Rowland's mind, but there is a
hope, held out at the end, for an end to her premature widowhood. Mallet visits Mary frequently in the home she shares with the woman who
would have been her mother-in-law; he tells his cousin Cecilia that he
is "the most patient" man. While a practiced James reader might see in
this statement futility, or impotence, the romantically inclined might
read promise, or the possibility that at some point in future, after she has
dutifully seen Mrs. Hudson into a peaceful grave, Mary might turn for
companionship to an enduring, patient Mallet.

The Question of Romance: *The Princess Casamassima*

In the March 1904 column mentioned above, Mabie can be found answering a second reader query with a James novel—this time around,
the reader has asked whether "any really great, enduring work of fiction

[has] been published in the last ten years." Mabie first replies that "[i]f you mean by 'great, enduring work of fiction,' novel-writing of the very highest order, such as is found in 'Vanity Fair,' 'Henry Esmond,' 'Quentin Durward,' 'The Mill on the Floss,' 'David Copperfield,' and 'Eugénie Grandet,' it cannot be said that such work has appeared in the United States during the last ten years"; however, he concedes that "those years have been peculiarly fruitful in thoroughly sincere, well-constructed and vital pieces of fiction" (March 1904, 16). He lists foremost short fiction, but has also a long list of novels he claims qualify, which include the fourteen-year-old *Hazard of New Fortunes* (1890) alongside the eighteen-year-old *Princess Casamassima* (1886).

Perhaps Mabie simply neglected to check publication dates when he was composing his column, or perhaps he was influenced by the theme with which he opened the month's reflections, "The American Romance." This mini-essay functions primarily to reclaim working-class subject matter for romance, insisting that "the romance of the workshop is as pure in quality as, and is perhaps greater in mass than, the romance of the castle and the palace." While he still celebrates the "old romance" of chivalry, Mabie wants to democratize nobility, to argue that "the profoundest interest in life is found in the struggles of the soul, and that pathos and grandeur are as often found in the experience of the peasant as in that of the king." Though his language remains archaic, speaking of peasants rather than industrial laborers, Mabie also claims this shift as a hallmark of modernity and, most important, as a reader-driven transformation. "So far has this movement gone that the figures which most intensely interest modern readers are those of men and women who are struggling against adverse external fortunes, or who, by reason of isolation or detachment from the larger movements, the main currents, of society, have a marked and homely individuality." I take up later the ways that this passage explicitly indicates the superiority of regionalism, but for now one can see how it begins to point directly to *The Princess Casamassima*, particularly as Mabie goes on to trumpet the storyline of "the escape of [the spirit of man] from narrow into large conditions"— in other words, the story of a protagonist's desire for upward mobility (March 1904, 16). Hyacinth Robinson, with his humble (even ignominious) beginnings but inherent nobility, is at first glance a perfect candidate for the "escape" Mabie suggests is the most "interesting" for modern readers—*his* readers.

Certainly, Mabie is here careful to couch his discussion in the pure language of spirit rather than in the filthy language of lucre, but a directly preceding discussion of the biographies of Abraham Lincoln and William Gladstone has paved the way for his readers to interpret his words in either register. And a reader who has been directed towards *The Princess Casamassima* just after digesting such a discussion will also be likely to read with such a trajectory in mind, rooting eagerly for, and probably expecting, Hyacinth Robinson's elevation from Lomax Place to a spot beside the titularly promised princess. In other words, through the power of proximity, such a reader might be inclined to view *The Princess Casamassima* as an exemplar of Mabie's "American romance" despite its English setting and James's refusal to follow the Horatio Alger storyline for which he lays the groundwork in the opening pages. Indeed, many of the critics who supported the romantic revival in the 1880s and 1890s targeted this novel as a particularly antiromantic abomination, perhaps because of the frustration of that readerly expectation.[18] *Lippincott's* 1887 review, for example, complains that "there is hardly any story," as James "carefully eschews the ideal characters, the romantic incidents, which the finer art of the modern novelist has taught him to abandon."[19] And yet, to return to Mabie, we can see that it makes sense that he would point his readers towards the most recent James novel to suggest "American romance" possibilities. In other words, if he were laboring under the expectation that he recommend something by James in response to a query about the best of recent American fiction, better *The Princess Casamassima* than *The Spoils of Poynton* or *What Maisie Knew* (the first eligible James novels of his post–*Guy Domville* [1895] period). One imagines him feeling compelled to do so, damning the consequences of readerly frustration with the eventual outcome.

Admittedly, this reading also runs counter to many current critical takes on the novel that, following particularly Michael Davitt Bell, see *Princess Casamassima* as an attempted "realist" offering from a James negotiating "competing versions of realism, impression, and naturalism."[20] At the same time, and in an argument by no means mutually exclusive with Bell's, Marcia Jacobson has convincingly demonstrated that *Princess Casamassima* saw James in intense dialogue with the popular genre of the working-class novel. Jacobson sees James recapitulating stock plots from contemporaries George Gissing and Walter Besant while rejecting their simplistically optimistic conclusions.[21] James rejected the ways that others worked out the formulae, but he retained the architecture—this extant echo, combined with Mabie's penchant for recommending novels in generic groupings, makes it all the more likely that a Mabie reader would take *Princess Casamassima* as another of these types of novels with which he or she was already familiar. Once again, this reader would naturally become aligned with the struggling working-class hero.

Princess Casamassima makes only one other appearance in Mabie's columns, this time as one of a long list of books under the heading "A Beginning in the Best Fiction," accompanied by James's *Roderick Hudson*. In this case, Mabie seems to be treating *Princess* as a later step in progressive weight training, the process to which he likens a reading program earlier in the column:

> Begin by reading the kind of books that interest you, but be sure that they are the best of that kind. If you have never disciplined your mind don't begin by trying to read Kant's "Critique of Pure Reason" or Spencer's "First Principles"; read something that aids you by the simplicity of its style. In physical training you begin by lifting light weights; the heavy weights come later, when the muscles have been strengthened by practice. If you like fiction don't be afraid of that irrational and ignorant condemnation of novels simply because they are novels. There are hosts of trashy stories, but there is also a host of novels which rank with the best literature. Don't hesitate to begin with novels, but be sure you read only the best. When you have reached the point where you can enjoy the finest fiction you will pass easily to history, to essays, to narrative poetry. (October 1905, 20)

After such a construction of the self-culture process, it makes sense that Mabie would recommend one of his proven favorite James novels first and then the closest thing to a "sequel" that James ever penned. The rest of the "Beginning in the Best Fiction" list follows a similar pattern. Mabie often suggests two works by an author, but they are not always listed in order of publication; rather, the first listed seems to be the title more commonly considered a "standard," and the second is either less well known or reputed to be more "difficult." For example, Scott appears first on the list, his *Ivanhoe* to be followed by *Waverly*. For George Eliot, *Adam Bede* prepares readers for *The Mill on the Floss*. Having read Thomas Hardy's *Far from the Madding Crowd*, one would apparently be more likely to appreciate (or follow!) *Under the Greenwood Tree*. All of these literary heavyweights share space on Mabie's list with Thomas Nelson Page, George Washington Cable, James Lane Allen, and Mary Noailles Murfree; the list is heavily weighted towards "romance" and regionalist works. The list also seems to be structured as a progressive program of reading; readers would start with Scott and arrive at Eliot via Jane Austen and Maria Edgworth; Mrs. Humphry Ward and Harriet Beecher Stowe directly precede Nathaniel Hawthorne, James Fenimore Cooper, Oliver Wendell Holmes, James, and Howells; a cluster of local color writers eventually make way for the last, and edgiest, writer on the list: Frank Norris.

Hyacinth Robinson is an autodidact in the Mabie mold, and he does finally refuse to commit a murder that would upend the balance of society, for he appreciates the cultural products that social and economic hierarchies have produced. He discovers that he values the "splendid accumulations of the happier few, to which doubtless the miserable many have also in their degree contributed."[22] He reflects that these cultural works, though they have been "based if you will upon all the despotisms, the cruelties, the exclusions, the monopolies and the rapacities of the past," still render "the world . . . less of a 'bloody sell' and life more of a lark," and despite his relative lack of funds, he still has access to them through books. "I smoke cigarettes and in the pauses of this composition recline on a faded magenta divan in the corner. Convenient to my hand in that attitude are the works of Leopardi and a second-hand dictionary. I'm very happy—happier than I have ever been in my life save at Medley—and I don't care for anything but the present hour."[23] Such is the ideal attitude of the Mabie reader, in blissful, concentrated study, and it is this attitude that ultimately saves Hyacinth from criminality.

An alternate reading, of course, is that Hyacinth kills himself out of grief over having been rejected by his princess in favor of Paul Muniment, coupled with the knowledge that he has lost his working-class childhood sweetheart, Millicent, to the false Captain Sholto. If this love quadrangle is read as the central focus of the novel, it is relatively easy to overlook the anarchist content, and the class commentary appears primarily in service of this romance plot. In other words, *The Princess Casamassima* can look like any number of traditional plots, and none of them need be troubling to a reader who is in search of a particular reading experience. It is a romance; it is a story valorizing self-culture; it is a tragedy; it makes itself available to a number of different Mabie readers with relative ease.

Romance Realized: *The Portrait of a Lady*

Roderick Hudson and *The Princess Casamassima* were both acceptable James novels, but Mabie recommended neither of them as frequently as he mentioned *The Portrait of a Lady*. Among professional critics, he was not exceptional in his appreciation of *Portrait*; in the early 1900s, the novel was already generally considered to be James's masterpiece, the hallmark against which all his other works were judged. To a certain extent this revisionary appreciation of *Portrait* could be attributed to the 1901 publication of the controversial *The Wings of the Dove*. Professional reviewers were divided about *Wings* and frequently tried to redeem James by recourse to *Portrait*—as did the reviewer for the *Chicago Evening Post*, whose article is worth quoting at length for its thorough detailing of the elements of *Portrait* that held primary appeal:

> The world moves and of course the growing artist must move with it; but that twenty-two years should have led us on from 'The Por trait of a Lady' to 'The Wings of the Dove' is a matter more for amazement than for pleasure. [. . .] Isabel Archer is just as attractive in her tender young dignity as Milly Theale, and rather easier to get at; and Lord Warburton is worth a dozen Lord Marks; and old Mrs. Touchett has much more definition and brio than Aunt Maud Lowder; and Henrietta Stackpole is just as staunch a friend as Susan Shepherd Stringham, and much better fun; and quaint, blessed Ralph Touchett is worth all the Merton Denshers that ever could be invented; and Gardencourt is vastly more of this world than is the vague Venetian palace wherein Milly Theale wore her ropes of pearls and held her pathetic little court.[24]

The *Post* reviewer goes on to lament that "Mr. James has gone along refining on his own refinements until the delicate has become the impalpable, and the elusive intangible, and the exquisite the all but imperceptible," and predicts that "[a]ll these characteristics . . . make it unlikely that, with the best will in the world, he will produce a book that the general reading public, even in its upper grades, can greatly care for." Books like *Portrait*, though, remain so important that "no fairly discriminating reader would wish to lose" them. James's adoption of a more rarefied style throws earlier works, like *Portrait*, into relief, and they are even more essential because James, now a captive to this new style, will probably never be able to produce a sequel.

In 1881, the reviews of *Portrait* had not been unanimously glowing, but even reviewers like the writer for the *New York Times*, who found the novel "unsatisfactory in its beginning and in its end," thought that the novel, if accepted on its own terms, probably marked James's "highest-water mark in fiction."[25] Even though there were many who, along with John Hay in the *New York Tribune*, would predict that the novel would "certainly remain one of the notable books of the time," both the resolution of the plot and the amount of text James had produced to reach that resolution came in for considerable critique in 1881 from reviewers inclined to celebrate James and those whose patience had clearly worn thin.[26] The reviewer for the *New York Herald* conceded that "Mr. James is always at a level of brilliancy in writing which defies a loss of interest, though it seems at time that he should have produced his effects with half the expenditure of force."[27] A more cynical reviewer for the *Chicago Tribune* complained that "Mr. James thinks that he is writing for a class to whom the simplest statements are enigmas, and he deems it necessary to explain at great length the most natural traits in human nature"; the review closes predicting that "to the general reader the volume will be found entertaining, and will be classed as the best, as it is the longest, Mr. James has yet written."[28]

Despite the relative absence of a "plot" in the novel, then, it was supposed that it would have appeal for a general readership and that readers would stick with the story to the (unsatisfactory) conclusion. "In spite of a certain amount of irritation which it will be likely to excite," wrote the *Times* reviewer, "in spite of not a little thinness and unnaturalness which belong to the characters . . . one is never quite content to lay aside the volume without knowing what has become of them so far as Mr. James is willing to let his reader know."[29] Even more, a reader bent on collecting James as a part of his or her mental furniture would figure out some way to maintain interest, even if this meant neglecting to read every word of the text. The *Chicago Tribune* review points to a dynamic of James fetishization that was already in place by 1881; the "general reader" so cynically evoked presumably makes his or her determinations based on a text's length, or perceived importance, and will embrace the novel on those points, if not on any substantive response to the text itself. And, indeed, a reader of *Portrait* could very easily skim over some of the slower portions of the text, could blur through long passages of reflection and description to arrive at dialogue, or action, or some key moment that would signal movement. Such a reader might well ignore the frustrating ending in favor of a more salutary possibility that sees Isabel somehow, sometime, finding romantic happiness away from Osmond—despite any Jamesian indications to the contrary—or might choose to console him- or herself with the one happy marriage plot in the novel, that between Henrietta Stackpole and Mr. Bantling.

The beginning of *Portrait* offers no signal that a romantically inclined reader would need to look elsewhere than to Isabel for interest. Isabel arrives, in the first scene, at a picturesque English country house and is immediately set upon by an eligible lord who is enamored of her American verve and freshness. She is Daisy Miller with better luck, but she also has something Daisy lacked: she has ideals, which have been fostered by her desultory youthful reading. By describing her aunt's library as "full of books with frontispieces," James pithily indicates the genteel romantic offerings from which Isabel draws her knowledge of history, politics, psychology, and philosophy.[30] It may in fact be going too far to say that Isabel derives "knowledge" of these topics from these books; Isabel is not a deep reader, but she does receive impressions from her books. She enjoys having the "reputation of reading a great deal" (*PL*, 41), a characteristic that would be attractive to and resonant for the *Journal* reader who aspires to a similar graceful reputation. But James short-circuits this admiration when he illustrates Isabel's inability to distinguish between the imagined world of the romance and the reality that surrounds her through her attitudes towards the American Civil War. "[S]he passed months of this long period," James writes, "in a state of almost passionate excitement, in which she felt at times (to her extreme confusion) stirred almost indiscriminately by the valour of either army" (*PL*, 41). Isabel has not formulated a politically nuanced opinion of the competing claims of North and South, but she thinks of the war in abstracted romantic terms. She is not unlike the feuding Shepardson and Grangerford families in Mark Twain's *Huckleberry Finn*, who act as if they are living in a Scott novel and have little apparent awareness of the life-or-death consequences of doing so. For the young Isabel, war is noble, because it is the occasion for nobility in Scott. James leaves little room, with such a portrait, for uncritical identification; at the very least, a reader as young and inexperienced as the Civil War–era Isabel should intimate from the narrative's tone a critique of such attitudes; older readers should easily acknowledge the youthful silliness and potential danger of Isabel's uncritical romanticism.

At the moment of her arrival in England, however, Isabel is not sufficiently aware of her naïve idealism, and she behaves in many respects like the heroines of her novels. She is a cheeky American girl, telling her lordly suitor Warburton: "In a revolution—after it was well begun—I think I should be a high, proud loyalist. One sympathizes more with them, and they've a chance to behave so exquisitely. I mean so picturesquely" (*PL*, 71). James has overdetermined his text in such a way that his reader should receive such a statement with bemusement, just as Warburton does; he sets up the reaction even more solidly in the New York Edition than in the original, in which Isabel declares her sympathy with a "conservative" (*PL* 1881, 502) instead of a "high, proud loyalist." In the revised version, Isabel is so clearly ventriloquizing stock romantic formulae that we can regard her statement as nothing but that of an inexperienced, but widely read, young girl from the provinces. But Isabel refuses to play the script as written; she rejects Warburton's proposal of marriage, preferring to gain the experience she knows she lacks. This turn of the screw is designed to paradoxically reengage the romantic impulses of even the most cynical of readers. Presented with a character who knows enough to know that she doesn't know enough, the unwitting reader, like Ralph Touchett, is supposed to be intrigued, and, like Ralph, the reader should eagerly anticipate the attractive and unpredictable Isabel's next move. James has set up a bildungsroman founded on an initial rejection of the romantic ideology of a bildungsroman, and he works to disarm his more realistically inclined readers to the point that they become willing to engage in the archetypal romantic form. The remainder of the novel functions to chasten the reader who has presumably conceded so easily to the romance, even under the guise of rejecting romance; the final rejection would come in Isabel's selfless, noble, but outwardly "conventional" return to her legal husband at the end of the novel.

At least, this is how the novel's complex engagement with the romance would ideally function; however, some indications exist to suggest that not a few readers would be likely to recast the novel's ending to conform with readerly desires for a happier, more hopeful, and more dramatic ending. The reviewer for the *Times*, for example, asserts that Caspar will have "the perilous and unlikely task of consoling the heroine for her first mistake in matrimony," and while that is not a particularly satisfactory post-Gilbert option for Isabel, he does at least envision a future for Isabel beyond this unhappy marriage.[31] The minor problem of how precisely that is to come about is easily dealt with—"by death or divorce, as the reader may elect"—and either possibility seems to comfort the reviewer, not to scandalize him or her. "The novel ends with Isabel refusing to run away with Caspar Goodwood and returning to her worthless husband in a manner suggestive of a sequel," writes the reviewer for the *New York Herald*, in a manner suggestive of wish-fulfilling revisionism.[32] One might contrast these efforts with Margaret Oliphant's review of the novel in the March 1882 number of *Blackwood's*; she is likewise sure that Isabel and Caspar will find their way back to each other, but she describes this likelihood as a "future stain" and finds this suggestion too similar to a sensation novel and beneath the dignity of James. "Let smaller workmen avail themselves of these easy means of startling the reader; from him we have a right to expect better things." For the *Journal* reader, who has not been a fan of James's tendency to leave his reader, as Oliphant puts it, "usually tantalized, half angry with an end which is left to our imagination," this more sensational approach may well be a welcome change.[33]

One imagines the assurance that the Isabel-Caspar reunion will come to pass is largely a result of Henrietta Stackpole's benediction to Caspar, which is presented in the original with much less editorializing than in the revised New York Edition. In the 1881 edition, Henrietta's "Look here, Mr. Goodwood . . . just you wait!" is followed simply by Caspar's reaction, "On which he looked up at her" (*PL* 1881, 575). In 1908, the reader would receive a bit more direction away from hoping for a Caspar-Isabel reunion; he still looks up at Henrietta, but now "only to guess, from her face, with a revulsion, that she simply meant he was young. She stood shining at him with that cheap comfort, and it added, on the spot, thirty years to his life. She walked him away with her, however, as if she had given him now the key to patience" (*PL*, 490). In this iteration, Henrietta is not only wrong about the possibility that Isabel will return to Caspar, she is self-deluded, and more than a bit silly in that delusion. It seems quite likely that James felt he needed to add this commentary because of readings like those of Oliphant and the *Times* reviewer; if a professional reader jumped to such conclusions, and entertained a variety of creative options that would bring about the more-desired conclusion, surely other readers would have done the same. We should not be surprised, in fact, to find readers of *Portrait* hoping throughout that Isabel might find her way clear to marrying her English lord or her American industrialist while setting aside James's engagement with the worldviews of aestheticism and the fineness of Isabel's final sacrifice. And just as surely, James's attempts to prevent readers from doing so would have made the resulting revision much less satisfactory to those who wanted a happier ending.

James was not looking to frustrate his readers when he revised *Portrait*. He actually predicted in a letter to his publisher that the revisions "shall have hugely *improved* the book—& I mean not only for myself, but for the public; this is beyond question."[34] Indeed, the preface to *Portrait* is the most reader-centric in the New York Edition, signaling that James cared a good deal about the reader reception of *this* novel in particular. When he talks about the *Portrait* reader, an anxiety over Henrietta Stackpole follows closely behind. His concern about the reader losing interest in the story segues quickly into a discussion of his "flawed" treatment of Henrietta, whose characterization he claims is a result of an "anxiety" over providing for "the reader's amusement." Henrietta haunts James's discussion of the novel; she reappears like the repressed immediately after he compliments himself on the part of the novel that he feels was most successful and most innovative. Almost before he can finish discussing the chapter in which Isabel's midnight meditation on the situation with Osmond and Merle "throws the action further forward than twenty 'incidents' might have done," James needs to finish "apologizing" for Henrietta:

> [S]he exemplifies, I fear, in her superabundance, not an element of my plan, but only an excess of my zeal. So early was to begin my tendency to *overtreat*, rather than undertreat (when there was choice or danger) my subject. (Many members of my craft, I gather, are far from agreeing with me, but I have always held overtreating the minor disservice.) "Treating" that of "The Portrait" amounted to never forgetting, by any lapse, that the thing was under a special obligation to be amusing. There was the danger of the noted "thinness"—which was to be averted, tooth and nail, by cultivation of the lively. That is at least how I see it to-day. Henrietta must have been at that time a part of my wonderful notion of the lively.[35]

James's prefaces are as concerned with creating a commanding authorial persona as they are about guiding the readerly experience, and in this case he does so at the expense of his younger self. The now older, wiser James represents a youthful self who is not entirely in control of his text, or of his textual effects. The desire to please a particular segment of an audience—the desire to appease an audience notion of "amusement"— drove the younger James to commit a sin against his own better aesthetic judgment, a sin to which the older James would apparently never fall prey. Even though his transgression was minor—an error in the direction of "overtreating" rather than "undertreating"—he still paid more attention to his reception, to his feelings of obligation towards the audience, than to his obligations to the material and to his project. Insofar as the preface offers a narrative in which he promises to correct the error of those ways, James reinforces the persona of the "Master," and he assures his audience that the text they are about to read in the corrected version has greater integrity than the former version.

James is of course also guiding readerly opinion in this passage about Henrietta by indicating, however subtly, the category to which readers should belong if they were to find themselves attracted to Henrietta's character. By suggesting that she was produced with a mass taste in mind, and to the end of offering a "lively" figure to entertain the less sophisticated of his readers, James inoculated his conscientious reader against too much affection for Henrietta. Who, after all, would want to be accused of seeking out the "lively" in a work by the Master? This would be, at best, evidence of an aesthetic understanding not fully formed—would evince a similarity to the inexpert young James's "wonderful notion of the lively." At worst, an attraction to Henrietta would reveal the reader as a philistine, the kind of reader who could not be expected to understand James's experiments in psychological narrative and who would need a crutch to get through chapter 42. The reader enters the text predisposed to see Henrietta as a silly character, a light "ficelle," as James terms her in the preface, rather than a figure who has something significant to offer the piece or something important to say about the central action. Her commentary in the novel becomes, for a reader thus prepared, little more than comic relief, and any comparisons with Isabel Archer would necessarily redound to Isabel's favor and Henrietta's detriment.

The fact that James spent so much time trying to steer his readers away from Henrietta suggests that he felt that the original audiences of the novel—whether this was a part of his intent or not—were far too attentive to Henrietta, too interested in her career and her commentary, perhaps even to Isabel's disadvantage. Perhaps readers were finding in Henrietta too much sensible critique of Isabel's actions, too many prescient warnings that the romantic Isabel should not have ignored. It is Henrietta, for example, who critiques Isabel for sounding "like the heroine of an immoral novel" and warns her that she is "drifting to some great mistake," long before Isabel has inherited money or met Gilbert Osmond (*PL*, 146). It is Henrietta who observes to a newly wealthy Isabel that "the peril for you is that you live too much in the world of your own dreams" and who cautions her that her "newly-acquired thousands will shut you up more and more to the society of a few selfish and heartless people who will be interested in keeping up those illusions" (*PL*, 188). By the time the reader witnesses Henrietta's latter offering, she has already been privy to Madame Merle's inchoate envy over Isabel's inheritance and has been told in that connection that Merle had "desires which had never been satisfied" (*PL*, 180). Henrietta is the voice of reason throughout the novel, and she is the one character who a reader can feel is always, uncategorically, on Isabel's side, who has no ulterior motives for helping her, whether invidious (like Merle or Osmond), romantic (like Warburton or Goodwood), or naïve and clumsy (like the two Touchetts, Ralph and his father).

In the New York Edition, while James does not evacuate the accuracy of Henrietta's observations, he does tweak the descriptors he uses for her in these key scenes in ways that subtly undermine her as an alternate exemplar in the text. In the scene cited above, in which Henrietta warns Isabel against "drifting towards some great mistake," the reader of the 1908 version sees Henrietta "glittering for an instant in dismay" (*PL*, 146) rather than simply "standing there with expanded eyes" (*PL* 1881, 516). Such changes do great violence to the Henrietta so attractive to readers like the *Chicago Evening Post* reviewer of *The Wings of the Dove*, who praises her as "as staunch a friend as Susan Shepherd Stringham, and much better fun."[36] The Boston *Literary World* reviewer found the 1881 Henrietta and Bantling "two of the most wholesome characters in the book" and would surely have been dismayed to find them, as Nina Baym has characterized it, the victims of a "systematic vulgarization."[37] Baym argues that the new dynamic between Henrietta and Isabel bolsters James's project of making self-awareness the success Isabel achieves at the end of the novel; after the revisions to Isabel and the attendant changes in Henrietta, the former is "no longer perceived as having failed."[38] This change is all the more reason for Mabie to avoid mention of the New York Edition altogether; such a "success" would hardly have been seen as one by his readership. The unromantic failure to imagine a way out of such a return—even in death, which would be tragic, and romantic, rather than quotidian—smacks of pessimism, and Mabie thought pessimism only justifiable in "the case of Roman satirists of the decadence, and the Russian novelists; but current pessimism is largely a pose or fashion, an affectation or a pretension" (March 1907, 22). Such are sentiments that could easily have been expressed by the no-nonsense Henrietta Stackpole, who utters the final, stubbornly optimistic words of the text: "Look here, Mr. Goodwood . . . just you wait!" (*PL*, 490). In the 1881 edition, these words are followed simply with the line, "On which he looked up at her" (*PL* 1881, 575), and the curtain closes on an ambiguous scene that could indeed promise a sequel chronicling Caspar's final success. In 1908, James adds a long qualification paragraph that seems intended to undercut Goodwood's hopes by characterizing Henrietta's phrase as formulaic, empty, "cheap comfort" (*PL*, 490). Such pessimism has no place in the Mabie universe; it is unproductive, unnecessary, and ultimately shortsighted. It is a telling coincidence that the 1881 *Literary World* reviewer wrote that "we hear in this book a semi-wail, as it were, of the latter Roman empire."[39] Without the 1881 Henrietta, that "semi-wail" would surely have been a shriek.

Portrait's success, in the words of one earlier reviewer, was a result of the novel's "combining a scientific value with romantic interest and artistic merit."[40] Some of the work of the revision was to distance the novel from the "romantic," and to this we may attribute the lack of interest in the New York Edition from critics like Mabie. Unfortunately for James, such critics had by 1908 established themselves as gatekeepers, if not for all fiction, certainly for "quality" fiction and the high-middlebrow market. Mabie never mentioned the exciting new versions of James's greatest novels, primarily because the features that made *Portrait*, *Roderick Hudson*, and *The Princess Casamassima* suitable for the general reader were weakened by the New York Edition changes. A more romantic Henry James, one who offered characters consistent with the culture of success promulgated by Mabie and the *Ladies' Home Journal*, was to be had in the original versions.

The Unrepentant Romance of F. Marion Crawford

After some selective rereading, James's oeuvre can indeed offer some of the same satisfactions as the work of another one of Mabie's perennial favorites, who Mabie frequently set alongside James in reading lists and reviews: F. Marion Crawford. Crawford enjoyed tremendous popular success in the 1880s through the 1910s, publishing forty-four novels over a thirty-year period, alongside numerous nonfiction pamphlets and monographs. As Crawford's biographer writes, "In open competition, Americans preferred Crawford's novels to the fiction of Howells, James, and even Mark Twain. Americans liked Crawford's stories well enough to purchase each of his forty-four volumes by the tens of thousands and to support three collected editions of his work during his lifetime."[41] Contra James, whose collected editions failed miserably in the marketplace, Crawford celebrated the entertaining in literature and wrote frequent critical essays combating the realist manifestos of Norris, Hamlin Garland, and Howells. He saw himself as a content provider whose primary duty was to give the public what it wanted. What it apparently wanted, and what it might have found through effort in James, was the swashbuckling romance of a novel like Crawford's 1885 *Saracinesca*.

The reader looking for advice from Mabie's columns as to what reading was most valuable or pleasurable would be able to discern only the slightest, and most indirect, judgment of relative merit between James and Crawford. Mabie occasionally classifies Crawford's work as "entertaining," as fiction "of today," rather than "enduring" fiction. But he just as regularly includes representative works of Crawford in lists of the "best fiction" or of works of "lasting value." It might even be said that Mabie favors Crawford over James; he mentions Crawford more—twenty-two times to James's eighteen mentions—and mentions *Saracinesca* eight times to *Portrait*'s six mentions. In the lists that provide the outlines of the Mabie canon, Crawford appears just as frequently as, and in easy proximity with, James (March 1903; June 1905; October 1905; September 1909). It is of course one of the novels listed in a series of "fiction based on the history of Italy" in the June 1910 column "Books about Europe for Home Reading and Travel." Unlike James, Crawford is a regular feature of Mabie's lists of books for younger readers; Crawford's fiction helps Mabie answer in the affirmative the question he asks in "Should the Young Read Novels?" (September 1907) and provides good options for girls fifteen to twenty years old (October 1907). Crawford is more broadly appealing than James, and his less-successful pieces are still "wholesome," if not classics. This assessment is in marked contrast with James, whose late pieces Mabie dismisses as "disagreeable" (March 1905, 21).

By 1902, when Mabie's tenure at the *Journal* began, Crawford had already written most of his most notable works—the *Saracinesca* trilogy (1887, 1889, 1892); *The Cigarette-Maker's Romance* (1890); *Corleone* (1896); and *Via Crucis* (1899)—but Mabie dutifully marked the publication of each new Crawford novel with a review and a recommendation. He usually also made reference to *Saracinesca* in these latter-day notices. In January 1903, in a column flanked by a photograph with the caption "Mr. F. Marion Crawford's Italian Home," he celebrates the publication of *Cecilia* under the heading "A Bunch of Good Stories." He qualifies his remarks with the acknowledgment that "the season has not been rich in novels which will be read by the next generation, but it has produced a number of well-written stories of wholesome tone and well-worth reading for refreshment and entertainment." *Cecilia* "has a novel plot with a suggestion of the Oriental doctrine of reincarnation, contains some very good character drawing," and, perhaps most important, "takes the reader back to Rome, the scene of some of Mr. Crawford's best novels; among which are 'Saracinesca,' 'A Roman Singer,' and 'The Cigarette-Maker's Romance.'" The last titles, one assumes, *are* novels "which will be read by the next generation," whose members are up to eighteen years old themselves (January 1903, 15). Mabie is still referencing *Saracinesca* in December 1909, when he welcomes one of Crawford's last novels, *Stradella*, as "one of the best of its kind." Acknowledging that "it lacks the literary quality of the 'Saracinesca' series," Mabie applauds the novel as an exemplary "stor[y] of incident and plot." "[I]t moves with rapidity, the characters are not submerged in the current of the story, and the atmosphere of artistic feeling, of daring individuality in crime, and of a religious devotion which makes it possible for two vigorously-drawn villains to make provision for prayers for the soul of the man they are about to murder, invest the adventures of the brilliant young singer from the South and the beautiful Venetian girl who elopes with him with something of the splendor of the Renaissance period" (December 1909, 32). A wholesome tone, an accurately observed atmosphere, and an engaging story, are all qualities that recommend a novel for "refreshment," and refreshment is just as important, and profitable, a goal for reading as "betterment."

Saracinesca offers the Mabie reader the perfect combination of entertainment and cultural value. Like the "reading up" version of *Roderick Hudson*, *Saracinesca* reads in many spots like a travel guide, a narrative interpretive history, and a companion to self-education. From the opening lines introducing the reader of 1887 to the Rome of 1865, which is the story's setting, Crawford takes an instructional tone, signaling that the previous generation's attitudes towards dress, aesthetics, and manners, while sometimes quaint, were overall far preferable to current attitudinal trends. The 1865 traveler to Rome, in particular, had a superior approach to the latter-day traveler:

> Old gentlemen then visited the sights in the morning, and quoted Horace to each other, and in the evening endeavoured by associating with Romans to understand something of Rome; young gentlemen now spend one or two mornings in finding fault with the architecture of Bramante, and "in the evening," like David's enemies, "they grin like a dog and run about the city": young women were content to find much beauty in the galleries and in the museums, and were simple enough to admire what they liked; young ladies of the present day can find nothing to admire except their own perspicacity in detecting faults in Raphael's drawing or Michael Angelo's colouring.[42]

The problem with contemporary Roman vacationers, it seems, is an unwarranted sense of entitlement to opinions—and half-baked ones at that—about an ancient civilization and complex culture that requires more respectful study than "handy text-books and shallow treatises concerning the Renaissance" (S, 3) can provide. The interested reader, however, may well turn towards some of those "handy text-books" to understand more perfectly what Raphael's drawing looks like or consult "treatises concerning the Renaissance" for further enlightenment on any extant debates over Michelangelo's palette. In a move that seems predictive of Mabie's own tendency to evoke, and then assuage, his reader's intellectual insecurities, Crawford solidifies his position as an observer of Italian life and culture by denigrating the critical practice of his philistine contemporaries:

> This is the age of incompetent criticism in matters artistic, and no one is too ignorant to volunteer an opinion. It is sufficient to have visited half-a-dozen Italian towns, and to have read a few pages of fashionable aesthetic literature—no other education is needed to fit the intelligent young critic to his easy task. The art of paradox can be learned in five minutes, and practised by any child; it consists chiefly in taking two expressions of opinion from different authors, halving them, and uniting the first half of the one with the second half of the other. (S, 4)

The chastening that Crawford's proleptic narrator offers in the opening pages of the novel would have hit very close to home for the reader of Mabie's columns who, perhaps, had arrived at *Saracinesca* through the helpful list of works offered in Mabie's January 1904 column under the heading "Travels at Home." Recalling their reading advisor's assurance that "in order to travel it is not necessary to go outside the walls of one's home" (January 1904, 17), the Mabiean reader of Crawford might easily disregard the comment on shallow, callow young critics as irrelevant to his position; he is, after all, following expert advice, subordinating personal judgment in the choice of texts to someone who has (presumably) more immediate experience. Or, perhaps, the reader reads Crawford's critique as directed towards his *literary* rivals, rather than his readership; this preamble would thereby function to legitimate the novel that follows as accurate, and properly observed, despite its more sensational passages.

Having gestured towards the necessity of intimate, immediate experience of a culture, Crawford proceeds to offer his readers—who perhaps put their trust in Crawford as a well-known expatriate and longtime inhabitant of Italy—an armchair traveler's romanticized version of prelapsarian (pre-"modern") Italy, replete with duels, political intrigue, and lovely aristocratic women who retreat to convents to avoid other women's diabolical schemes. *Saracinesca* tells the story of Duke Giovanni Saracinesca's courtship of Corona d'Astradente, who we first meet as the unhappy but faithful and dutiful child bride of an elderly fop.

Aside from this marriage, Saracinesca's affection for Corona is complicated by the attentions of Donna Tullia, a wealthy young widow who has set her sights on the noble title of duchess. Her desire to snare Giovanni, once met with frustration, turns to contempt and a desire for revenge, in which she is joined by the malevolent Ugo del Ferice, a social climber who loathes Giovanni and who attempts to better his social status through deception and manipulation. Though the novel includes some minor complications that ostensibly threaten to imperil the happy match between Corona and Giovanni (the aforementioned elderly husband, a duel with a malevolent nemesis, and a trumped-up polygamy charge based on a case of mistaken identity), the reader knows intuitively that none of these will present any permanent barrier to their happy match. Corona's elderly husband is dispatched in the first third of the novel, leaving her open to marry after a year of modest retirement; the malevolent nemesis cheats during the duel, but Giovanni is the superior fighter and triumphs at the end (mercifully stopping short of killing his opponent); and the accusation of bigamy is easily disproven. Crawford's novel is, in short, orchestrated throughout to achieve the maximum of romantic readerly pleasure; drama and complications add just enough angst to make the sigh of resolution thoroughly satisfying.

Crawford is an unabashed meritocrat, and one of the central lessons of the text is the surety that aesthetic beauty is inseparable from moral superiority and that such well-matched inner and outer perfection will always triumph over the poseurs who connive against it. There is never really any doubt that things will turn out fine for our hero and heroine, because their nemeses are internally inconsistent from the very start of the novel. While moral and aesthetic superiority are mapped most clearly onto the most aristocratic characters in the novel, there are also bad aristocratic characters, just as there are bad social climbers. We are told, for example, that Donna Tullia's "indescribable air of good breeding, the strange inimitable stamp of social superiority which cannot be acquired by any known process of education," cohabits uneasily with her "distinctly vulgar" dress, voice, and manner. Likewise, the social climbing del Ferice, whose outward appearance is subtle refinement itself, must "perform[] the daily miracle of creating everything for himself out of nothing" (S, 14–15). Both of these villains dabble in revolutionary politics, but again, what seems to bother Crawford is not revolutionary impulses in themselves but the lack of sincerity behind this particular revolutionary moment, both as a whole and as manifested in Donna Tullia and del Ferice.

> When [del Ferice] had begun talking of revolutions to Madame
> Mayer and to half-a-dozen hare-brained youths, of whom Gouache
> the painter was one, he had not really the slightest idea of accom-
> plishing anything. He took advantage of the prevailing excitement
> in order to draw Donna Tullia into a closer confidence than he
> could otherwise have aspired to obtain. [. . .] Del Ferice had hopes
> that, by means of the knot of malcontents he was gradually drawing
> together, he might ruin Giovanni Saracinesca, and get the hand of
> Donna Tullia in marriage. (S, 85)

Donna Tullia plays at revolution because she enjoys the intrigue; she has
no real ideological agenda, and her sympathies are easily swayed. Crawford himself seems to have felt some compunction about placing his villains, however superficially, in the revolutionary camp, and he offers a
retraction of sorts in his epilogue, where he explains that he was not
painting all revolutionaries with the same brush through del Ferice, who
he says "represented the scum which remained after the revolution of
1848 had subsided" (S, 450). Like the false revolutionaries in *The Princess
Casamassima*, the revolutionaries of *Saracinesca* are driven by personal,
not world-historical, motives.

Between the Corona/Giovanni and Tullia / del Ferice extremes, a
fifth character with an independent storyline offers an interesting, and
not immediately explicable, counterpoint. This figure is the expatriate
French painter named Anastase Gouache, who initially caucuses with
del Ferice and Donna Tullia but who comes to see the error of his ways
and joins the Papal Zouaves to fight against the revolutionaries. Gouache
is an aristocrat of a sort, a revolutionary aristocrat, with a long pedigree:
"His grandfather had helped to storm the Bastille, his father had been
among the men of 1848; there was revolutionary blood in his veins, and
he distinguished between real and imaginary conspiracy with the un-
erring certainty of instinct, as the bloodhound knows the track of man
from the slot of meaner game" (S, 237–38). He thinks revolutions are
aesthetically useful—good subject matter—but he does not really sub-
scribe to a political viewpoint, despite long hours spent in the confidence
of the purported conspirators. "It was a good thing for him to paint a
portrait of Donna Tullia, for it made him the fashion, and he had small
scruple in agreeing with her views so long as he had no fixed convictions
of his own" (S, 236). What separates Gouache from his associates is his
combination of innate talent and dedication to craft; Donna Tullia observes, in a moment of self-awareness, that "the part she fancied herself

playing was contemptible enough when compared with the hard work, the earnest purpose, and the remarkable talent of the young artist" (S, 92). Gouache is the genuine article, but he has fallen into a bad set—probably just because he is from out of town.

When he finally enters into prolonged conversation with a truly principled man, the Cardinal, Gouache readily understands that a "true republic" is not socialist—America and the Netherlands, for example, qualify (as does the ancient Roman Empire)—and that the church is consistent with that kind of republicanism. A "hierarchy existed within the democracy, by common consent and for the public good, and formed a second democracy of smaller extent but greater power" in the early church, insists the Cardinal (S, 242), an explanation that satisfies Gouache and leads him to the conclusion that "if the attack upon the Church were suddenly abandoned, your Eminence would immediately abandon your reactionary policy ... and adopt progressive ways" (S, 244). Whether Crawford's political gymnastics here are valid is beside the point; the turn that Gouache makes brings him in line with his true nature, makes his talent and his ethics consistent with each other, and aligns him, finally, with the natural aristocrats of the novel. He appears in the closing scene of the novel, in pursuit of a fugitive del Ferice. After riding for a bit with Giovanni and Corona, he stops to admire their beauty, and then the beauty of the landscape:

> Gouache dropped behind, watching the pair and admiring them with true artistic appreciation. He had a Parisian's love of luxury and perfect appointments as well as an artist's love of beauty, and his eyes rested with unmitigated pleasure on the riders and their horses, losing no detail of their dress, their simple English accoutrements, their firm seats and graceful carriage. But at a turn of the grade the two riders suddenly slipped from his field of vision, and his attention was attracted to the marvellous beauty of the landscape, as looking down the valley towards Astrardente he saw range on range of purple hills rising in a deep perspective, crowned with jagged rocks or sharply defined brown villages, ruddy in the lowering sun. He stopped his horse and sat motionless, drinking in the loveliness before him. So it is that accidents in nature make accidents in the lives of men. (S, 444–45)

Gouache's aesthetic reveries cause him to miss del Ferice when Corona and Giovanni meet him around the bend. Corona begs Giovanni to have mercy on the villain, and del Ferice escapes to wreak havoc in the sequel.

Gouache's artistic preoccupations are the reader's own; his reveries on the fine aristocratic couple and on the landscape are part of the romance that might attract a reader to the novel in the first place. It is fitting, then, that they facilitate continued romance.

While Gouache is like James's Sam Singleton, admirable because of his dedication to craft and standing in the reader's position as an observer of the fascinating personages around him, he is *not* an alternative hero; indeed, his career turns more markedly unheroic in the sequels. Gouache does not need to fill that role because, frankly, the central characters already do so admirably. What female reader would not want it said about her, as it is said about Corona, that she "wielded magnificent weapons, and wielded them nobly, as she did all things" (*S*, 18)? What man, or boy, would not want to imagine himself, like Giovanni, to be "honest and constant in nature, courteous by disposition, and considerate by habit and experience" (*S*, 17)? The production of exemplary characters is Crawford's stated, explicit aim in writing, as he very plainly explains in his 1893 treatise *The Novel: What It Is*. Written in direct response to the publication of William Dean Howells's 1891 *Criticism and Fiction*, Crawford's manifesto holds as a central tenet that "the first object of the novel is to amuse and interest the reader," in opposition to what he saw as the practice of literary realism.[43] To do so, the author is to present his readers with "characters whom they might really like to resemble, acting in scenes in which they themselves would like to take a part" (*NWI*, 23). Readers, Crawford contends, use the resemblance between themselves and the characters in a book as a principle of selection: "The reader knows one side of life, his own, better than the writer possibly can, and he reads with the greatest interest those books which treat of lives like his own" (*NWI*, 81). With circular logic, Crawford explains that the novel also offers its readers exemplary figures, whose resemblance to "real" people apparently makes them available as models: "[The novel's] object is to make one see men and women who might really live, talk, and act as they do in the book, and some of whom one would perhaps like to imitate" (*NWI*, 82).

Crawford's primary contention against realism is that it presents a dull version of life; the novel, he insists, should "represent the real, but in such a way as to make it seem more agreeable and interesting than it actually is" (*NWI*, 46). The benefit of a novel is that it can present to its readers life lived to the extreme, with extraordinary circumstances and events: "The great emotions are not every-day phenomena, and it is the desire to experience them vicariously which creates the demand for fiction and thereby and at the same time a demand for emotion" (*NWI*, 98). And so, Crawford questions the distinction between "realism" and "romance": "Why must a novel-writer be either a 'realist' or a 'romantist'? And, if the latter, why 'romanticist' any more than 'realisticist'? Why should a good novel not combine romance and reality in just proportions? Is there any reason to suppose that the one element must necessarily shut out the other?" (*NWI*, 45). Crawford hits here, unintentionally, on the crux of the matter: the ideologies of genre are irrelevant, after all, to the broad audience, and the semantics seem petty and ridiculous when one begins playing with the words. Crawford appears similarly radical in his unstinting embrace of the novel's status as at base a "marketable commodity, of the class collectively termed 'luxuries,' as not contributing directly to the support of life or the maintenance of health" (*NWI*, 8). Authors are "fiction-makers [. . .] heavily backed, as a body, by the capital of the publisher, of which we desire to obtain for ourselves as much as possible" (*NWI*, 7–8). He rails against the authors and publishers of what he calls "purpose-novels" and speculates that someone who finds he has unwittingly purchased "somebody's views on socialism, religion, or the divorce laws" masquerading themselves as a novel should be able to seek restitution and damages (*NWI*, 14). But he moves, quietly, away from this rhetorical focus on financial capital as he turns his gaze to the promises of a true novel.

> What we call a novel may educate the taste and cultivate the intelligence; under the hand of genius it may purify the heart and fortify the mind; it should never under any circumstances be suffered to deprave the one nor to weaken the other; it may stand for scores of years—and a score of years is a long time in our day—as the exposition of all that is noble, heroic, honest, and true in the life of woman or man; but it has no right to tell us what its writer thinks about the relations of labour and capital, nor to set up what the author conceives to be a nice, original, easy scheme of salvation. [. . .] Lessons, lectures, discussions, sermons, and didactics generally belong to institutions set apart for especial purposes and carefully avoided, after a certain age, by the majority of those who wish to be amused. (*NWI*, 17)

The true novel belongs to the realm of leisure, outside the scrabbling of capital, and above ideological debates about capital; readers do not want to be reminded of that world when they are cultivating themselves through reading. Such rhetoric, of course, obscures the material conditions for such readers' leisure time, just as it works to mystify the cultural object and elevate the author, who stands to profit directly from the notion of the novel as a luxury object.

In the end, Crawford would certainly have been just as uneasy with certain segments of his Mabiean audience as James was; his argument against utilitarian reading of fiction, like James's against those who would be attracted to Henrietta Stackpole, seems a reaction against witnessed phenomena. While Mabie frequently insists on the recreational element of literature—"To rest and to refresh the reader, to stimulate and to enrich him, to enable him to look out over a wide field of life—these are the services which books should render to men; and if a book does not do one of these things for the person who reads it, the reader wastes the time he gives to it" (September 1902, 17)—he also explicitly argues on several occasions that reading teaches one transferable skills that will lead to "success" in no uncertain terms: "Very few people have learned to think, and yet a writer and thinker of high importance has said that success is measured by the power of applying ideas to life. [...] The best way to learn to think—that is, to concentrate the mind on a subject and hold it steadily there—is to read books" (1 November 1910, 36). Reading, presumably even novel-reading, teaches one "ideas" that can be "applied," and it works like mental calisthenics to sharpen the mind for other tasks. Such assertions of fiction's utility to the world of work are what markedly differentiate Mabie from the genteel literary idiom that Crawford represents, as much as they separate him from the realists who would reserve a less utilitarian role for the novel. Crawford comments in his treatise that "the point upon which people differ is the artistic one, and the fact that such differences of opinion exist makes it possible that two writers as widely separated as Mr. Henry James and Mr. Rider Haggard, for instance, find appreciative readers in the same year of the same century—a fact which the literary history of the future will find it hard to explain" (*NWI*, 10). The simultaneous popularity of James, Haggard, and Crawford is less difficult to fathom once one considers not the aesthetics of all three but the readerly orientation that renders all the ostensible aesthetic differences irrelevant.

4 / Misreading *The House of Mirth*

Evidently the "big public" does not shut the door against strong, earnest,
high-class stories if those stories deal with vital subjects in a vital spirit.
The crux of the matter lies at this point: No story can be too good in
literary quality for popular liking provided it deals with the fundamental
passions, relations, and experiences of men, not in a philosophical,
scientific or academic manner, but freshly, vitally.

—HAMILTON WRIGHT MABIE,
"ARE THE BEST-SELLERS WORTH READING?"
(NOVEMBER 1911)

With her first best-selling novel, *The House of Mirth* (1905), Edith Wharton came face-to-face with a reading public determined to have a happy ending for its upwardly mobile heroines. A story has frequently circulated of one indignant friend who chastised Wharton as she was walking in her adopted hometown of Lenox, Massachusetts: "[I]t was bad enough that you had the heart to kill Lily. But here you are, shamelessly parading the streets in a red hat!"[1] For this reader, Wharton's insufficient grief over the death of her heroine is confirmed by her public appearance and underscored by her preference for red over black. In the ostentatious hat, Wharton may even have appeared complicit in the social and economic structures that created Lily's painful final days in the milliner's shop. Wharton's Lenox neighbor was not alone in her dismay. The death of Lily Bart seems to have fundamentally affronted Wharton's 1905 readership, and there were many readers to affront. The book sold 30,000 copies during its first three weeks on the market, a figure that doubled to 60,000 within a month. The numbers then increased exponentially: after ten more days, sales had reached 80,000, and after another ten days, 100,000. The book was soon one of the three most requested adult fiction titles at the New York Public Library.[2] Such figures would be more than respectable for a literary author today; for Wharton's time, they were astonishing.

Astonishment at *The House of Mirth*'s popularity has become a common feature of Wharton criticism, and every critic seems to have a favorite explanation for the novel's appeal. Why indeed would a vast reading public, attracted primarily to escapist romances and rough-riding adventure stories, feel drawn to the story of a socialite's disenchantment, marginalization, and eventual suicide? And why would middle-class readers—who made up the bulk of Wharton's audience—take a critique of high society to heart, given the general culture's fixation on and idealization of upward mobility?[3] *The House of Mirth* was published during Hamilton Wright Mabie's tenure at the *Ladies' Home Journal*, and he wholeheartedly embraced the novel as a "literary" success that could also translate into popular success. Mabie regularly endorsed Wharton as a serious literary producer, albeit one whose focus on craft sometimes rendered her works more austere than her contemporaries' (and he rarely mentioned her without offering another author as a foil). Her works, especially *The House of Mirth*, were tailor-made for his sometimes paradoxical project of simultaneously validating and elevating his audience's tastes; as Mabie would write in a late column about the relative value of "best sellers," the commercial success of Wharton's novels signaled that "the 'big public' does not shut the door against strong, earnest, high-class stories if those stories deal with vital subjects in a vital spirit" (November 1911, 30). Wharton's novels were perfect for Mabie's audience because they fulfilled both the desire for engaging (even sensational) storylines and the status requirements of an upwardly mobile population.

As we shall see, when those two desires were countermanded by the text, readers were also ready, and willing, to perform acts of interpretive legerdemain. Lily's tragic fate may well have touched Wharton's early twentieth-century readers, moving them to tears and eliciting resolutions to thrift. But these readers just as surely imbibed the novel's lush descriptions of Lily's surroundings, the details of the lives of her wealthy friends, and the particulars of the elaborate social rituals by which members of the *haute bourgeoisie* could recognize one another. So one must wonder whether Wharton's contention that "a frivolous society can acquire dramatic significance only through what its frivolity destroys" also reflected the attitude of her readers.[4] Perhaps for most readers, the novel's tragedy was not Lily's destruction itself but her inability to remain in the society in which she nearly had a foothold.

In this light, Lily's tale may be an admonitory one only insofar as it instructs young social climbers what situations they should avoid—or avoid getting caught in—at all costs. Lily is thus a sacrificial lamb not only in the realm of Wharton's novel but also in the world projected by the readers who would take its lessons to heart. Although Wharton scorned the reader who focused on "getting the most out of books," disdaining these "sense-of-duty readers" as a destructive force in American literature ("VR," 514), Lily's story became a flashpoint not for critique of high society but for lengthy debates in several newspapers' editorial pages over Wharton's cruelty in refusing to imagine a different end for her heroine. Contemporaneous discussions of Lily's fate were concerned less with descrying the evils of a high society that devoured its margins than with condemning Wharton for refusing to imagine other options for her heroine. The thematics of the novel and the debates it occasioned present a compact, yet complex, portrait of the practice I have been calling "reading up," which approaches all books as how-to manuals and rewards so-called misreadings that would enable vicarious participation in the lives of wealthy protagonists.

Mechanical Readers and the Reading Habit

By the time Edith Wharton's scathing essay "The Vice of Reading" appeared in the October 1903 issue of the *North American Review*, Hamilton Wright Mabie had already expended considerable energy convincing his *Ladies' Home Journal* audience that any of them could become true readers if they would take their reading practice more seriously, approach it more systematically, and pursue a more refined reading list. It is tempting to think that Mabie's columns were in the front of Wharton's mind when she wrote her piece excoriating "sense of duty" readers, unworthies who had cultivated the "habit of reading" by approaching literariness as an adjunct to "such seasoned virtues as thrift, sobriety, early rising and regular exercise" ("VR," 513). But even if Mabie was not the specific target of her attack, his readers certainly were, as was the foundational assumption of his column: that anyone, regardless of income or education, could come to a reasonable approximation of erudition through application and diligent attention to approved texts. The rhetorical parallels between Mabie's columns and Wharton's essay are extensive; they address the same issues, use the same metaphors, and contest the same key phrase: the "habit of reading." At every point, they stand opposed on principle. And yet Mabie embraces Wharton's fiction as a necessary component of his readers' mental bookshelf, contributing to the production of Wharton as a popular, and financially successful, highbrow author. Reading Mabie's columns against Wharton's essay, we can easily see how both constructed the notion of "elite" literacy in ways that served both parties well; Wharton's elites could appreciate popular highbrow texts without losing their sense of superiority to the masses, and Mabie's readership could congratulate itself on successfully achieving the precincts of the literati. Wharton's essay is a moment at which we can see quite clearly the dynamic I discussed in the introduction, in which elite literature is produced as a brand that relies on a perception of tension—or mutual exclusivity—between mass and highbrow culture.

Though she was notoriously fixated on the marketing and sales of her novels, Wharton presents herself in "The Vice of Reading" as an author terribly concerned about the probability of her work being read inaccurately by an increasingly active mass of readers who were not "born readers" but who, under the tutelage of advice-manual authors and columnists, had "renounce[d] their innocuous dalliance with light literature for more strenuous intercourse" ("VR," 514). Wharton's abiding concern about the proliferation of "sense-of-duty readers" suggests that self-interested misreading was one of the more likely of available ways for an upwardly mobile, middle-class reader in the first quarter of the twentieth century to have approached any text, particularly the "quality literature" to which he or she was being pointed by Hamilton Wright Mabie and other elite cultural arbiters. Wharton dubs this menace to literature the "mechanical reader," her vituperative attack suggesting not only that the practice of mechanical reading was widespread but also that she felt her own work vulnerable to readers of this type:

> It is when the mechanical reader, armed with this high conception of his duty, invades the domain of letters—discusses, criticizes, condemns, or, worse still, praises—that the vice of reading becomes a menace to literature. Even so, it might seem in questionable taste to resent an intrusion prompted by motives so respectable, were it not that the incorrigible self-sufficiency of the mechanical reader makes him a fair object of attack. The man who grinds the barrel-organ does not challenge comparison with Paderewski, but the mechanical reader never doubts his intellectual competency. As grace gives faith, so zeal for self-improvement is supposed to confer brains. ("VR," 515)

The "mechanical reader," Wharton fears, can influence the marketplace and alter the shape of American literary production. Because mechanical readers go about looking for "the book that is being talked about, and [their] sense of its importance is in proportion to the number of editions exhausted before publication," popular books become potentially more important to publishers, Wharton argues, than "the best in literature" ("VR," 517, 520).

The "best in literature," though, was precisely what Mabie was encouraging his middle-class, upwardly mobile audiences to read, even as
he vigorously promoted the "habit of reading" as something all of his
readers should cultivate assiduously. In his third column for the *Journal*,
appearing in May 1902, Mabie features both Wharton and the "reading
habit" in a juxtaposition that might well have left Wharton fuming. In the
centerpiece image, a serene Wharton peers off into the distance beside
the promising subhead "How to Form the Reading Habit." Mabie advises
his time-strapped readers that "[i]n order to organize odd minutes into
fruitful hours one must have a consistent scheme," while cautioning that
"reading ought to be a resource as well as a recreation." Mabie emphasizes that his readers should be decisive and directed in their reading and
that once they have decided on a "scheme" they should be careful at all
costs not to "take up with those [extraneous books] which drift in your
direction." He also advises his readers to ease their way into directive
reading, because a too-ambitious "scheme" will be discouraging and will
probably fail. The key to success lies in beginning with the types of books
towards which you are already inclined: "[I]f you are drawn toward fiction," he writes encouragingly, "plan to read half a dozen novels of the
best kind." And then, organization is the key. "When you have made
your plan, keep your book so near that when the odd ten minutes come
you need not lose one of them" (May 1902, 17).

In his discussion of the "habit of reading," Mabie is explicitly addressing readers who have intellectual ambitions but who do not have
the leisure or the financial wherewithal for a more formal education. In
the description he offers of the moments in which his readers might be
able to benefit from an organized plan of reading, we can see precisely
the class fragment to which Mabie is addressing his column; these are
readers who work, who use public transportation, who are not masters
of their own time but who must wait for and on others, and for whom
reading may provide a rare moment of self-care in the midst of an other-
directed life:

> When you have formed the reading habit in the right way the time
> you spend on the street cars, in ferryboats, on journeys, in waiting
> for others, will constitute your chance for going to college, or of keep-
> ing up the education begun in college. Nine-tenths of those who are
> bewailing absence of opportunity are simply blind to the opportuni-
> ties which lie within their reach; for the chief difference between men

does not lie in difference of opportunity but in difference of ability to recognize an opportunity when it appears. (May 1902, 17)

There are unmistakable promises of escape in this passage, but it is not escapism of the variety against which the eighteenth- and nineteenth-century moralists railed; in this case, the moment of reading offers the escape, as the book becomes an oasis on a crowded streetcar or ferry. "When you have your book in your hand, forget that there is any world outside its pages, for the educational value of reading depends largely on the habit of attention." In the midst of a busy life, a book is a means for solitude, the book reader becomes "independent of his surroundings" by virtue of his ability to concentrate on the book.

And while that promise of escape is enticing, even more so is the implicit result of reading. While obliquely referred to as "opportunity," it is clear from the passage that the reader will, by reading, improve first the self and then the self's material surroundings. Mabie evokes Gladstone as a master of concentration and insists that the focused individual "can do his work four times as well, and he can do four times as much of it." More work, better work, more opportunities—all are code words for professional and financial success, for upward mobility of a material sort, which Mabie implies will directly follow the formation of a "reading habit." He does not come right out and say that one can "read and grow rich," but the connection is certainly there to be made by the desiring reader; it has been implicit from the column's opening discussion of "profitable reading," and the assertion that "the man who knows the value of ten minutes has gone a long way toward making himself rich in mind"—"in mind" sounding here somewhat like an afterthought demanded by propriety. It can be no coincidence that, having written extensively on the opportunities afforded by books, Mabie next turns his attention to two memoirs very much in the "rags-to-riches" mold: Jacob Riis's *Making of an American* and Booker T. Washington's *Up from Slavery*. Both men, Mabie argues, "have formed themselves on American models and developed themselves by means of American opportunities"—the same "opportunities," one imagines, of which Mabie has just been apprising his readership (May 1902, 17).

Wharton also deploys the image of public transportation in discussing aspirational readers in "The Vice of Reading," but with a dramatically different valence. The "ambitious" reader, she contends, is far too familiar with, and too accepting of, uncouth modes of transportation: "The desire to keep up is apparently the strongest incentive to this class of readers:

they seem to regard literature as a cable-car that can be 'boarded' only by running; while many a born reader may be found unblushingly loitering in the tea-cup times of stage-coach and posting-chaise, without so much as being aware of the new means of locomotion" ("VR," 514–15). The "born reader" is genteel, unhurried, and something of a Luddite; the "ambitious" reader is a product of a streetcar culture, which waits for no man. The class differences between "born reader" and "ambitious reader" are quite clearly marked by this image, and Wharton makes no apology for the implication. She finds fault with the practice of reading at a set time every day, likening this to a housekeeper's practice of scheduling a certain time each day for going to the store, and observes that "he who reads by time often 'has no time to read'; a plight unknown to the born reader, whose reading forms a continuous undercurrent to all his other occupations" ("VR," 515). Wharton seems utterly oblivious to the possibility that there might be readers whose "other occupations" are not conducive to an undercurrent of reading, whose schedules may not be so fluid as to accommodate a more ad hoc approach to literature. Of course, this is all rhetorical polemic; Wharton, an astute businesswoman, read and wrote at scheduled times on a regular basis. But the polemic offers comfort for the reader who feels assailed by the encroachment of mass audiences; by ignoring the structures of education and of leisured lives, the self-congratulating "elite" reader can differentiate his or her reading practice from that of the reader in the cars and can presume that his or her reading is more in line with the demands of a highbrow text.

In a May 1905 question-and-answer column, Mabie confronts directly a letter that ventriloquizes the position Wharton staked out in "The Vice of Reading." "You attach great importance to the reading habit," a correspondent identified only as "Inquirer" observes, "You have spoken of it many times. Ought not reading to be spontaneous rather than mechanical?" (May 1905, 18). As I have discussed previously, there is no way of confirming or denying the "reality" of this reader letter; the *Journal* did solicit reader letters actively and frequently editorialized on its superior responsiveness to reader queries, but there is no documentary evidence that a single letter like "Inquirer's" ever existed. The generic quality of this letter likewise points away from any single source for the query. The most likely scenario is that Mabie was aware of the critique his variety of advice was receiving in the elite literary press; that he had perhaps received a number of letters asking generally the same question about the "reading habit" from the same skeptical, even hostile, perspective; and that he then chose to address the issue in a dialogue format to acknowledge the presence of concerned or opposing readers and critics. The letter-response dynamic functions to signal his openness to the readership and enables him to counter his critics more directly and more decisively. "Certainly," he answers, "but the value of habit is to lay a better foundation and give a wider range for spontaneity." After a lengthy detour though false analogies to musicians who must practice in order to improvise, and artists who must learn the characteristics of their materials before attempting innovative techniques, Mabie asserts that only after working to develop a reading habit can a reader turn "spontaneously" to a book: "When you have formed the reading habit you no longer have to plan times and places when you can take up your book; you take up your book automatically. To develop spontaneity you must keep yourself in the mood in which spontaneity is generated" (May 1905, 18). Here Mabie is of course answering the letter, but not the spirit, of the query; he is thinking about a spontaneous decision to read at a particular point in time, not about the spontaneity of one's general orientation towards reading, which was of course the attitude about which the original letter was asking.

Taken in the aggregate over his tenure at the *Journal*, Mabie's comments on the "reading habit" do offer a remarkably consistent philosophy of reading, though it can seem internally contradictory, or at least paradoxical. He repeatedly asserts that careful, studious preparation is the condition of possibility for readerly spontaneity and mastery. He closes his January 1904 column with "six rules for those who read," rules that encapsulate the points he offers (frequently in piecemeal fashion) throughout the columns:

    I Do not read at random; select your books in advance.

    II Read intelligently and with foresight; make a scheme for the season, not too large to be worked out.

    III Read books that interest you; follow the line of your taste unless your taste is wholly untrained; if it is, read good books in different fields until you find out what you care for most.

    IV Have a book always within reach and make the most of your spare minutes.

    V Read only good books and put your mind on them. To get the best out of books you must be able to remember them.

    VI Do not make a task of reading; read for enjoyment. (January 1904, 17)

Though it seems counterintuitive, Mabie does repeatedly insist that the last rule not only can coexist with all the previous rules but that it also follows from the proper implementation of rules one through five. In his November 1907 column, for example, he offers the cautionary tale of an "intelligent man" who, after being stricken with poor health that left him in a lengthy convalescence, "spoke regretfully of the fact that he could not enjoy books during his enforced illness because he had never formed the habit of reading, and getting through a book was a slow and laborious process for him." Despite this man's intelligence, he was not yet a reader because he had not trained himself. Reading, Mabie insists, "does not come by nature as some people imagine" (November 1907, 28)—and this is not just true for some people, it is true for everyone. This insistence directly contradicts the position Wharton takes in "The Vice of Reading" that some readers are just "born readers," who "read as unconsciously as [they] breathe" ("VR," 513). Mabie insists that every reader must practice, must allow his or her eyes to become "accustomed to rapid transit across lines of print" (November 1907, 28) and must cultivate the proper capacity for attention and focus. "To enjoy books and gain their friendship a man must form the habit of being frequently with them, and must learn how to keep his mind on the page before him, amid all kinds of distracting sounds and sights, for hours at a time." Mabie's approach is adamantly democratic; he gives his audience a sense of enfranchisement by describing the reading habit as something within reach of everyone willing to work at it. Contra Mabie, Wharton does not think that just anyone can become a good reader through practice and application. In "The Vice of Reading," she does concede that "the gift of reading is no exception to the rule that all natural gifts need to be cultivated by practice and discipline," but she adds an important caveat that "unless the innate aptitude exist the training will be wasted. It is the delusion of the mechanical reader to think that intentions may take the place of aptitude" ("VR," 515). Wharton does not deny the right to read to any of this audience; she contends that these folks are fine as long as they stick to the kind of literature that best suits them—"the novel of the day"—and do not try to encroach the precincts of "letters."

The "mechanical reader" who dares to pick up a belletristic text endangers letters by dumbing down the critical conversation, either through bolstering the careers and visibility of "mechanical critics" or by offering their own assessments of literature to the public discourse. Wharton has unkind words for the critics consulted by, and (she claims) produced by, the mechanical reader. Unlike the born reader, who she

disingenuously describes as indifferent to critical assessments of literature, the mechanical reader uses a particular type of critic as a crutch,
relying on his thumbnail plot summaries as aids in book selection:

> The born reader may or may not wish to hear what the critics have
> to say of a book; but if he cares for any criticism he wants the only
> kind worthy of the name—an analysis of subject and manner. He
> who has no time for such criticism will certainly spare none to the
> summing-up of the contents of a book: an inventory of its inci-
> dents, ending up with the conventional "But we will not spoil the
> reader's enjoyment by revealing, etc." It is the mechanical reader
> who demands such inventories and calls them criticisms; and it is
> because the mechanical reader is in the majority that the mechani-
> cal plot-extractor is fast superseding the critic. ("VR," 520)

In this passage, one of the more convoluted in the essay, not only has
Wharton created a chicken-and-egg causality paradox (do mechanical
readers create mechanical critics, or vice versa?), but she also dances
dangerously close to a statement that the purest of "born readers" is and
perhaps should be indifferent to even the most sophisticated of critical
conversations. Individual readerly interaction with a text is, she has already argued, the chief marker of a "born reader," and this exemplary
individual's ability to enter into dialogue with a text is in turn a marker
of the text's greatness. Wharton's discussion of this point is so remarkable for our purposes that it is worth citing at length:

> What is reading, in the last analysis, but an interchange of thought
> between writer and reader? If the book enters the reader's mind just
> as it left the writer's—without any of the additions and modifica-
> tions inevitably produced by contact with a new body of thought—
> it has been read to no purpose. In such cases, of course, the reader
> is not always to blame. There are books that are always the same—
> incapable of modifying or of being modified—but these do not
> count as factors in literature. The value of books is proportion-
> ate to what may be called their plasticity—their quality of being all
> things to all men, of being diversely moulded by the impact of fresh
> forms of thought. Where, from one cause or the other, this recipro-
> cal adaptability is lacking, there can be no real intercourse between
> book and reader. In this sense it may be said that there is no ab-
> stract standard of values in literature: the greatest books ever writ-
> ten are worth to each reader only what he can get out of them. The

best books are those from which the best readers have been able to extract the greatest amount of thought of the highest quality; but it is generally from these books that the poor reader gets least. ("VR," 513–14)

The moment of reception is, then, the moment in which the book happens—Wharton here looks like a proto-Jaussian.[5] But to maintain her notion of readerly hierarchies, she tries to claim that the best books will not "work" for the worst readers, and we can then see why she is so concerned about the moment when the mechanical reader "discusses, criticizes, condemns, or, worse still, praises" a text. This reader's cultural purchase—after all, a whole genre of "plot extraction" has arisen to serve such a reader's needs—makes it likely that the world of publishing will similarly shift to his or her tastes. En masse, mechanical readers become a daunting social force. Other readers will listen to mechanical readers' discussion, criticism, condemnation, or praise. Their preferred books will become popular, and will crowd out offerings that have not caught the eye of these improperly responsive readers.

Wharton scorned the impulse to read popular books even as she goaded her publishers to advertise her books more actively: "Here is a book that every one is talking about; the number of its editions is an almost unanswerable proof of its merit; but to the mechanical reader it is cryptic, and he takes refuge in disapproval. He admits the cleverness, of course; but one of the characters is 'not nice'; *ergo*, the book is not nice; he is surprised that you should have cared to read it" ("VR," 517).[6] We might bracket for the moment the paradox here—if popularity is predicated upon the support of the uniformly responsive "mechanical reader," the scenario Wharton paints here of such a reader's rejection could never take place—to note again that Wharton's greatest objection to mechanical reading was the possibility that its practitioner would be unable to "discern the 'fine issues' of any book. [. . .] To those who regard literature as a criticism of society, nothing is more puzzling than this incapacity to distinguish between the general tendency of a book—its technical and imaginative value as a whole—and its merely episodic features" ("VR," 519). The mechanical reader, in other words, tends to have a tough time appreciating a novel that might run counter to his or her worldview, and tends to reject such novels out of hand.

A contemporary might have reminded Wharton that she had already celebrated the interchange between reader and book as the defining constructive moment of the book's existence; in retrospect, we might be able to cut through the tangle of paradox by reading "The Vice of Reading" as a drama of Wharton's ambivalence about publication and popularity. It perhaps reflected her fear that her fictional work might be misread by a large public of new, aspirational readers who would have been following her career because of notices like Hamilton Wright Mabie's in the same May 1902 column that introduced the "reading habit" to his audience. Praising Wharton as "the accomplished artist, to whom the art of writing is an end in itself," he is careful to designate her as a writer who "deal[s] with the subtleties of experience rather than with its decisive moments"—in other words, she is not an architect of dramatic plots, and the partisan of the adventure story would not likely be satisfied by her novels, however important they may be. And yet there is an avenue to appreciating Wharton through the acknowledgment of her craftsmanship, a characteristic which Mabie frequently praised as analogous to a reader's careful application to a reading "program." Wharton was the authorial equivalent of a dutiful reader, her work important to such a reader's advancement. Little wonder, then, that such readers might pursue her work and might focus on her "picture of a society polished, urbane, cultivated, and elegant, and, at the same time, frivolous, heartless, corrupt and helpless in the face of the great Revolutionary movement which was filling all Europe with restlessness and which broke like a tempest in France at the close of the eighteenth century" (May 1902, 17). Pulse racing from that description, a reader might well overlook Mabie's qualifications and go on to ignore anything in Wharton's novel that veered away from the costume drama he backhandedly promises. Looking, desiring, and burnishing her intellectual credentials, the "reading up" reader could approach any Wharton novel as a window into society, past or present, and could register any critique as a cautionary tale. As we shall see, such readers did also "discuss, criticize, and condemn" Wharton's text for failing to deliver the vicarious success they desired.

Desirable Surfaces

Wharton had the aspiring reader in the forefront of her mind, and she explicitly rendered Lily Bart a surrogate for the upwardly mobile reader throughout *The House of Mirth*. Lily's goal is to "fight against ['dinginess'], dragging herself up again and again above its flood till she gained the bright pinnacles of success which presented such a slippery surface to her clutch" (*HM*, 34, 39), which is also the goal of the reader who has been taught to idealize the "escape of a human spirit, by sacrifice, toil, and courage, out of narrow into generous conditions of life; out of ignorance and lack of training into knowledge and skill" (March 1904, 16). As Lily looks and desires, so does the reader, as in the scene where Lily peers over the banister into the hall of the Dorsets' country home, Bellomont:

> The hall was arcaded, with a gallery supported on columns of pale yellow marble. Tall clumps of flowering plants were grouped against a background of dark foliage in the angles of the walls. On the crimson carpet a deer-hound and two or three spaniels dozed luxuriously before the fire, and the light from the great central lantern overhead shed a brightness on the women's hair and struck sparks from their jewels as they moved. There were moments when such scenes delighted Lily, when they gratified her sense of beauty and her craving for the external finish of life; there were others when they gave a sharper edge to the meagreness of her own opportunities. (*HM*, 24–25)

As a guest at Bellomont, Lily is able to experience the accoutrements of the hallway, to see the dogs on the carpet, in much the same way that a reader can "see" the richly described scene. And while her current mood renders her an outsider, her straitened circumstances brought into relief by the wealth she surveys, in other moods her ability to appreciate such a scene—her aesthetic sensibility—renders her an insider. Lily's position while peering over the banister is thus very much like that of Michel de Certeau's "reader as poacher": "[The reader's] place is not *here* or *there*, one or the other, but neither the one nor the other, simultaneously inside and outside, dissolving both by mixing them together, associating texts like funerary statues that he awakens and hosts, but never owns."[7] Lily, too, "never owns" the scenes she surveys; she is a perpetual guest in other peoples' houses and purchases her clothing with donated or borrowed funds. Like the intermingled dogs piled on the crimson carpet, Lily and the reader become for a time indistinguishable. Even without the similarities of vulgar financial situations, the aspiring middlebrow reader and Lily, by virtue of the phenomenology of reading, occupy the same position.

In many ways, Certeau's economic metaphors suggest that the middle-class aspirer is the prototypical reader: somewhere in between entitled and dispossessed, the reader attempts a wish fulfillment very like that of the striver who imitates the actions of higher social classes. But the historically specific valences of reading up cannot be ignored. No one was to enter a text without the expectation of being changed by the experience of reading. When Certeau argues that consumption, and in turn reading, should be understood as "'making something similar' to what one is, making it one's own, appropriating or reappropriating it," he is translating into contemporary terms the implicit message of Mabie's *Journal* columns: that identification with fictional characters could enhance and better the self. Reading up was not a passive activity; only through engagement with the text could a socially aspiring reader hope to achieve his or her goals. And within the value structure of class aspirations, active engagement with a society novel meant making the practices and attitudes of high society "'similar' to what one is."[8]

Such practices might have been the impetus behind the negative reviews that met *The House of Mirth* in some circles, particularly in newspapers and journals priding themselves on catering to popular taste. These reviews pointed out that the overwhelming negativity of Wharton's "smart set" was an exaggeration unworthy of the novel's technical accomplishment. A critic for the *Chicago Daily Tribune* who applauded the novel in October 1905 as "clever, piquant, and vastly entertaining" changed her mind by the time she made up her list of holiday book recommendations in December: "Gloomy and pitiless, the tale was a picture of the New York smart set at something worse than its puerile actuality."[9] The novel was clearly not appropriate for gift giving. Wharton's determination to indict the "smart set" robs the book of its potential "exploding point," according to the *New York Daily Tribune*'s reviewer: "It is conceivable, for example, that Gerty Farish might live in a cramped flat and still find wallpapers which were not 'hideous.' . . . [A] broadening of the canvas to permit the introduction of some of the more normal phases of our social system would have helped to give the work a richer quality, and would only have served, we believe, to put Miss Bart in a truer perspective."[10] Gerty might have found tasteful wallpaper; Lily might have found a less odious partner, or at least a corner of American society outside the "smart set" in which there was no "dinginess." Indeed, this reviewer's concern seems to be that the monochromatic "dinginess" of life outside society only serves to make Lily's rejection of that life all the more understandable, and by extension, to make the reader all the more awed by the contrasting brilliance of the wealthy. Wharton makes such misreading available by neglecting to show Lily in a "true perspective"; notwithstanding the fact that "Lily's [high society] associates, as Mrs. Wharton paints them, make appalling company," the *New York Daily Tribune* reviewer still expects that "much of [the novel's] certain popularity will be due to its vivid pictures of the little world of wealth and pleasure."[11]

Hamilton Wright Mabie, on the other hand, is happy to recommend Wharton's novel as an accurate indictment of "fast society everywhere"— missing the point a bit as he strives to assert that it is only a *segment* of high society that comes in for Wharton's strongest critique and that the novel is, overall, "true to life."

> Society novels are rarely written by people who know society, and are usually full of exaggeration, misleading characterization and lurid descriptions; they are as far from the truth as the reports of society affairs in the sensational newspapers. "The House of Mirth" is important not only because it is a work of art, but also because it is true to life. It is not a picture of society as a whole, but of one phase of society found in every city in the world. (December 1905, 21)

Mabie cannot condemn all of "high society"—his forum is, after all, dedicated to popularizing reading through suggesting its instrumentality for social advancement. By isolating the "fast set" as the target of Wharton's criticism, Mabie preserves the greater part of high society as an ideal. The "fast set" is only a subset that has gone overboard, its members the only ones who experience the "decay of character brought about by idleness, love of luxury and pursuit of pleasure as the chief occupation of life." This group is not the refined society one might still hope to join, but is a "vulgar set" in which "life is pathetically empty of all real interests and true pleasure; and . . . its inevitable drift is toward the tragedy of immorality." In fact, the "fast set" counts as its members those who have not hewn to the solid, substantial society practices—like reading excellent, morally sound literature—that made high society superior in the first place. Wharton's novel is a corrective to high society—albeit a scathing one—not a wholesale condemnation of the social hierarchy. Mabie's final word on the novel drives this point home as it praises Wharton's technical achievement: "The story is told with very great skill; it is absorbingly interesting and deeply pathetic, and its moral significance, never obtruded, but never blurred, gives it high importance in an age of mushroom social growths and cheap social ambitions." Reading *The House of Mirth*, it seems, can work as a corrective to "cheap social ambitions." While it thematizes the perils of superficiality, the reader is already working against superficiality in his or her own life by reading a "quality" novel.

Mabie thereby deftly avoids the potential pitfall of criticizing the novel too much. With his warnings safely in place, his audience can still appreciate elements of the "vivid pictures of the little world of wealth and pleasure" with the assurance that they have the proper orientation towards the materialism Mabie has already warned them about. One such vivid picture is Lily's *tableau vivant* at the Brys' party, in which she imitates Joshua Reynolds's portrait of Mrs. R. B. Lloyd. This moment is frequently examined in Wharton scholarship, yielding infinite interpretive possibilities because of the endless regression of interpenetrating images: Lily as Mrs. Lloyd, Mrs. Lloyd as dryad, Lily as socialite, Lily as herself. Lily is not only imitating the painting, however, but also "banishing" it (*HM*, 134) through her seamless skill at "'making [it] similar' to what [she] is." In her identification with it, she creates something wholly other than the original. Nancy Bentley notes that Wharton's forte lies in "reproducing on the page the spectacularity of a Nouveau Luxe social world,"[12] and it takes little to imagine that a reader predisposed to imitative practice would draw inspiration from Wharton's lush descriptions of social scenes—the opera, the ball, the society wedding.

That Wharton implicitly condemns the position of the spectator does not mean that her reader, once drawn in by the beauty of her world's glittering surfaces, would follow her into the realm of critique. But it cannot be denied that Wharton thematizes the improbability (if not impossibility) of acquired cultivation. Even one, like Lily, to the manner born cannot thrive on artifice; the *tableau vivant* can certainly be read as an emphatic argument about the dangers of self-presentation and the possibility of misappropriation. As Bentley contends, "[R]ather than secure her real identity and value, the staged appearance subjects Lily to the speculations of a group of wealthy men. . . . Lily is eventually caught and framed, as it were, by the forces of social speculation, which are ultimately fatal."[13] This scene marks, for Bentley and others, the pivotal instance of Lily's publicity, particularly as the painting she "banishes" represents a moment of writing.[14]

The question before us, however, remains: how might a reader schooled in the practice of reading up, whose reading is dictated by the desire for social and financial success, approach the *tableau vivant*? This reader is, after all, not likely to be concerned with Wharton's underlying interest in the possibilities of female authorship. If we read the scene primarily as a moment of reading rather than writing, we can see that Wharton anticipates a reader who is unfamiliar with this kind of amusement. By extension, as *tableaux vivants* were typical fare at high-society parties in the early part of the century, it also seems likely that she was in fact anticipating a reader who is not of the social set about which she writes. And by noting the ways that Wharton uses the familiar language of the society column (despite the fact that she disdained society journalism), we can see that, regardless of her bluster about the problems of popularity in literature, she actively instructs her audience how to read not only this scene but also the whole of her novel.

Gerty Farish is the most likely candidate for a reader's guide in the scene of the *tableau vivant*. As she sits next to the blasé Selden before the beginning of the festival, she displays the awed alertness of one unaccustomed to glamour and intent on taking everything in, "lost in that indiscriminate and uncritical enjoyment so irritating to Miss Bart's finer perceptions" (*HM*, 132). Gerty babbles happily to Selden, in part because of her infatuation with him but also because she is fascinated by her surroundings. Although she seems critical of the wasteful expense of Mrs. Dorset's pearls— "I suppose the smallest of them would pay the rent of our Girl's club for a year"—she immediately censors herself for thinking uncharitably about these conspicuous consumers: "Not that I ought to complain about the club, everyone has been so wonderfully kind." She makes no demands on the performers in the social spectacle and is merely grateful when they deign to make contributions to her quiet charity work.

When Wharton notes that Gerty's attitude would be "irritating to Miss Bart's finer perceptions," she is seeing Gerty not through Lily's eyes (Lily is still offstage) but through Selden's detached and vaguely cynical perspective. While Selden makes pretence to being above the social whirl, including himself and absenting himself at whim, he excuses his presence at the Brys' party by noting that it was likely to meet his standards for opulent entertainment: "[H]e enjoyed spectacular effects, and was not insensible to the part money plays in their production: all he asked was that the very rich should live up to their calling as stage-managers, and not spend their money in a dull way" (*HM*, 131). Though he does not have the means to create his own entertaining *tableaux vivants*, Selden is not an uncritical and thankful audience like Gerty is; he reserves the right to judge the actions of the wealthy as "dull" and to refuse to spectate if they disappoint. In a world where wealth must signify through conspicuous consumption, then, Selden as the critical observer of society has the power to shut it down: if he refuses the role as audience, there can no longer be a social performance.

The loss of Selden seems on the surface more potentially disruptive than the loss of any other spectator to the social scene. He has refined tastes, he can discriminate, and most important, he is somewhat a part of the thing he watches. He is the informed observer. His ability to comprehend the *tableaux* echoes his ability to read the society whose borders he has learned so strategically to navigate:

> *Tableaux vivants* depend for their effect not only on the happy disposal of lights and the delusive interposition of layers of gauze, but on a corresponding adjustment of the mental vision. To unfurnished minds they remain, in spite of every enhancement of art, only a superior kind of wax-works; but to the responsive fancy they may give magic glimpses of the boundary world between fact and imagination. Selden's mind was of this order: he could yield to vision-making influences as completely as a child to the spell of a fairy tale. (*HM*, 133)

Selden has the "responsive fancy" Wharton extols, and so he can read the *tableaux* properly, noting the way they play with the "boundary world between fact and imagination," the fuzzy realm between fiction and nonfiction—in short, he understands the complexities of identification. Wharton's attempts to describe the qualifications of the ideal readers of the *tableau vivant* and the mental processes they perform in the act of reading resonate powerfully with the rhetoric of the reading manual. While in one respect constructing a difficult criterion for the reader (one must somehow acquire a "responsive fancy"), Wharton is also delineating the goal of reading, much as Edwin L. Shuman in *How to Judge a Book* (1910) distinguishes the meaningful from the meaningless experiences of reading a sentimental novel: "The trouble with the uncultivated taste is that it does not distinguish between the false and the true emotional appeal. While reading emotional novels, then, it will be well to pause occasionally, become critical, and see whether we are laughing and weeping over characters and events true to life or merely over wooden puppets dangled on a string." [15] After reading Wharton's description of the proper reaction to a *tableau vivant*, her reader might, or should, be able to effect the same kind of self-check that Shuman's reader is taught to perform when reading an emotional novel: Am I focusing simply on the effect of this *tableau*, on the accuracy with which the actors approximate the original? Or am I more keenly aware, more fully participant in the spectacle, cognizant of the play between the personalities of the actors and the scenes, of the space between "fact and imagination"?

In this scene, Wharton's role as a guide to the activities of the upper class and the preferred responses of the cultured runs contrary to her frequent criticism of the society journalists who perform the same function in the gossip pages of newspapers. As Maureen Montgomery notes, Wharton's assertion of a "privileged gaze"—she is both a writer of "serious fiction" who disdains the popular novelist and a critical chronicler of society who denigrates "the part of [society journalism] that legitimizes the ostentatious display of wealth and mistakes 'conspicuousness' for 'distinction'"—is "to some extent undermined by the discussion of her novels on the society page and the appropriation by the very forces she criticizes."[16] Evoking Pierre Bourdieu's observation that the attempt to distinguish between authentic and imitation culture masks their ultimate collusion, Montgomery briefly acknowledges the "'educative' function of society journalism" albeit without drawing the logical conclusion that Wharton's fiction performed a similar educative function. Montgomery contends that "in making visible old New York at a time of heightened publicity for those who had millions to spend on leisure and mansions, Wharton contested the new hegemony of the latest class of 'world-compellers.'"[17] And yet because Wharton's fiction can be seen as, in effect, approximating the instruments of publicity that have produced Lily's world of "Nouveau Luxe," *The House of Mirth*, as it was read by its vast popular audience in 1905, finally functions to validate and perpetuate this machinery. For such validation to be the result, however, readers had to perform a selective misreading of the substance of Wharton's text, or at least the spirit in which Wharton wrote.

Lenox and Newport

One of the more prolonged published debates over *The House of Mirth* occurred in the *New York Times Saturday Review of Books*. Beginning innocuously enough with a letter asking whether "the gentlemen who dwell in Fifth Avenue palaces, own splendid country seats, and wear purple and fine linen every day, [are] truly represented by the Trenors, the Dorsets, and Rosedales of Mrs. Wharton's story," the debate became so heated that it hijacked the *Times* readers' forum for nearly three months.[18] Writers initially took sides based on whether they believed the smart set of Wharton's novel accurately mirrored contemporaneous New York society, particularly after a reader signing "Newport" wrote, "I never met the prototypes of Mrs. Wharton's motley crew in society, and can recall a pretty wide experience." Newport concludes that "[t]he motive of the book is low."[19] For this reader, "inaccuracies" in Wharton's portrayal of society leave the rest of the novel's plotting open for critique. Though not identified by name in the column, Newport is also quick to claim "wide experience" from which to speak regarding the true situation of New York society. The source of Newport's anonymity is perplexing: the letter was sent to the paper signed, but whether the writer was given a pseudonym by request or by the decision of the *Times* editors is unclear.

Both the substance and the anonymity of Newport's letter seemed to distress the *Times* readership. In the following week, a reader objected: "If the book 'misleads outsiders,' to which Newport, in spite of . . . 'pretty wide experience,' must belong, without a comprehension of the entire scheme and purpose of 'The House of Mirth,'—the inner circle of society which it portrays will be quick to see and to recognize." This letter, signed "Lenox," also denigrates the right of "one unsympathetic critic" to express "harsh, badly-expressed, and uncalled-for" remarks against the praises of "an army of reviewers."[20] Lenox's choice of pseudonym closely identifies with Wharton's chosen home, and indeed Lenox's whole letter works to validate the superior discernment of the insider and the hopeless outsiderness of the outsider. Paradoxically (but logically, for Lenox), only members of society can "see and recognize" the critical nuances of Wharton's text. Only the insider can recognize the validity of the critique of society, whereas the outsider is forever hopelessly blinded by the performance.[21] By criticizing Wharton, Newport has demonstrated outsiderness. Lenox also defends the text against those who, unauthorized, would offer opinions of literature against "an army of reviewers." The sense-of-duty reader, it seems, is close kin to the social arriviste.

The social and critical posturing takes a sharper turn once the editors of the *Times* begin to offer comments on the letters in their "Reader's Forum" exchange. "Topics of the Week," a regular column usually devoted to reporting the news of the literary world, not the vagaries of their own readers' letters, becomes a place for the *Times* to clarify the positions and the identities rhetorically obscured by the letters. On [25] November, the *Times* editors make the unusual gesture of prefacing Lenox's letter (published on the page facing "Topics of the Week") with the assertion that the publication of an unsigned letter was a onetime departure from custom, indulged in on this exceptional occasion because "[the] letter is obviously sincere, and an authentic expression of opinion." The *Times* editors also take great pains to identify the genders of these letter writers, asserting that "we may reasonably assume" that the writer they have dubbed Lenox is a woman, and then clarifying that the writer signed Newport is

... a mere man, of mature years, who, we doubt not, has "heard the chimes at midnight" and has, off and on, mingled in fairly good society. He is a correspondent from whom we would be glad to hear frequently. So, for that matter, is "Lenox," whose communication we cheerfully print, although she has neglected to send us her name and address, "not necessarily for publication," but as a guarantee of good faith.[22]

Clearly, Lenox did not understand that letters published pseudonymously were not necessarily sent to the paper pseudonymously. While the editors of the *Times* are ostensibly indulging the "sincere" objections of the feminine Lenox—"for her sake we break a rule, which shall not be broken again"—the *Times* editors are in fact preempting her letter, which starts out by "attribut[ing] the feminine gender [to 'Newport'] without hesitation, as women are not apt to spare each other!" But this is not so much about assigning gender to a reading practice as it is about refusing Lenox's assumption of Newport's gender as a preliminary to refusing her other more pressing assumptions about Newport. The editors undermine her criticism of Newport as neither an insider nor a credentialed and sanctioned commentator; as it turns out, he is not only a veteran of "fairly good society," but he has also been invited to contribute literary commentary to the *Saturday Review of Books*. Even though his letter had been contrary to the official *Times* critics' positive reviews, the editors insist that "it, too, was obviously sincere, and ably expressed."[23] After this type of official support, Lenox's condemnation of Newport's letter as "harsh, badly-expressed, and uncalled-for" looks simply petty. Even though she writes with a knowledge of current literary debates surpassing Newport's, chiding his comparison of Wharton and Henry James as "wearisome," Lenox seems to typify her own stereotype of the woman "not apt to spare" another, her arguments shrill rather than thoughtfully provoked.

The *Times* editors may well have been encouraging contrarian views like Newport's in order to foster the sort of lively dialogue that followed and filled the reader's forum until early in 1906. "Such things," they write, "increase the gaiety of living and tend to the development of literary culture by stirring up trains of thought where thought has previously been sluggish."[24] The fact that they so thoroughly undercut the stance of insider for a writer like Lenox primarily suggests the importance to the *Times* of outsiders' identifications with the heroine. Lenox wants to foreclose such identification, but the literary debate, the *Times* editors argue, would suffer from such exclusivity. Their intervention seems to have been successful. By 9 December, the discussion had grown so active that the *Times* gave it a whole section in the *Saturday Review of Books*, with the headline "The Strong Impression Made by *The House of Mirth* Shown in the Discussion It Provokes." In this issue, Newport responds that his critique had been not just that *The House of Mirth* is an inaccurate portrayal of society but also that Wharton stacks the deck too harshly against Lily. Not only are there too many coincidences in the novel, but "[i]t seems to the plain American that, as Lily and Selden often met for years, and as frequent reference is made to her reliance upon his complete power of comprehension, they might have 'become known to each other' without waiting until she was dead." The writer's plea to the logic of the "plain American" here is unprovoked by any calls to national identity in previous letters, and his assumption of the designation "plain" seems slightly out of synch with the editors' previous reference to him as a person not unaccustomed to very good society. "Plainness" and "Americanness" are either not inconsistent with good society or they refer to some other register of identity that has little to do with social standing.

Given the prior discussion of the relationship between insiderness and the capacity to read properly, "plain" may well be a nod to a type of reading practice—perhaps, in conjunction with "American," a popular one—which decries the machinations of an author who "draws her creations so fine that her own personality shines through," unlike Henry Harland or Elinor Glyn, whose *Three Weeks* would become the "most talked about book in America" three years later.[25] In a similar vein, Joseph Holmes writes from on board the *S. S. Crette*: "[W]e are not told till nearly the last chapter that Lily was 'heir expectant' to about four hundred thousand dollars. Given this fact earlier, Lily had married Selden and spoiled the story. (Better so.)"[26] It is impossible to fathom where Holmes gets this amount (Lily's total settlement from her aunt's estate was only ten thousand dollars, and we are aware of this amount during the whole of Lily's post–Monte Carlo decline), but the wishful imposition of this plot twist, and the righteous indignation with which Holmes protests its perceived omission, aptly illustrates the degree to which some readers were ready to fault Wharton for arbitrary cruelty.

The final scene of the novel, Lily's deathbed and Selden's belated discovery of the truth of her relations with Trenor, is heavily contested by the *Times* readers. Newport's opening letter complains, "Even the proverbial sanctity of the dead is not regarded [by Mrs. Wharton], for it is unheard of that a man should shut himself up in a room with the dead body of a girl in the bed." Lenox scoffs at this "blunted vision, which sees only, in this dramatic termination to the tragedy of two souls who have in this last supreme moment become known to each other, a lack of 'les convenances,'" and calls the last chapter an "artist's proof." "New York" writes on 30 December that it is unclear whether Lily "intended" to commit suicide and that "after reading such a very painful story, it seems too bad that she was not allowed to 'live happily ever after' as a reward for her virtue," though such wishes do not keep this reader from being generally complimentary of the novel.[27] "Jax" writes, "I have not read Mrs. Wharton's book, and . . . I have no present intention of reading it—" and then, breaking into verse, observes: "In the work-a-day world—for its needs and woes / There is place and enough for the pains of prose."[28] Jax writes, however, not primarily to take issue with Wharton's narrative (though it is clear that he or she does not want to read the novel because of the widely revealed tragic ending) but to take issue with a writer who generalized about the state of the "average reader":

> I wish to point out to "E. D." as courteously as possible . . . that this department of the *Saturday Review of Books* is sacred to the "average reader." Here, if anywhere he should be able to say his say without exciting suspicion that he thinks himself a "literary limelight." He should be courteous, but it is his right and duty to be frank. We most of us want to know what the "average reader" thinks of a book. . . . Upon the "axe-swinging" opinion of the "average reader" depends the fate of every book. According to his verdict it stands or falls, lives or dies, both in the present and in the future.[29]

Jax's letter plays into Wharton's anxiety that the "mechanical reader," by virtue of collective financial might, would become the single most powerful force in literature. And this aggressive response to a reader who essentially suggested, like Wharton, that criticism should be left to the experts indicates that the advice manuals and popular magazine columns that increasingly permitted their readers to select books that would give them pleasure were prevailing. The last letter about *The House of Mirth* was published in the *Times* on 20 January 1906, shutting down the debate with a suggestion that the previous forum participants should "'hire a hall' and fight it out by word of mouth and not waste so much valuable space in your excellent paper."[30]

Loving Lily

Few would deny that misreaders exist. There are no assurances that the same message is accessible to or even desirable to all of a narrative's readers, and a work's popularity, as evidenced by sales figures or library borrowing rates, is also shaky ground on which to base the cultural dominance of the ideas expressed therein. (Who can say that books purchased were also books read?) Few critics go as far as John G. Cawelti, who at least allows that "[n]ovels may be best-sellers because readers find the story or the characters interesting irrespective of the attitudes expressed by the author."[31] But Wharton's keen attention to the figure of the misreader demands that we pay attention to the possibility of imperfections in the reception of her text, particularly from readers attempting to make their reading of Lily cohere with a sentimental economy of identification in which Lily herself seems caught.

Wharton describes Lily early in the novel as a partisan of "pictures and flowers, and . . . sentimental fiction" (*HM*, 35), and this reading material can be deemed in large part responsible for the misguided belief that her refined taste uniquely qualifies her for "worldly advantages":

> She would not indeed have cared to marry a man who was merely
> rich: she was secretly ashamed of her mother's crude passion for
> money. Lily's preference would have been for an English nobleman
> with political ambitions and vast estates; or, for second choice, an
> Italian prince with a castle in the Apennines and an hereditary of-
> fice in the Vatican. Lost causes had a romantic charm for her, and
> she liked to picture herself as standing aloof from the vulgar press
> of the Quirinal, and sacrificing her pleasure to the claims of an im-
> memorial tradition. (*HM*, 35)

Lily's musings sound like the options among which Isabel Archer must choose in Henry James's *Portrait of a Lady*, but we could say that her preference for sentimental novels has led her to misread James.[32] She dreams of a suitor like Lord Warburton, the "English nobleman with political ambitions," or even for a "lost cause" who somewhat resembles Gilbert Osmond. Lily insists that, as neither the faux aristocrat with an Italian castle nor the true English aristocrat with vast, though dilapidated, estates had any money at all, she would be content to "sacrific[e] her pleasure to the claims of an immemorial tradition." But she overlooks the realistic aspects of James's novel—the fact that there must be money to keep that tradition afloat or the possibility that the man in the

Italian castle is an effete tyrant. Again, Lily conflates a moment of reading with a moment of contemplated performance; what she reads (or what Wharton wants us to imagine she may have read) is a potential blueprint for what she does, or for what she yearns to do, an echo of the success manual. And in treating her "text" like a success manual, Lily indulges a desire to separate the aesthetic and the romantic from the vulgarity of finance. Such behavior is symptomatic of Lily's actions throughout the novel and is symptomatic as well of the practice of reading up—of separating the desirable surface of a glittering society from Wharton's insistence that it is frivolous and destructive. In other words, the desires that enable Lily to idealize Isabel Archer's choices are the same as those that would enable Wharton's readers to idealize Lily's environs.

Identification was key to the practice of reading up. We have already seen in chapter 1 the ways in which Mabie promulgated readerly identification through his fiction recommendations. One of his lengthier and more poetic defenses of novel-reading appears in September 1907, in a column devoted to answering the titular question, "Should the Young Read Novels?" Mabie's answer is an emphatic "Yes!" which he elaborates with a meditation on the psychic value of fiction, and its anthropological role:

> Every normal man and woman would like to see life on a large scale, to know cities and people, and let experience draw out what is in them. This is simply a craving for self-expression, for getting out one's power, and it is this craving which prompts men and women to read eagerly stories which describe those who have had experience of life on a great scale. [. . .] The sense of tragedy haunts the imagination of every normal man and woman; and when it does not come to the individual as a matter of experience it always comes as a matter of imagination or of sympathy. (September 1907, 28)

While Mabie does not use the term *identification*, it is implied through his evocation of "sympathy," and it is reinforced by his discussion of the story he pinpoints as the most archetypal of the time; the story of "the rise of the man out of poverty and ignorance into affluence and knowledge." "In our part of the world," he asserts, "the story of the self-made man has been told a thousand times, and will be told a thousand times more, because it is the romance of industry, honesty and resolute purpose." It is writ large in fiction and, the reader hopes, writ small in his or her own life. Reading is an escape, but it is the best kind of escape: it enhances the self.

> [I]n the greatest fiction, as in the greatest plays, the sense of life is
> deepened and heightened, the imagination trained and enriched,
> and the vision of what life means enlarged; because it takes its read-
> ers into the society of the most interesting, stimulating, and capti-
> vating men and women; [. . .] because in the best novels another
> world is opened to the jaded reader, who escapes from the pressure
> of his work, the routine of his duties, the tyranny of his own expe-
> rience, and gets a vacation from himself. (September 1907, 28)

Identification here bears only slight resemblance to nineteenth-century
"identification with the progressive possibilities of liberal political
agency and . . . submission."[33] Indeed, the practice of reading up relies
on a shift to identification as a means of wish fulfillment, which leads to
an "enlarged and clarified" life because it is an identification of the self
with a character who is a social better. A maid can enjoy the novel of high
life because it enables vicarious participation; presumably, she would get
no pleasure out of a novel whose heroine was a maid because she already
knows about (and wants to escape) her life of domestic service. But by
identification with a maid who has risen into "affluence and knowledge"
she might find a way to follow, perhaps through more reading.

A wishful and willful identification can, however, lead to misreading, though not necessarily the kind of righteous misreading Wharton
scorned. The desire, in Certeau's phrase, to make the text "'similar' to
what one is" can lead to self-interested misreadings and to selective identification. Lily participates in such an oblique misreading, as we have
seen, when she seems to identify herself with an Isabel Archer whose
marital choices are all idealistically romantic. But this mode of misreading need not wholly serve ambition. When Lily is nearly raped by Gus
Trenor, her penchant for self-dramatization makes her place herself at
the center of the third play in Aeschylus's *Oresteia*:

> She had once picked up, in a house where she was staying, a trans-
> lation of the *Eumenides*, and her imagination had been seized by
> the high terror of the scene where Orestes, in the cave of the oracle,
> finds his implacable huntresses asleep, and snatches an hour's re-
> pose. Yes, the Furies might sometimes sleep, but they were there,
> always there in the dark corners, and now they were awake and the
> iron clang of their wings was in her brain. (*HM*, 148)

Candace Waid notes that "[t]he appearance of 'a translation of the *Eumenides*' and Lily's identification with Orestes . . . is puzzling and complex,"

and her analysis of these thematics in terms of Wharton's "preoccupation" with Greek mythography is compelling.[34] But it is also puzzling that the partisan of sentimental fiction should take up such a weighty text for the casual, time-killing kind of reading one expects she would be pursuing "in a house where she was staying." Of course, Wharton placed the *Eumenides* in Lily's hands to make her story resonate for her classically trained readership, but she also specifies the conditions under which her heroine became familiar with such a text, and in thus drawing attention to the scene of Lily's reading forces us to consider that this reference to Aeschylus is potentially mediated by Lily's disposition. As in her previous reading, Lily misses significant points in the *Eumenides*, though in this case her desire to recall "high terror" makes her forget that in the scene she cites, Orestes is watched over and aided by Apollo and Hermes, and she perhaps has not read far enough to note that the Furies are ultimately tamed by a diplomatic Athena bent on restoring justice to her city. Lily thinks that the Furies are "always there in the dark corners," and she is immune to any potential Hermes or Apollo in the form of Gerty Farish or Lawrence Selden. She cannot, because of her sentimental reading practice, go beyond an interpretation of the scene that both inspires dramatic sentiment and works as a textual version of the pathetic fallacy: I am eternally pursued, and so then is Orestes.

Lily's identification with Orestes may indeed replicate the identification Wharton's readers feel with Lily, though Wharton finally frustrates the latter by giving her readers a Lily with whom they should not ultimately be able to identify—a beautiful corpse. But just as Lily, perversely, would not be able to identify with the pardoned Orestes at the end of the *Eumenides*, so too might Wharton's readers be unwilling to identify with the Lily who burns Bertha Dorset's letters and overdoses on chloral. Their protestations against Wharton's cruelty fueled sales of the book, which became the "most talked-about book of the year," and it is not difficult to imagine, from the slight documentary record that does exist, that a vast public, in the interests of reading up, chose to see Lily's career not as a warning against social aspiration but as a road map to the potential pitfalls of a still very attractive existence in high society.

Apart from the "Reader's Forum" in the *Times*, we know that *The House of Mirth* occasioned a flood of letters addressed directly to Edith Wharton. While none of this fan mail, unfortunately, seems to have survived, we do know of its existence from Wharton's letters. She writes, tantalizingly, to Edward Burlingame: "I sent Mr. Scribner only the *serious* letters, but I have a trunkful of funny ones which I will bring to town with me. One lady is so carried away that she writes: 'I love, not every word in the book, but every period & comma.' I hope she meant to insert an 'only' after the 'not.'"[35] It seems that *The House of Mirth* was, in fact, as numerous Scribner's advertisements crowed, "the book every one is reading," and although Wharton tells Burlingame she finds the attention "great fun," as early as 31 October 1905, she pleads with Charles Norton to stop giving out her address, as she was "so persecuted by letters since the appearance of this book."[36] The "funny" letters may very well have come from readers of the "mechanical" type, but in any case, Wharton's bulging mailbox is yet further material evidence of her burgeoning popularity.

In November 2007, the *New York Times* reported the rediscovery of a letter that Wharton had sent to a physician friend and that had lain interleaved with a first edition of *The House of Mirth* for one hundred years. In the letter, Wharton writes that "[a] friend of mine has made up her mind to commit suicide, & has asked me to find out . . . the most painless & least unpleasant method of effacing herself." The letter's recipient, Dr. Francis Kinnicutt, did not have much of a chance to be horrified, because Wharton quickly explained that this friend "has just started on a seemingly brilliant career in the pages of Scribner's Magazine, but the poor thing seems to realize that she is unequal to contend with the difficulties which I have heartlessly created for her, & she is determined to escape from them by self-extinction."[37] Wharton's ironic language anticipates the charges of "heartlessness" she will face upon publication of the novel, and though it does not necessarily jettison the ambiguity of Lily's final scene, the letter does suggest that at one point in the composition, at least, Wharton was consciously constructing Lily's death as a suicide. Accompanying this letter in the same copy of *The House of Mirth* was another interleaving, a poem dated February 1906 that eulogizes Lily in seven hackneyed and inelegant stanzas. Stephanie Copeland, then president of The Mount, speculated in the *Times*: "My guess is that the author is one of those people who just didn't want to believe in the suicide, and that, knowing of his interest, Kinnicutt gave him the letter, or the first part of it. It breaks off just where Wharton starts to talk about Teddy's health."[38] After marking the sorrows of the other flowers in the garden at Lily's passing, the poem laments, "Ah Lily! Boundless possibilities / Might your creator have accomplished here!" The "creator" is doubtless more Wharton than divine, Wharton again becoming the target of a frustrated reader's condemnation. Wharton did not see the potential in Lily, or did not allow it to come to fruition; in the final line of the poem,

the author notes strangely and parenthetically that "(And here all Rea-
soning must turn to Fear)." This reader's ability to approach life—or at
the least literature—rationally has been shaken by Lily's death, enough
to compose, and then to preserve, this poetic rejoinder, which was likely
shared with Wharton's partner in crime.

Amy Kaplan reads Wharton's famous statement about the objective
of *The House of Mirth*—to expose the tragedy of what a "frivolous society" destroys—as self-justification. Wharton, Kaplan writes, "fear[ed]
that a novelist indeed endorses society's wastefulness and even produces
more waste when she preys on society's glamour and transforms it into
a marketable commodity in the form of a novel."[39] Just before her discussion of Lily Bart's genesis, Wharton also takes the opportunity in
A Backward Glance to once again criticize some of her readers: "There
can be no greater critical ineptitude than to judge a novel according to
what it ought to have been about."[40] Wharton undoubtedly thought that
both sides of the debate in the *Times* were talking past her novel, that
all had indulged a conception of "what it ought to have been about" that
bore little resemblance to the text she crafted. And yet such impositions
of meaning onto the text were also the source of the novel's success—it
could be "all things to all men" ("VR," 99) and all women—and one of
those things was a guide to the potential pitfalls of an upwardly mobile
career built on cultural prowess.

Pointing out the affinities between the descriptions of interiors in *The
House of Mirth* and the language of women's guidebooks for home deco-
ration—which, like reading manuals, instructed their middlebrow readers in highbrow aesthetics—Melanie Dawson has argued that Lily's career demonstrates the ineffectiveness of attempts to wield cultural capital
as a means of upward mobility. But Dawson also points out that in the
writing of this fable, Wharton "cannily invites her readers to claim the
abilities Lily lacks, to take precedence in a reading of the politics of cultural hierarchy." Dawson concludes that "while Wharton's middlebrow
readers stand to benefit from the lesson of Lily Bart's fall, the text simultaneously points to the futility of attempting to step out of a middlebrow
position by exercising cultural knowledge," finding in the text "embed-
ded warnings to those who wished to traverse cultural boundaries or to
glamorize positions outside of their own realms."[41] Dawson's analysis is
indispensable in its assertion of Wharton's engagement with the middlebrow advice genre, but she maintains (paradoxically, I would argue)
that Wharton has ultimate agency in determining the meaning of the
text. While Dawson reads such warnings as thwarting the middlebrow

reader desiring upward mobility, I would argue that the reader trained in the school of reading up would see Lily's career as a lesson by negative example.

Even before approaching the regrettably meager existing documentary evidence of reader reactions to the novel, it is easy to see how Lily would be a particularly compelling figure of identification for an aspiring middle-class reader. Joan Lidoff argues that Lily's story is charming because it is a story of failed identity, that "Lily charms the reader as she does the other characters in the novel (and as she has her creator). . . . Irrationally, we wish with her for a prince to transport her from her troubled poverty to the paradise she craves; we concur in her yearning to live happily ever after." Lidoff locates the sympathy readers feel with Lily in her appeal to "those sustained remnants of narcissism in adults."[42] While I favor a historical approach over Lidoff's psychoanalytic model, many of Lidoff's sensitive readings speak to the identificatory dynamic of reading up. Contrary to Lidoff's analysis, which tends to see Lily as a static model of narcissistic and libidinal pleasure, however, Wharton's contemporaneous, striving, middle-class readers would have noted not just Lily's charm but also its instrumentality. Her liminal position in her social set would not have escaped them; indeed, it would have been crucial for their identification with her. Although Lily does not have the wealth or position required for full membership in high society, her accomplishments make her an indispensable member of her set. By arguing that the choices she makes, which in the rhetoric of the novel ostensibly speak to her free will, are in fact constrained by an unaccountably sadistic author, the readers of *The House of Mirth* who want to identify with Lily while maintaining social ambitions can overlook Wharton's criticism of those who already occupy the heights. Lily asks herself: "What debt did she owe to a social order which had condemned and banished her without trial?" (*HM*, 300). But the reader who reads up replaces "social order" with "pessimistic author," weeps for Lily's waste, and continues to cultivate an upwardly mobile lifestyle.

From Lily Bart to *Ethan Frome*

Mabie in his November 1911 column "Are the Best-Sellers Worth Reading?"—a column written near the end of his *Journal* tenure that reads at all points like a capstone—works hard to distinguish the "quality" best seller, or "steady seller," from the "manufactured fiction" that is generally thought of when one talks about best sellers. He notes that Scott, Dickens, and Thackeray, among others, were best sellers in their own day, and that they are now thought of as "classics." Indeed, it seems that Scott is better appreciated in 1911 because this "new generation of readers" does not "hang breathless on the plots, as did the young readers of the third decade of the last century," but rather recognizes that Scott's novels are "rich in human interest" (November 1911, 30). This is the column in which Mabie dismisses *Charlotte Temple*, *The Lamplighter*, and *The Wide, Wide World* as unfortunate missteps in taste, while celebrating the brisk sales of *Uncle Tom's Cabin*. Mabie wants to suggest that most of the "classics" were best sellers at the time of publication and to suggest by extension that the most exemplary "best sellers" of the first decade of the twentieth century might be likewise destined for such esteem.

Mabie lists the "best sellers" of the previous six years, to see what kinds of conclusions he and his readers might draw from the collection. Of his list, only *The House of Mirth* and *The Jungle* are immediately recognizable in the twenty-first century; Thomas Dixon's *The Clansman* is there, but holds current significance largely insofar as it was the source text for D. W. Griffith's *Birth of a Nation*. And while Mabie signals in other columns his opinion that *Conquest of Canaan*, *Beverly of Graustark*, and *The Garden of Allah* are destined for spots in the pantheon, they are of course waiting in oblivion for the moment when they become the subjects of a recuperation project for middlebrow literature. Mabie recognizes that the list is a mixed bag; while "perhaps six" will endure, "there are four or five stories of no lasting value, but of a pleasant flavor, a passing charm; and there are fourteen or fifteen which bear well-known trademarks and are to be classed with what are known in business parlance as spring or autumn "offerings." As long as his readers have a proper relationship to them, such texts will do no harm. But it is disconcerting to see Wharton grouped in such company; her novel is unusual in that regard, and Mabie almost certainly wants to keep her an exception here. *The House of Mirth*, while it is well known as a quality text, is here presented en masse with books one might reach for more lightly, books that do not seem to require the same kind of intellectual commitment that Wharton's book would. This is precisely the point: Wharton's book is within reach of the reader who might have previously only considered *The Awakening of Helena Ritchie* or *The Masquerader*. Mabie's list works just as well to promote the reading of Wharton as it does to make his readers reflect on whether they really should be spending their time with *The Millionaire Baby*.

Aside from this mention and the initial review Mabie offers for *The House of Mirth*, the novel appears in his column six times, nearly always as an item in a list of reading programs. In an April 1906 question-and-answer column, a reader (or Mabie posing as a reader) glosses the term "analytical novel" with reference to *The House of Mirth*, and in his response Mabie reinforces this classification by noting that the novel is one of several "striking studies of character and society modified by the materialism of the day" (April 1906, 26). In the following month's column, Mabie lists Wharton alongside Mary E. Wilkins Freeman, Sarah Orne Jewett, and Mrs. Humphry Ward, among others, in response to a reader's query about the "ten leading women authors of today." He lists *Sanctuary* and *The House of Mirth* as Wharton's representative texts, offering the caveat that "[i]t is impossible to say definitively that any one book is *the* best of any particular writer; that is a matter of taste" (May 1906, 18). In the same column, Mabie offers his version of the "three tests of a good novel" and uses *The House of Mirth* as an illustrative example of a novel that "describe[s] a character with such insight and feeling as to create genuine dramatic interest." In his November 1908 course of reading, "Novels Descriptive of American Life," *The House of Mirth* is listed in company with Hawthorne's *The House of the Seven Gables*, Norris's *The Octopus* and *The Pit*, Owen Wister's *The Virginian*, and Howells's *The Rise of Silas Lapham* (see appendix B). And finally, the novel is one of the representative "novels of realism" in Mabie's compendious September 1909 "Courses of Novel-Reading" column. In one of his benedictory columns, Mabie explains why *The House of Mirth* stands out among Wharton's works: it is the novel in which she lets herself be the most romantic:

> Mrs. Wharton writes with a quick artistic conscience and is greatly concerned with the form of her work, and one suspects that she is indifferent to the general verdict. It is her limitation that she always makes us aware that she is an expert. She lacks humor, but she is well-stocked with wit, and the intellectual quality of her work is always high. In "The Valley of Decision" she was the expert rather than the creative artist; in "The House of Mirth" she wrote with conviction and emotion, and the story came to life. (February 1912, 42)

When Wharton lets herself go, when she writes in a way that is more responsive to "the general verdict," she is a better writer—more "emotional," more evocative of the responses a Mabie reader might want to enjoy while reading a novel.

Mabie mentions other Wharton novels along the way, but the only one he mentions repeatedly is *Sanctuary*; with four appearances, it seems to be his go-to Wharton novel when he wants to recommend something with a less ambiguously happy ending, or with a greater affinity for sentimentality. Mabie no doubt concurred with the assessment of the original *New York Times* review of *Sanctuary*, that "it is good, ethically and artistically, to read and read again a book with such a lift";[43] with the reviewer from the *Independent*, he may have felt that the book attested to "a beautiful, tender sentimentality peculiar to women, whether they are writers, mothers, or missionaries."[44] He chooses *Sanctuary*, for example, as the suggested Wharton novel in a list that closes the column "Should the Young Read Novels?" (September 1907). This novel of renunciation and maternal devotion would have played very well with a large part of Mabie's demographic, who would never have described it, as Hermione Lee does, as a "claustrophobic study in maternal possessiveness."[45] Mabie's time at the *Journal* ends before he can shape a nuanced response to Wharton's *Ethan Frome* (1911); *Frome*, one imagines, would have posed a dilemma for Mabie, a dilemma he was perhaps facing across the board with the more naturalistic turn in her work and the work of many of his other favored authors. He praises it as "a noble piece of penetrating analysis, close characterization and atmospheric effectiveness," and praises—or perhaps breathes a sigh of relief for—Wharton's craftsmanship: "In hands less skillful it would have been not only a depressing but also a sodden domestic tragedy." As it is, the novel is still tragic because of the "general sense of futility which pervades it," but "the situation is saved from moral squalor by the acceptance of the results of an impossible break for freedom." Still, *Frome* is a tough book to recommend, and Mabie himself seems glad for his section break and the turn to another text: "However one may enjoy the fine workmanship for this story it is a relief to open Mr. F. Hopkinson Smith's 'Kennedy Square' and find one's self in the genial air of an old-time Southern home, surrounded by people who believe in their emotions, but do not analyze them" (December 1911, 30). *Frome* does not offer the respite of *The House of Mirth*, and it needs to be followed with a palate cleanser, both in reading and in criticism.

Kennedy Square seems a relief for many reasons, not the least because it offers a more nostalgic, rose-tinted version of regionalism, which was the variety Mabie vastly preferred. *Frome* was artistic, yes, but it was regionalism with a bleak and critical bent; no one, reading *Frome*, would want to visit the Berkshires anytime soon. As we shall see in the following chapter, Mabie turned to regionalist fiction more frequently than to any other form, because it was there he was able to locate for his readers the last vestiges of romanticism. In his final column, "Which Way Is Literature Going?" (April 1912), Mabie writes hopefully of a trend that might run counter to the excesses of Zola and his ilk, who Mabie accuses of wielding "tremendous sledge-hammer force" to artificially suppress literary romanticism.

> Romanticism, which had taken on new forms from time to time, was held in many quarters to have had its day, and to have disappeared finally from the field of writing. Thereafter society was to be content with nothing short of the bare fact. The world had grown impatient of the graces of style, the flights of imagination, the pleasant interpretation of the hard facts of life, presented by romanticism. Realism had planted fiction on an immovable basis of fact, and life was thereafter to be presented unadulterated and without disguise. So it seemed at the moment. (April 1912, 42)

Readers revolted, however; Mabie uses the example of England, where "Mr. Locke, who is more popular [than hard-core realist Arnold Bennett], is writing romances with as brave a heart and as free a hand as in the days before Zola came and went, and Mr. De Morgan is as far removed from realism and veritism as is 'The Arabian Nights.'" When he shifts to the American context, though, Mabie speaks more gently of the readership of realism. He concedes that Frank Norris's *The Octopus* and *The Pit* are "both youthfully defective novels, but both novels of genuine power, dealing with real things and expressive of forces now making themselves felt in a supremely powerful way on this continent." Mabie goes on to predict, and to hope, that a novelist will write the decisive romance of business, will take the tone of *The Scarlet Letter* and turn it to business in the same way that Mary Johnston has "use[d] the history of the Civil War in an epical, romantic spirit."

In this benediction, Mabie includes Wharton as one who is "breaking away" to write "beautiful art" like, yes, *Ethan Frome*. He tellingly refrains from using any precise terminology to describe from what she is "breaking away," but one might read him as critiquing either derivative sentimental literature ("refined, delicate, and imitative") or realism ("bold, original, and crude"). His vagueness, his convoluted diction, and his conflation of seemingly rigorous technical terminology yet again sustains his project of rendering certain works, or certain authors, of high-capital "realism" palatable for his mass audience. Edith Wharton, a valuable intellectual commodity, must not be lumped with the less-valuable Norris, or with the abjured Zola, as a naturalist; she must continue in the minds of Mabie's audience, particularly after he has ceased to offer monthly advice, to signify the future of American letters.

5 / The Comforts of Romanticism

*It is a good thing to succeed honorably in one's business, but it is a better
thing to succeed in one's life; to be not only an efficient man or woman, but
to be full of interest in large matters, to think about great subjects, to know
and love the best the world has taught and said, to make life interesting,
refreshing, and worth living for others. [. . .] To the man in the right
place, as much as to the man in the wrong place, a door must open into a
larger world; and for most men that door is private reading.*
—HAMILTON WRIGHT MABIE, "MR. MABIE SUGGESTS COURSES FOR
PRIVATE READING" (NOVEMBER 1908)

William Dean Howells, Henry James, and Edith Wharton—in the early
twentieth century, having read these authors was a significant marker
of cultural sophistication. And despite these authors' tendency to criticize the culture of social mobility that undergirded the existence of the
Ladies' Home Journal, familiarity with their work was just as desirable
for that magazine's readers as it would have been for the readers of the
North American Review or the *Atlantic Monthly*. Hamilton Wright Mabie, as we have seen, finessed his recommendations of these authors to
focus on texts that would have been amenable to a particular type of
self-interested misreading, which I have termed "reading up": reading
with an eye to social advancement, with the hope of material advancement, that makes it possible to ignore a work's social critique if such a
message would rankle. We have seen that, with regard to Howells, readers could easily see *The Rise of Silas Lapham* as a romance and, indeed,
as a reinforcement of the reader's own ambitious reading. We have also
seen how *Roderick Hudson* and *Portrait of a Lady* could be read in a
manner consistent with an upwardly mobile mind-set. We have seen that
Edith Wharton's *The House of Mirth* infuriated readers who wanted a
happy ending and turned readers against a cruel author rather than a
cruel society.

While Howells, Wharton, and James were among the most frequently
mentioned authors in Mabie's columns, they were not dramatically more
prominent than many other authors, certainly not in statistically significant ways. *The Rise of Silas Lapham* and *The House of Mirth* are two of

the top twenty-eight most frequently mentioned single works, but there were others that made repeat appearances in the columns (see appendix A). Alongside perennial (and conservative) entries like *The Scarlet Letter*, *David Copperfield*, and *Uncle Tom's Cabin*, we find contemporaneous offerings that do not fit comfortably within a "high realist" rubric: *Hugh Wynne, Free Quaker*, by S. Weir Mitchell; *The Virginian*, by Owen Wister; *The Choir Invisible*, by James Lane Allen; and *The Grandissimes*, by George Washington Cable. For the Mabie reader, these texts functioned as literary comfort food, refreshing romanticism after the sterner realism one needed to read for the sake of cultural capital. These were novels of romance and "local color," and the Mabie audience could turn to them if they needed a distraction from, say, the depressing starkness of *Ethan Frome*.

For many years the romantic literature of the 1890s and early 1900s was ignored by scholars, who were focused on a linear narrative in which realism segued into naturalism and spawned modernism. In the 1990s, scholars like Amy Kaplan and Nancy Glazener renewed interest in the so-called romantic revival by paying long-overdue attention to the works that accompanied some realists on the popular books lists. Instead of dismissing these latter-day romances as "nostalgic retreat to a simplified past away from contemporary strife at home and abroad," Kaplan argues that romances complexly reconfigured the contemporaneous U.S. foreign policy situation as chivalric theater.[1] Glazener describes the ways that elite literary publications embraced the romance because of the serious financial straits that attended a waning readership.[2] Consumerism ceased to be anathema to periodicals that had once sniffed at the "popular" as unrefined and primitive. These corrective studies force us to recognize the messy fracturing of the literary landscape at a very early point in the 1890s and 1900s, and to picture literary history not as linearity but as simultaneity. The romantic revival, the vogue for regionalist and "local color" writing, and the persistence of realism and nascent naturalism were all fomenting at the same moment, each mode perhaps taking relative precedence at various points, but all under contestation in the same periodicals, on the same shelves at libraries and bookstores, on the same lists at women's clubs and in self-culture publications. We can see this simultaneity quite clearly in Mabie's columns, and we can mark there the cultural tensions as readers negotiate modes, searching for the text that can maximize both profits and pleasures. As we have already seen, Mabie had a vested interest in appealing to a wide range of tastes while attempting to direct his readers towards the most culturally advantageous literature. Mabie presumes a romantic bent on the part of his audience (a safe assumption, as the majority of "best sellers" from the early 1900s were historical romances), but he hopes to somehow channel that audience towards at least some subset of literary realism. Regionalism, or "local color" literature, becomes a kind of intermediary step for him; he offers such texts as a bridge between the contemporaneous romance and "high realism," repeatedly and consistently, from the first column in March 1902 through his final columns of 1912. When entertaining the question asked in the column "Are the American Novelists Deteriorating?" (September 1911), Mabie is able to answer in the negative because of the wealth of neo-romantic, regionally focused literature that he sees being published. Ticking off each region of the country, Mabie praises western author Owen Wister, New Englander S. Weir Mitchell, southern writers Ellen Glasgow and Mary Johnston, and Mary Watts and Mark Twain of the "Central West." The last is, Mabie argues, "the best field for fiction in America," because it "affords the largest field for observation of human character and occupation in this country, as it holds the political control of the country as well." The Midwest is, Mabie claims, the repository for all the good independent spirit that migrated westward after the Revolution, and in addition to the quirky individualism chronicled by Twain, one may find there "a reincarnation of the refinement and distinction of the old Colonial aristocracy." Ripe fodder for romance, that; as is the South, which produces authors who "imbibed early that spirit of idealization of the past which was not without justification, and is the expression of a sensitive and responsive imagination to the appeal of a vanished social order" (September 1911, 24).

Regional literature afforded Mabie an opportunity to champion nominally "realist" texts that nonetheless straddled the line into romance; they are atmospheric, their characters are noble and picturesque, and they typically resolve themselves more neatly than ambiguous James, ambivalent Howells, or aggrieved Wharton. Taking Mabie's inaugural column as a template, we can look at two representative regional authors, Sarah Orne Jewett and George Washington Cable, as prototypical Mabie favorites. Their preferred novels offer avenues for sympathetic identification, and opportunities for romantic flights, that Mabie resists terming "sentimental" because of the social dishonor of that term. Mabie is able to present his readers with the kind of reading experience they prefer, with texts that accommodate more easily that practice, when he turns to regionalism; in so doing, he also feeds into and reinforces the critical process by which regionalism was coded a more degraded variety of realism. By examining how Mabie promotes the reading of regionalism, we can easily see that literary regionalism's fluctuating critical fortunes are a result, not of anything inherent in regionalism, but of its attractiveness to "reading up" readers.

Identification Crisis: *Deephaven*

By the time Mabie began his stint at the *Journal*, regionalism was already a genre with an identity problem. One of Mabie's favorite regional writers, James Lane Allen, had registered pleasure in 1897 that "Refinement, Delicacy, Grace, Smallness, Rarity, [and] Tact," which he saw as hallmarks of the "Feminine Principle" and a particular subset of literature with a regional focus, were finally giving way to the "Masculine Principle" qualities of "Virility, Strength, Massiveness, Largeness, Obviousness, and Primary or Instinctive Action."[3] Donna M. Campbell has read Allen's curious criticism alongside commentary from Brander Matthews, Charles Dudley Warner, Hamlin Garland, and others, as a symptom of an ideological tug-of-war in the 1890s in which regionalism was "fragmented while it was almost simultaneously promoted as the key to a 'national literature, rejected as a literary fad, reworked as a variety of proto-naturalism, and, most damaging of all, redefined and marginalized . . . before it disappeared into a host of other movements, including historical romance."[4] In the "literary" magazines, like the *Critic*, the *Atlantic*, and the *North American Review*, regionalist writers were coming out in force to denounce regionalism as an effete form, as the victim of its success, bastardized by market forces that had led authors to mass-produce texts that looked like regionalism, but which did not have the true connection to place, the "veracity" of description and characterization, as the purer, earlier form. Warner offered a eulogy to "local color" in the May 1896 *Harper's Monthly*, explaining that "so much color was produced that the market broke down."[5] The backlash against regionalism was so strong, in fact, that Sarah Orne Jewett and Mary E. Wilkins Freeman turned away from their previous subject matter towards the more marketable historical romance.[6]

We join both of those authors in the midst of this self-refashioning in March 1902 when Mabie makes his first explicit book recommendations: Jewett's *The Tory Lover*, a historical romance, and Wilkins's *The Portion of Labor*, her return to New England after *The Heart's Highway: A Romance of Virginia in the Seventeenth Century* (1900). While both novels were relatively recently published, both had been out for several months, so the choice was not made solely on the basis of novelty—clearly, other considerations were at work. In chapter 1, we saw how Mabie's treatment of Wilkins's text was symptomatic of his tendency to emphasize feeling and character over other critical concerns when recommending fiction, and we noted that the Jewett discussion was largely an opportunity to discuss her earlier work, which is always evocative of "delicate sympathy" from her readers. Jewett is, in fact, an ideal author for Mabie because of the ways that his two favored novels, *Deephaven* and *The Country of the Pointed Firs*, model appropriate sympathies through narrators and characters that very closely resemble a main portion of the *Journal* audience. Mabie seems patently unconcerned about the terminological battles over "regionalism" and "local color"—he is happy to continue to embrace both the more "refined" and the more hackneyed offerings of the genre. But tellingly, he never mentions either term when discussing regionalist fiction, preferring instead to note its "romantic" or "sympathetic" capacity. Mabie again sidesteps the controversies swirling about in the highbrow periodicals so that he may offer his readers access to the texts that will confer status.

In March 1904, when asked to name candidates for the "best three American novels," Mabie chooses *Deephaven* as Jewett's contribution. He also recommends *Deephaven* two months later, when a mother asks, "What six books, standard or modern, calculated to benefit, can I purchase for reading by my daughter of sixteen, with the taste and intelligence of the average girl, who up to this time has done practically no reading of a general sort?" (May 1904, 24). *Deephaven* is the "starter" Jewett book, *Country of the Pointed Firs* the more advanced, in Mabie's October 1905 list "A Beginning in the Best Fiction," and both represent Jewett in his September 1907 "Some Standard Novels" list. In the September 1909 column "Courses of Novel-Reading," *Deephaven* appears in the "Novels of New England Life" list alongside *A Country Doctor*, Holmes's *Elsie Venner*, Stowe's *Oldtown Folks* and *Minister's Wooing*, and Hawthorne's *The House of the Seven Gables*. In all, Mabie recommends *Deephaven* six times, as many times as he recommends *The Country of the Pointed Firs*, and he recommends Jewett's late historical romance *The Tory Lover* thrice.

Even when it was first published, *Deephaven* was not a critical favorite. Readers were generally underwhelmed by the novel's episodic structure, seeing in the series of vignettes a failure of plot and, therefore, a violation of generic conventions. This critical consensus extends into the present day; one generally finds *Deephaven* described as a good first effort, but hardly a success. Paul R. Petrie locates the relative failure of the text in Jewett's inability to fully realize her transformation of what he terms "linear Howellsian literary mediation into a more evocative, reader-participatory narrative mode that was fully able to grapple with Jewett's spiritualized sense of temporal social realities."[7] It may be this precise "failing," however, that makes *Deephaven* a more appropriate text in certain circumstances, to Mabie's mind, than *Country of the Pointed Firs*. His lengthiest treatment of Jewett occurs in his inaugural column, in which he also discusses Wilkins's work. Mabie's treatment of Jewett's subject matter provides a good framework within which we can "read" his future recommendations of Jewett without being influenced by twenty-first-century critical arguments over regionalism.

> Miss Jewett's field is also in New England, but it rarely touches Miss Wilkins's territory; between them one can get a fairly complete impression of New England life outside the large cities. It is the simple, old-fashioned home, with its air of having sent boys and girls to college, whose interior Miss Jewett has often studied and sketched with the most delicate sympathy and the most sensitive skill. She understands also the hidden idealism of the plain people in farmhouses and farming towns, and she knows their humor as well.
> (March 1902, 17)

Mabie promotes Jewett as half of a diptych through which the reader can get a "fairly complete impression" of a region—this is the touristic, ethnographic model of regionalism that has been discussed by Richard Brodhead and Sandra A. Zagarell, among others.[8] While we may reasonably object that such may not have been the intention of regionalists such as Jewett and Wilkins, this is clearly the use to which Mabie was putting their works, and the use to which he suggested his readers put their works. He likewise introduces a clear position for identification when he comments that the homes in Jewett have the air "of having sent boys and girls to college." Certainly, some of the homes have such an air—the homes of the cosmopolitan visitors, though not those of the "local" inhabitants they visit. In *Deephaven*, for example, Kate's brothers are meeting their "classmates" for a school vacation trip to Lake Superior and come to meet the girls while "waiting until it was time for them to go back to college," but in the town of Deephaven itself there is no mention of anyone having gone to school save a shadowy, disappeared uncle of Kate's whose path towards the Catholic priesthood renders him persona non grata in the small group of Deephaven gentry from which he has sprung.[9] College is never mentioned in *The Country of the Pointed Firs* or in the most recommended of Jewett's short story collections, *The Queen's Twin*; in *Tales of New England*, the Reverend Dobin of "The Dulham Ladies" is a less-than-attractive college graduate. But explicit textual references are, after all, not Mabie's main concern—he is interested in "selling" his readers on Jewett, or at least, on specific texts of Jewett's, and this tactic is a useful one. Homes with the air "of having sent boys and girls to college" are the kind of homes one presumes Mabie imagines a majority of his readers coming from, or the kind of home he imagines his readers wanting to create for themselves, and therefore the kind of home about which they would be interested in reading.

Mabie's readers of Jewett, then, might be more likely to identify with the intercessory narrator and, perhaps aspirationally, with her wealthier friend Kate, than with the "locals" about whom Jewett was writing—even in *Country*, which by all accounts is the work that brings her closest to realizing an insider standpoint. Zagarell contends that the intrusive invocations of readers in *Deephaven* are addressed to "either cultivated, upper-class, and primarily Anglo-Saxon New Englanders like Kate Lancaster and members of Jewett's circles, whose sense of origins New England regionalist literature articulated, or, like Helen Denis, members of the newly professionalized upper middle class that identified with the class and ethnic standing exemplified in the book by Kate." Zagarell continues, "In introducing elite-identified readers to Deephaven, the narrative makes Anglo-Saxon Deephaven available to the population that carries on the ethnic traditions attributed to Deephaven."[10] This dynamic would certainly hold true for a large number of the readers of the *Journal* to whom Mabie was writing, but there would also be a good number of rural readers, and perhaps even some urban working readers (particularly young women) who would be inclined to pick up Jewett because of the frequent mentions of her work as "always worth reading." When they pick up the text, they are pushed into identifications with characters they do not resemble, and they construct sympathies that function more as wish fulfillment and which work to buttress the social order while rendering "realistic" works fantasy works.

One of the more complicated scenes of identification in *Deephaven* occurs when the two Bostonians, Kate and Helen, end up showing a group of tourists around the Deephaven lighthouse and one of the tourists, mistaking the genteel, cosmopolitan Kate for a simple lighthouse-dweller, offers to give Kate a reference for a job in Boston. When Kate's true class identity is revealed by her leisure-class hands and her expensive ring, the working girl, whom Jewett has until this point described as a paragon of manners, backtracks apologetically: "I ought to have known better; but you showed us around so willing, and I never thought of your not living here. I didn't mean to be rude" (D, 38). Zagarell notes that in this episode, "foregrounding an urban worker's anxious respect for a member of the superior class, *Deephaven* signals distress over contemporary challenges to upper-class authority," and certainly it does so.[11] But it likewise signals distress over the difficulty one might have in telling the difference between a member of the superior class and a lighthouse-dweller once the former has taken up so seamlessly with the latter, in an act of such complete sympathy that she begins to resemble the lighthouse-keeper, or at least to act just like her. Perhaps it also cautions the reader against too much vacationing in the other's identity—the lines should remain drawn as clearly as possible, and a reader should not become too clearly identified with any character who is too far outside the bounds of the reader's original identity.

Another avenue into *Deephaven* for the Mabie reader comes through Kate and Helen's reading, though there is little explicit evidence of their reading during the main body of the text. At the beginning of the novel, during her narrative of the meeting that sets the stage for the trip to Deephaven, Kate makes reference to a number of texts that locate her and Helen's literary life firmly in the realm of juvenilia. First, Kate accompanies a giddy, teasing announcement of her intentions to remove to Deephaven with "a few appropriate bars of music between," at which point Helen is "suddenly reminded . . . of the story of a Chinese procession which [she] had read in one of Marryat's novels when [she] was a child: 'A thousand white elephants richly caparisoned,—ti-tum tilly-lily,' and so on, for a page or two" (D, 12). Helen easily recalls the literature of childhood, and Kate's piano playing is probably meant to recall it, but both girls are clearly entering into this reference with their tongues firmly in cheek. Less critical is the friends' propensity for citing the popular poetry of Jean Ingelow, a member of John Ruskin and Christina Rossetti's circle, whose literary career was founded on her popular juvenile novel, *Mopsa the Fairy*, and on a number of collections of children's verse.[12] Kate punctuates her invitation to Deephaven with an Ingelow reference, which Jewett is careful to have Helen flag for the benefit of her readers:

She seemed to have finished her story for that time, and while it was dawning upon me what she meant, she sang a bit from one of Jean Ingelow's verses:—

"Will ye step abroad, my dearest,
For the high seas lie before us?"
and then came over to sit beside me and tell the whole story in a
more sensible fashion. (*D*, 12)

The lines are from "The Days without Alloy," a rhythmic and nostalgic tribute from the point of view of an ex-sailor to the siren call of boats being rigged in port. Though Helen marks Kate's invocation of the romantic and fanciful Ingelow as not entirely "sensible," it is a part of Kate's allure for Helen, an allure towards which Jewett is not at all ambivalent. Both references underscore what Ann Romines identifies as the fundamental childishness of Helen and Kate's plans in this opening chapter: "[N]ever do they seem to feel that they are doing more than *playing house*, building a sandcastle."[13] They self-identify as "girls," and they are "twenty-four, unmarried, genteelly unoccupied; at the edge of an adulthood they are not wholly eager to claim."[14]

Not unlike Catherine Moreland in Jane Austen's *Northanger Abbey*, the girls like to imagine the presence of romantic—even gothic—secrets in Miss Brandon's and Miss Chauncey's houses. They do not like to use the "best parlor" of the house: "[A]ll the portraits which hung there had for some unaccountable reason taken a violent dislike to us, and followed us suspiciously with their eyes" (*D*, 25). At an earlier point in her description of Miss Brandon's house, Helen remarks that "[i]t is very remarkable that there seem to be no ghost-stories connected with any part of the house," but when no mysteries present themselves legitimately, the girls work to create them:

The wide window which looks out on the lilacs and the sea was a favorite seat of ours. Facing each other on either side of it are two old secretaries, and one of them we ascertained to be the hiding-place of secret drawers, in which may be found valuable records deposited by ourselves one rainy day when we first explored it. We wrote, between us, a tragic "journal" on some yellow old letter-paper we found in the desk. We put it in the most hidden drawer by itself, and flatter ourselves that it will be regarded with great interest some time or other. (*D*, 24)

Though Helen as narrator treats these instances with a degree of self-mockery, Jewett's hand is so gentle that it is easy to read them as charming evidences of youth and high spirits rather than to see them, as in Austen's novel, as evidence of youthful imaginations run amok under the influence of too many novels. Indeed, the girls leave the journal despite having found two "legitimate" romances already—a stash of Kate's grandmother's old love-letters, which Helen barely mentions, and "a little package of letters; ship letters mostly, tied with a very pale and tired-looking blue ribbon" (D, 31), found alongside a faded miniature and dried flowers in Kate's maiden aunt's escritoire. The former seem unromantic because, of course, we know how they turned out—Kate's grandmother married her grandfather, gave birth to her mother, and lived a standard domestic existence. The latter, on the other hand, by their very existence give Kate and Helen a new perspective on Miss Brandon. "So there was a sailor lover after all, and perhaps he had been lost at sea and she faithfully kept the secret, never mourning outwardly" (D, 31–32). Even though they put the letters aside, intending to read them, they eventually accord them the privacy they do not give to other letters from Miss Brandon's school friends, and herein lies some room for readers to critique Helen and Kate's conclusions. First, we do not know whether the sailor was indeed a lover—nor do we know that he was lost at sea. Perhaps, instead, affections on one side or the other were alienated? The presence of another packet in the drawer renders an explicit counterpoint to this blue-beribboned package—another one, tied with black ribbon, which "had evidently been untied and the letters read many times" (D, 32). Which is the more important relationship?

Mentions of reading or books are fewer during the "body" of the text, but they come back at the end when Helen starts mentioning the things they did that summer that do not make the cut into the rest of the narrative. And as it turns out, their plans for summer reading far outpaced their accomplishments (a familiar phenomenon, indeed):

> We are fond of reading, and we meant to do a great deal of it, as every one does who goes away for the summer; but I must confess that our grand plans were not well carried out. Our German dictionaries were out on the table in the west parlor until the sight of them mortified us, and finally, to avoid their silent reproach, I put them in the closet, with the excuse that it would be as easy to get them there, and they would be out of the way. We used to have the magazines sent us from town; you would have smiled at the box of books which we carried to Deephaven, and indeed we sent two or three times for others; but I do not remember that we ever carried out that course of study which we had planned with so much

interest. We were out of doors so much that there was often little time for anything else. (*D*, 248–49)

Helen then mentions a number of books in what seems less like a definitive list of the things they brought with them to *Deephaven* and more like a "greatest hits" of Helen and Kate's library. In fact, Helen does not list any of the books which would seem to have instituted a "course of study," or any book for which the friends would require the services of a German dictionary. Instead, we are told that Kate "said one day that she did not care, in reading, to be always making new acquaintances, but to be seeing more of old ones" (*D*, 249); as it turns out, such is the actual practice, as opposed to the well-meaning intentions, of the two friends in between their interactions with the Deephaven locals. We find that Kate and Helen are not "highbrow" readers by any stretch of the imagination—they are in fact somewhat immature in their reading and cling to books generally considered "juveniles."

In Mabie's May 1904 list to the young girl whose mother sought his recommendations, *Deephaven* becomes a category representative; since her mother has not given Mabie any specific guidance about the "natural bent of the reader's mind," he offers her a list of books "chosen not because they constitute an ideal list but because they are all of the best quality, are in different fields, and are interesting to young people of average intelligence" (May 1904, 24). Alongside Jewett on the list appear Charles Lamb's *Essays of Elia*, Charles Kingsley's *Westward Ho*, John Greenleaf Whittier's "Snow-Bound," Washington Irving's *Sketch Book*, and Alfred Lord Tennyson's *Idylls of the King*. Jewett is a young girl's transition into realism; it is light, it ends with a return to urbanity and the world of courtship and colleges, and it affords an opportunity to exercise the idealizing and sympathizing impulse.

Creole Sensibilities: *The Grandissimes*

In his inaugural column, Mabie refers to George Washington Cable as one of "three popular authors of to-day." He praises Cable's early works for "show[ing] the most delicate feeling and art," and identifies *The Grandissimes* and *Doctor Sevier* as works possessing consummate "fineness and charm." Though Cable seemed to have lost his touch with the clunkily titled *John March, Southerner* ("it seemed to be the product of hard work, and no book is really successful unless it gives the impression of having been written easily"), Mabie is happy to welcome him back to form with his new novel, *The Cavalier*.

> In "The Cavalier" the charm has come back; the narrative is stir-ring, the incidents crowd fast upon one another; movement, ac-tion, variety carry the reader on from chapter to chapter. There are delightful bits of description, charming scenes, the old air of romance. It is a story of the Civil War. There are two love stories, and the novel suffers somewhat from excess of incident and lack of clearness in the narrative. (March 1902, 17)

Until the final line of this thumbnail review, *The Cavalier* seems an ideal romance—clearly, though, there were limits to the amount of adventure one text could contain. *The Grandissimes*, however, remained superla-tive, a perennial favorite recommendation for Mabie. A highly wrought, romantic novel of French Creole life in New Orleans just after the Loui-siana Purchase, *The Grandissimes* is one of the novels in the running for the "best three American novels" in the March 1904 column. It also appears consistently in Mabie's fiction reading lists: in March 1903, he includes much of Cable's oeuvre, including *The Grandissimes*, in a list of "the freshest and sincerest" American fiction of all time (March 1903, 17), and it is present with *Old Creole Days* in the October 1905 column on self-culture. Mabie's judgment of *The Grandissimes*' staying power seems to have been a bit off the mark, but his equating it with novels that have tended to pass the canon tests, like *Portrait of a Lady* and *The Scarlet Letter*, can be seen as symptomatic of his desires for his readers, of his assessment of their desires, and of their readerly and social expectations. Mabie does not have to sell *The Grandissimes* to his audience in the same way that he might have needed to promote or explain "high" realism; he needs simply to mention it, sometimes to classify it, and then to sit back while his readers pursue it.

In truth, the qualifications Mabie offered about *The Cavalier* apply very well to *The Grandissimes*; Cable's prose is highly wrought, there is hardly a direct statement in the whole of the novel, and the plot is labyrinthine. The circumlocutions not only add to the sense that all the social and racial identities in the novel are complicated and partially ob-scured but also make it exceedingly difficult, if not impossible, for the casual reader to follow all the tangled lines of relation. A reader must be dedicated to figuring out *The Grandissimes* from the moment he or she opens the text, because if not, the opening scene at a costume ball will be entirely impossible to read. For not only do we see the maskers primarily through snippets of dialogue from other observers, but much of that dialogue is rendered in dialect, and layered on top of that is Cable's own indirect style. The maskers are, moreover, gender-bending in their costumes—Dr. Charlie Keene is dressed as the Native American queen Lufki-Humma, the matriarch of the Fusilier family—and unknown to the majority of the people present are two female maskers, one of whom is gender-bending in a monk costume.

> The passing maskers looked that way, with a certain instinct that there was beauty under those two costumes. As they did so, they saw the *Fille á la Cassette* join in this over-the-shoulder conversation. A moment later, they saw the old gentleman protector and the *Fille á la Cassette* rising to the dance. And when presently the distant passers took a final backward glance, that same Lieutenant of Dragoons had returned and he and the little Monk were once more upon the floor, waiting for the music.
> "But your late companion?" said the voice in the cowl.
> "My Indian Queen?" asked the Creole Epaminondas.
> "Say, rather, your Medicine-Man," archly replied the Monk.[15]

And so on. The circumlocution and propensity for convoluted epithets continue, as in this passage where Cable ostensibly "explains" the family trees of the two clans whose stories set the background for the action of the novel:

> Thus, while the pilgrim fathers of the Mississippi Delta with Gallic recklessness were taking wives and moot-wives from the ill specimens of three races, arose, with the church's benediction, the royal house of the Fusiliers in Louisiana. But the true, main Grandissime stock, on which the Fusiliers did early, ever, and yet do, love to marry, has kept itself lily-white ever since France has loved lilies— as to marriage, that is; as to less responsible entanglements, why, of course—(G, 31)

The 1907 edition, fortunately, is full of helpful illustrations by Albert Herter, none of them with captions, but all placed at key points in the text to assist readers in understanding that, indeed, Lufki-Humma is "the daughter of the Natchez sitting in majesty, clothed in many-colored robes of shining feathers crossed and recrossed with girdles of serpent-skins and of wampum, her feet in quilled and painted moccasins," and so on, at great length (G, 28). The epithet "daughter of the Natchez" is here used for the first time to describe Lufki-Humma, and the picture helps us know that indeed we are still talking about the same person. Last names multiply and interweave, as the two founding families marry Nancanous and De Grapions. The basic outlines of relations, in other words, are labyrinthine, and the names exotic; this text is a far cry from the clarity and reticence of Wilkins or Jewett.

Cable's anthropological diction likewise distances his audience from the identifications that are much more available in Wilkins and Jewett. The language surrounding Lufki-Humma is in part respectful, in part anthropological, as in this florid passage describing her mental capacities:

> And as to her brain: what can we say? The casket in which Nature sealed that brain, and in which Nature's great step-sister, Death, finally laid it away, has never fallen into the delighted fingers—and the remarkable fineness of its texture will never kindle admiration in the triumphant eyes—of those whose scientific hunger drives them to dig for *crania Americana*; nor yet will all their learned excavatings ever draw forth one of those pale souvenirs of mortality with walls of shapelier contour or more delicate fineness, or an interior of more admirable spaciousness, than the fair council-chamber under whose dome the mind of Lufki-Humma used, about two centuries ago, to sit in frequent conclave with high thoughts. (G, 26–27)

The anthropologists, while here vaguely critiqued for their fetishizing and clinical ways, are yet closer to Cable's audience than they are to Lufki-Humma herself; the intercessory narrator through whom we access their diggings is more of an ethnographer than perhaps he would like to admit. And when the omniscient narrator is not available to offer such reflections on the older families, Dr. Charlie Keene, by name alone identified as an outsider in New Orleans, serves as the mediator between the normative Anglo audience and the exotic Creole Grandissimes and Fusiliers. In a lengthy bit of exposition, he lays out the family trees for another outsider, the German immigrant Joseph Frowenfeld (one expects this name is an anglicization of "Frauenfeld" and wonders why, when so many French Creole names in the novel have not been anglicized, Cable normalizes the German). The identifications in *The Grandissimes*, in other words, lie firmly with the non-Grandissime general public; these wealthy and exotic personages are the objects of investigation, not the stand-ins for the *Ladies' Home Journal* reader.

At the opening of *The Grandissimes*, it seems clear that the novel should fit clearly in the category of romance, and it seems unashamed in its tendency towards literary tourism. But as Donald A. Ringe explains, this romantic pose was strategic on Cable's part, an attempt to make palatable a story that had already been rejected by the editors of a number of the major literary magazines of the day, "including Richard Watson Gilder of *Scribner's Monthly* and George Parsons Lathrop of the *Atlantic*."[16] The story at "both the physical and the intellectual center of *The Grandissimes*" is the complexly narrated but rather straightforward history of an African prince sold into slavery and married off to his master's illegitimate mixed-race daughter.[17] At his wedding banquet, the prince, now called Bras-Coupé, has too much to drink and after provoking his master runs away to hide in the swamp while placing a voodoo curse on the house of Fusilier.

At a key stress point in the novel's romance plot, Aurora (Nancanou) evokes Bras-Coupé's situation as a parallel to her own—on the verge of eviction, without a picayune to her name, she and her daughter must make a last stand against the scion of the Grandissime family, who has fallen in love with Aurora and who we, as readers, know will save her. This evocation, while it could function to keep the antislavery thematic at the front of many readers' minds, ultimately undermines that plot by relegating it to the status of a symbolic mirror. Do readers who come to Cable's novel with the hope of getting some "local color" of New Orleans, a healthy smattering of Creole patois with their culture, really pause to consider the plight of the enslaved as they root for Honoré Grandissime to hand over Aurora's wrongly seized land? Do the same readers really take seriously Clementine's heavily accented, but utterly accurate, indictment of the system that undergirds the attractive, if quirky and backward, New Orleans society? Even the emotionally brutal description of Clementine's torture and murder near the end of the novel can be forgotten in the wake of the comedic resolution, in which the two couples who were meant to marry do marry, and all the problematic mixed-race characters, with whom readers have not really been induced to sympathize, are scuttled off to foreign lands to languish or else to commit suicide. These were certainly the reading experiences of Cable's contemporaneous readers in the 1880s, and there is little reason to believe that much had changed by the 1900s. If William Dean Howells and his wife, for example, entertained themselves after reading *The Grandissimes* by speaking to each other in the Creole patois of Aurora and Clotilde, what kinds of reactions might other readers have had, following Mabie's lists and noting his celebration of the "refreshment" that can be afforded by the perusal of regionalist literature?[18]

Romancing the Revolution: *Hugh Wynne, Free Quaker*

While Mabie spent a lot of time teasing out the romantic elements in realist fiction, he did not ignore bona fide romances entirely. Aside from *Vanity Fair* and *The Rise of Silas Lapham*, the single work that Mabie recommends most frequently is S. Weir Mitchell's historical romance, *Hugh Wynne, Free Quaker* (1896). The story of a young Quaker who rails against the restrictive rule of his observant father, is expelled from the Society of Friends (on 4 July 1776!), and eventually finds his niche fighting for George Washington in the Revolution, *Hugh Wynne* was serialized in the *Century* from November 1896 to October 1897 and was among the best-selling books of 1898 after being released in novel form.[19] The popularity of the book was such that Mabie would reference it six years later when answering a "reader letter" that wondered about the reason for the brisk sales of "the latest novels." "Is this due to increased intelligence or skillful advertising, or is it because we are giving up more solid reading?" asks a questioner signed only "Reader." In responding, Mabie reminds his audience that

> The novels which have attained very wide popularity, and the sales of which have been sensationally advertised during the past few years, have been for the most part well worth reading. When it is remembered that among them are to be counted "The Choir Invisible," "Richard Carvel" and "The Crisis," "The Virginian," "Hugh Wynne" and Miss Johnston's stories of adventure in Colonial times, it is clear that the interest in these books is not an indication of degenerate taste, or of a taste for cheap reading.
> (March 1904, 16)

All of the titles he mentions in this reply are repeat recommendations of his, and all fit the rubric of neo-romance, or quasi-romance, with a local color or regionalist inflection.

All are also *historical* fictions, which "serious" critics like Brander Matthews and William Dean Howells had spent the last years of the nineteenth century condemning with broad brushstrokes as escapist and inartistic, "as untrue to the complexion of the past as to personality in any time, or rather as crudely tentative and partial."[20] Matthews leveled extensive charges of irreality against the historical novel in an influential essay in the *Forum* for September 1897:

One of the foremost merits of the novel, as of the drama, is that it enlarges our sympathy. It compels us to shift our point of view, and often to assume that antithetic to our custom. [. . .] We learn not merely what the author meant to teach us: we absorb, in addition, a host of things he did not know he was putting in—things he took for granted, some of them, and things he implied as a matter of course. This unconscious richness of instruction cannot but be absent from the historical novel—or at best it is so obscured as to be almost non-existent.[21]

Because the author of the historical novel must do so much backward projection, Matthews argues, there is no more incidental depth to the novel; this quality renders *Uncle Tom's Cabin* a good "historical novel" about the South before the Civil War, but Cable's fiction would be dreadful in Matthews's eyes.

We can therefore understand why, when Mabie praises *Hugh Wynne* as an exemplary specimen of historical fiction, he does so not because of its facticity but because of its atmospheric accuracy. As he writes in a 1909 column, "An historical novel does not necessarily follow the lines of history. If it deals with historical events it must not distort or misrepresent them; but historical novels, as a rule, deal with a period or a man with integrity of truth rather than with integrity of fact" (September 1909, 28). Even when he discusses the presence of Washington in the text, Mabie focuses more on the quality of character drawing than on the historical accuracy. Terming Mitchell's portrait "very engaging and bear[ing] many marks of fidelity to its subject," he seems to prefer it to Thackeray's more demonstrably researched version in *The Virginians* (November 1905, 20). He takes a similar stance when referencing the book's historicity in an October 1908 column that addresses the approaches book clubs might take to the reading of history, as well as in March 1909 when he offers *Hugh Wynne* as a book though which a reader might "pass beyond the bounds of . . . personal experience into the larger experience of the race, to see how other men and woman have lived" (March 1909, 42). Historical books, in this formulation, are most useful because they "make us acquainted with the experience of our ancestors," not because they are expected to be historically accurate. Like the original reviewer of *Hugh Wynne* in the *New York Times*, Mabie directly addresses Matthews by accepting his definitions of successful novels and insisting that they apply to Mitchell's text. The *Times* review, appearing as it did only one month after Matthews's *Forum* essay, addresses Matthews directly: "Although it presents a permanently interesting picture of the Revolutionary time, to call it a historical novel would be to narrow its scope, and might perhaps suggest the type of fiction against which Mr. Brander Matthews has made so brave an assault, and in which 'humanity is choked by archaeology.'"[22] Both Mabie and the *Times* reviewer need to offer more intellectually legitimate validations of Mitchell's novel, and both hit on his ability to evoke the "human element" through characterization as the means of doing so.

Other critics with a predilection for realism took a similar approach to the genre-bending novel. The portrait of Hugh's mother was the highlight of the novel for Willa Cather, who reviewed the novel under the pseudonym of "Helen Delay" in the *Home Monthly*. Hugh's mother is "certainly a much finer woman than the blushing Dorothea [*sic*] whom the young hero goes daft over and finally marries," Cather writes. "But then, I wonder are men's sweethearts ever so good as their mothers?" Second only to Mrs. Wynne is "his reckless old Aunt Gainor, who read with avidity all the novels published in England and France, and drank a great deal of claret, and could lose at cards until four o'clock in the morning without flinching. Not an admirable character by any means, but a clear cut one and thoroughly alive." Next to these two, Cather finds the historical component in the novel—and the chivalric romance elements—superficial and even irritating.[23]

It is indeed possible to read *Hugh Wynne* with an eye to the family romance and only scant attention to the Revolutionary War plot. The subtitle of the book, which is really the extended title of Wynne himself ("Sometime Brevet Lieutenant-Colonel on the Staff of His Excellency General Washington"), promises more exposure to the Revolution and George Washington than the text really delivers; Wynne does not meet Washington until the halfway mark of the novel, by which point the battleground-minded reader may well have put the book aside. Zelig-like, Hugh is the person who informs Benjamin Franklin about the Battle of Lexington; he hears John Nixon read the *Declaration* in front of the Philadelphia Statehouse, has a battle wound dressed by Benjamin Rush, and witnesses General O'Hara deliver Cornwallis's surrender at Yorktown. But the Revolution provides little more than a backdrop for the tensions within the Wynne family. Hugh's grandfather had been the squire of a large Welsh estate, but he had forfeited the title when he converted to Quakerism. His middle brother, William, died childless, and the proprietorship of the estate had fallen to the youngest brother, Owen. Hugh Wynne's grandfather immigrated to America shortly after his Quaker conversion, and Hugh is raised in a household whose stiff Quakerism is leavened only by his lively French mother. When Hugh is a young teenager, he meets his elder cousin Arthur, Owen's grandson, who has been stationed in America as an officer with the Scotch Grays. Hugh's admiration for Arthur ends quickly when both fall in love with the enchanting Darthea Peniston. They become tense rivals, a situation exacerbated by their competing political inclinations. Hugh gradually comes to sympathize more openly with the Revolutionary cause, and after the death of his mother and his expulsion from the Society of Friends, he leaves his home to fight for the rebellion.

After Hugh joins Washington's army, he is wounded and taken prisoner; Arthur sees him in the prison at the moment when he is near death and abandons him, telling no one in the family that he has seen him. When Hugh finally escapes from prison, his aunt (not Arthur's mother) suggests that Arthur might be nervous about his right to the old Wynne estate in Wales. As it turns out, Aunt Gainor is right; Hugh's uncle William had ceded the land back to Hugh's grandfather; Owen Wynne, suspecting the existence of a later deed, had dispatched Arthur to search for it and destroy it. The events of the Revolution interposed, and it was only after the cessation of international hostilities that the Wynne family drama could be played out. By this point, Darthea, who had been engaged to Arthur, discovers her fiancé's treachery and consents to marry Hugh. The ambitious Aunt Gainor, with the purest of aristocratic intentions, pursues the land case and presents the evidence to the prospective future Lady of Wyncote; Darthea promptly burns the deed, horrified that she might be responsible for turning even someone as odious as Arthur out of his home. Hugh had never intended to leave America for an ancestral manse in the Welsh countryside, anyway; he reprimands Darthea for distrusting his resolve, she apologizes, and they live happily ever after on a sizable estate in the Pennsylvania countryside.

Hugh's story was certainly intended to be a metaphor for the new nation—any doubts on this score evaporate when one reads that his dismissal from the Society of Friends takes effect on 4 July—but some scant reader-response evidence from the letters page of the *New York Times Book Review* suggests that this was far from the central concern of all of Mitchell's readers. Instead, contra Matthews, they worried about historical accuracy and, on a metafictional level, about whether the novel was "original" or imitative of prior Revolutionary War novels. As we noted above when discussing the *House of Mirth* controversy, *Times* letter writers—and the subset of those whose letters were actually published—are probably not representative of a cross-section of the thousands of people who read *Hugh Wynne* at the turn of the century. But their responses, and the fact that they were sustained enough to prompt correspondence, can be read as symptomatic of a particular nexus of reading, in which generic divisions were simultaneously porous and politically very important.

In April 1898, apropos of nothing, the *New York Times Book Review* published a letter from "Frederica Edmunds" of Trenton, New Jersey. Admitting that her review was "somewhat belated," Edmunds contradicted the *Times* review by complaining first that *Hugh Wynne* contained too much period detail—"why give us every alley and footpath of old Philadelphia?"—and then that some additional detail could have been lavished on the "great events of the day." "It is true this is realistic treatment, but the reader is not satisfied without some artistic perspective, or the compensating conviction that the characters are working out some strong plot of their own." After praising the character drawings, the letter closes with a lament that "the author has told us no story, that the plot possesses no cumulative interest, and is continually impeded by the dragging in, without due warrant, of early Philadelphia celebrities of whose patriotic virtues we are quite ready to hear when not thrust upon us as romance."[24] The novel, it seems, has offered its historicity in all the wrong places for this reader, and in approximating a realist mode it has become considerably less satisfying. The intermodal text, in other words, fails to satisfy either expectation.

After this letter, *Hugh Wynne* is absent from the *New York Times Book Review* pages until November 1899. The occasion for its return is the publication and review of Winston Churchill's Revolutionary War novel, *Richard Carvel*. In a provocative letter, a reader signed "Similia Similibus" details a number of significant plot parallels between the Churchill and Mitchell novels. "Hugh had an always present fairy aunt—Richard's grandfather was his protecting angel. In his youth Hugh's aunt presented him with a mare, 'Lucy,' fleet as the wind, and he became a masterful rider, which served him well later in the war—Richard's grandfather brought him 'Firefly,' a mare of lively disposition, and he learned to ride like a centaur, which afterward served him very well when challenged to ride the wild stallion on the London streets."[25] Similia Similibus continues with the comparison for some time, then registers regret that she had read *Carvel* first, rather than its "prototype." Once this gauntlet is thrown, readers are eager to weigh in on the possibility that Churchill has engaged in unethical borrowing. "Charles H. Young" ups the ante by citing Thackeray's *Virginians* as another source text for *Carvel*, and a poorly executed one at that. To any of these texts, Young vastly prefers Paul Leicester Ford's *Janice Meredith*, which "is original; it has more life; it is more picturesque than a chromo and strong enough for a Turner oil painting." If its heroine is silly, "she has the merit of being silly through-out, and, according to accepted literary tenets, all heroines of that period in America seem to have been silly."[26] In the same issue, "Desdichado" offers the blanket critique that "[a] slight sense of proportion would hardly hurt some of these writers, and the lack of it is perhaps what gives the strongest ground to enemies of fiction in general."[27]

The following week, the *Book Review* editors published a clarification that may well have been prompted by a flurry of letters on the plagiarism controversy. "It seems necessary to emphasize the point that 'Richard Carvel' was conceived, mapped out, and mostly written several years before 'Hugh Wynne' was published."[28] This seems an adequate refutation, and a clear one; when the editors go on to try and argue for the necessary overlaps between works that deal with the same historical epoch, they get into trouble. Certainly, the two novels could mark similar historical landmarks, like Lexington and Yorktown, but these were not the elements that Similia Similibus and Young delineated. What the editors do not want to entertain is the highly formulaic quality of the Revolutionary War novel; they cannot validate "mechanical fiction" in their pages. To their aid comes "L.," whose letter on 23 December offers several examples of other literary "coincidences," plot resemblances between *Quo Vadis* and *The Last Days of Pompeii*, and between *Reds of the Midi* and *Ange Pitou*.[29]

After this skirmish, the *Review* again falls silent for a month, until a slow February spurs a challenge. "A.U." writes in to introduce a parlor game of sorts: "Which of these three books [*Richard Carvel, Hugh Wynne*, or *Janice Meredith*] is the best?" The prompt suggests that they be "considered both as literary productions and as historic studies of the men and times of the Revolution," in other words, along the fault lines that have already demarcated the debate over the "value" of a historical novel.[30] The discussion becomes a referendum on the form and on the possibility that one text could fulfill all the requirements of literary and historical excellence. Mrs. E. J. Moore weighs in early that *Carvel* is superior, followed by *Hugh Wynne*, and that *Janice Meredith* is not only immoral (the heroine is engaged three times!), but "the mixture of history, mostly imaginary, and romance is exceedingly crude, and at no times rises to the plane of literary excellence."[31]

"Veritas" wants more like *Janice Meredith* because "[t]here is no mawk-ish sentimentality; there is no vulgar sensuality; there is no fashionable self-analysis; but it is just a plain, healthy novel . . . ."[32] "J.T.H." thinks that *Carvel* "presents the most picturesque picture," but that between the three plots "it is the toss of a cent which we take. They are all good and worth preserving."[33] George Middleton votes for *Richard Carvel* because it has more action, while *Janice Meredith* is "slow, and 'Hugh Wynne' slower." This writer also compares the climax of the romance plots for relative gratification: "Hugh wins Darthea while riding on horseback, and there is nothing beautiful about it at all; in 'Janice Meredith' the final scene is very pretty, though it did not impress me half as much as the scene in 'Richard Carvel,' where Dorothy kisses the forehead of her lover, Richard."[34] "L.A.M.," on the other hand, predicts that most readers would find *Hugh Wynne* more gratifying because of its intimate por-traits of historical personages and because "many people prefer the story of the struggle for liberty on the land rather than on the sea." This reader is unbothered by "superficial" similarities among the novels, arguing that these "would naturally occur in any American historical fiction of that period."[35]

I have offered the key points of these selected letters in scattershot fashion to emphasize a point: the responses to the question are as varied as they are impassioned, though they mark for each letter writer a par-ticular alignment with the terms of professional critical debates over the historical novel. A reader who prefers a fast-paced plot will balk against a perceived focus on self-investigation, as will a reader who seeks out historical detail. A reader who is drawn to "intimate portraits," on the other hand, finds fault with more encyclopedic treatment of characters and events. "Literariness" is attributed to whichever characteristic is more positively connoted, and there is no clear consensus on the pre-ferred mode—neither is there consensus on the quality that each novel exemplifies. The editors of the *Times* surely had a role in the selection of the letters, and most likely they chose to offer a number of letters in sup-port of each novel, both for the sake of author relations and to keep read-ers from feeling marginalized. Such ecumenicalism, though, implies the presence of all "faiths" among the readership. There was neither realist nor romantic orthodoxy when it came to the historical novel. The plas-ticity of the historical novel served Mabie well in his recommendations because it was so easily assimilable to preexisting personal preferences. As literary "comfort food," the historical romance, like regionalism, could be justified, but it could also be a guilty, escapist pleasure.

The Varieties of Literary Experience

An attentive reader will have already objected that even the texts I have identified as the most frequently mentioned in Mabie's columns are hardly ubiquitous, appearing perhaps a dozen times in one hundred columns. The truly remarkable thing about Mabie's writing for the *Journal* is, in fact, the profound *infrequency* of repetition. Writing ten columns a year for ten years, one might expect him to return to the same favorite authors and texts more than once or twice a year. But Mabie was truly ecumenical in his recommendations, covering a wide range of nonfiction as well as fiction, and touching on many authors only once or twice. On the other hand, reading Mabie regularly, one gets a strong sense of his preferences, and certain novels seem to figure even more prominently than the sheer numbers would suggest. I have chosen, for the sake of this study, to focus on Mabie's recommendations of works of "high realism," because these were the core of his project: in encouraging his readers to sophisticate their reading, he needed to package realism along with the older "romantic" works with which they would already be familiar, and which they would already embrace (e.g., *The Scarlet Letter*); to avoid alienating his readership, he needed to put "high realism" on a continuum with other literature that was "quality" literature, "of lasting value," but not as bleak or, ultimately, as valuable in terms of cultural capital. If a Mabie reader can come to speak as readily of Howells, James, or Wharton as he or she does of Thackeray, F. Marion Crawford, or Kate Douglas Wiggin, then he or she may enter the precincts of the educated and enjoy all the (vaguely suggested) benefits thereof. We might consider, for example, the case of a reader who has come to *The Grandissimes* after having read Mabie's November 1908 column, "Mr. Mabie Suggests Courses for Private Reading." This column, immediately following an October 1908 column about reading lists for women's clubs ("When a Club Can Do Good Work"), offers some of the most unambiguous expressions of his philosophy regarding the benefits of reading to the upwardly mobile man or woman:

> Private study is especially the resource of those whose occupations and surroundings are dull. Instead of breaking away and seeking fortune at a distance it is often wiser to stay by a task for a time and make ready, by study, for something more congenial. A man who can make a good horseshoe has mastered an honorable and difficult craft, but sometimes a youth is at the anvil who belongs somewhere

else; it is not a question of the relative dignity of occupations, but of finding the occupation which Nature had in view for the particular boy. Here, for instance, is a young man striking vigorous blows on an anvil, whom Nature intends shall become a distinguished lawyer. How shall he find his way from the workshop to the courtroom? Not by abruptly leaving his trade, but by reading law at night. In one particular case the young man read through fifty volumes of reports and cases and kept up his work at the same time. Here is a boy reading law in an office whom Nature plans to do the work of an engineer; how shall he make the change? By giving up every spare minute to private study of books on engineering and the working out of problems in the seclusion of his own room. The country is full of able and spirited young men who are supporting themselves by hand-work by daylight, and getting ready for their life-work by brain-work by candlelight. The stories of these quiet workers who, by intelligence, persistence and self-denial, build bridges from the occupation most accessible to that most desirable are chapters in the great, unwritten romance of American life. (November 1908, 36)

Epilogue: Reading Up into the Twenty-first Century

Both Oprah and I want the same thing and believe the same thing, that the distinction between high and low is meaningless.
—JONATHAN FRANZEN, 26 OCTOBER 2001[1]

We have a little history.
—OPRAH WINFREY, 17 SEPTEMBER 2010[2]

While I have structured this study around Hamilton Wright Mabie and his *Journal* writings—a book historian's treasure trove that would certainly repay further scholarly attention—it is important to note that although he had the largest bully pulpit, he was not unique among critics and literary popularizers at the beginning of the twentieth century. The *Atlantic*, for example, had Agnes Repplier, who "led the charge against high realism" during that publication's flirtation with more popular tastes.[3] Mabie himself refers frequently to manuals of "self-culture" that his readers might want to use to supplement his columns, such as James Freeman Clarke's *Self-Culture*, Philip Gilbert Hamerton's *Intellectual Life*, and Noah Porter's *Books and Reading; or, What Books Shall I Read and How Shall I Read Them?* Matthew Arnold's *Essays in Criticism* and *Culture and Anarchy* had become a textbook for the self-culture movement, and the Chautauqua movement was flourishing.[4] Everyman's Library, which began production in 1906, was making the "classics" mentioned by Mabie affordable, and it was constructing its own canons along similar lines as Mabie. A particularly salient example of this dynamic is the Harvard Classics series Five-Foot Shelf of Books, published with inspirational synergy by P. F. Collier from 1910 to 1961. The Five-Foot Shelf combined a reading advisor sensibility—these are the texts you should read, and this is what you should get out of them—with an impressively bound edition of the works themselves. Unlike Everyman's Library, the Five-Foot Shelf was remarkable for its fixity: the contents of the collection did not change at all over its fifty-year publication history. One selling point of the Five-Foot Shelf was its programmatic efficiency—following the daily reading guide in a bound pamphlet with the promising title "Fifteen Minutes a Day," you could learn all you needed to know to succeed socially or professionally. What better assurance for the beginning reader than to know that, really, the only texts that required attention could fit in fifty bindings?

In her treatment of the Five-Foot Shelf, Joan Shelley Rubin discusses the ways that "the early rhetoric surrounding the Harvard Classics satisfied the need for access to 'the best' while simultaneously addressing the desire for information and making it consumable."[5] But why would a reader want to read "the best" books? The conflation of reading and financial success that is nascent and implied in Mabie is fully formed and explicit by Collier's early 1920s advertising campaign for the Five-Foot Shelf series. On 23 January 1921, the reader of the *New York Times* was confronted with a picture of a typical daily scene: the interior of a train during the morning commute, seated men in business suits and fedoras (and one well-dressed woman), noses buried in their newspapers. One lone, standing passenger, eschewing the newspaper, is engrossed in a book. The banner caption crows, "Which Wins Out?"[6] The book reader, it seems, will have a competitive business advantage over the newspaper readers because he is acquiring "'the essentials of a liberal education'—the power to think straight and talk well." The ad promises that such knowledge will "lift men to distinction and success," and encourages readers to send off for a free reading-plan booklet.

A little over one month later, the reader of the *Times Book Review* would find a Harvard Classics ad appealing to a different set of aspirations, keyed perhaps to the recently passed Valentine's holiday. A lovely woman sits at a dinner table, flanked by two men in evening dress. She has turned her back on one concerned-looking gentleman while she lavishes the other (who, by the way, is also the younger and more attractive of the two) with a winning smile. The headline asks, "Which of these two men has learned the secret of 15 minutes a day?"[7] The ad continues:

> Here are two men, equally good looking, equally well dressed. You see such men at every social gathering. One of them can talk of nothing beyond the mere day's news. The other brings to every subject a wealth of side light and illustration that makes him listened to eagerly. He talks like a man who had traveled widely, though his only travels are a business man's trips. He knows something of history and biography, of the work of great scientists, and the writings

of philosophers, poets, and dramatists. Yet he is busy, as all men are, in the affairs of every day. How has he found the time to acquire so rich a mental background? When there is such a multitude of books to read, how can any man be well-read?

The Five-Foot Shelf is, of course, the answer to this conundrum, with its helpfully condensed and programmed plan for reading. This project is "the answer to this man's success"—a success in this case not professional, but personal, if the illustration is any indication. In 1922, Collier's ad writers tied marital contentment to well-read-ness, with a comparative picture of two couples, one pair staring blankly at the reader over cards, a card table separating them physically and spiritually; the second pair, with legs crossed towards each other, a book in front of each, are smiling as they discuss their respective reading. This couple has "learn[ed] the secret of eternal youth. They are constantly acquiring fresh, new interests. Their evenings are a delight to themselves when they are alone; and their company is eagerly sought by their friends."[8] Marital, social, and professional success—all would presumably result from reading the right books. The center part of the equation is never filled in; it is never quite clear *how* such results will come from the reading project. And there was no need to fill in that blank; the culture of success had already folded the notion of "reading up" into the general cultural understanding.

From Mabie forward, the idea that a particular type of reading—reading "the best books"—was desirable, and would produce material results, was unquestioned, self-evident, "natural." Founded soon after Mabie's tenure at the *Journal* were the Modern Library (1916), the Book-of-the-Month Club (1926), and the Reader's Subscription (1951), to name just three of the myriad taste-making ventures of the early twentieth century.[9] Cultural capital became big business—but this was only possible because at some point, the idea became general that reading "good" books would somehow be good for you, both socially and financially. Mabie was an agent of the production of that "reading up" ideology, but the traces of his influence have been obscured, his presence effaced.

Oprah v. Franzen, 2001–10

Fast-forward to September 2001, as Oprah Winfrey announces that her forty-second Oprah's Book Club selection will be Jonathan Franzen's *The Corrections*. Franzen's book had just been published to considerable critical fanfare, Franzen's publisher, Farrar, Straus and Giroux, having produced a glossy promotional package to prep book reviewers for "the most important book of the last fifteen years."[10] It was already on its way to best-sellerdom; Oprah's selection promised to catapult it into mega-best-sellerdom, putting it, in Franzen's words, "into Wal-Mart and Costco and places like that."[11] Oprah celebrated the novel, and her faithful book club followers on the message boards at Oprah.com were ready to agree after reading the opening lines, which several quoted in posts from 2 October 2001. "I completely agree with you about the beginning of the book," writes "Jonanna." "I read reviews when it came out a month or so ago, and had planned to read [it] in the future. When Oprah made it her book this month, I was overjoyed. It is superb. I look forward to participating in a discussion."[12] It is important to note, in light of what follows, that this reader and many others on the discussion boards report that they had already planned to read the novel. This reader had seen the novel's generally positive reviews, perhaps like Francine Prose's in the September 2001 issue of *O: The Oprah Magazine* (an issue devoted to "Success!"): "These complex, marvelously drawn characters—and their closely interwoven stories—are enough to keep us reading attentively, and with pleasure. [. . .] But what makes the novel so truly electric are the multiple jolts of recognition it delivers as Franzen gets so many different scenes eerily right."[13] The subtitle for Prose's review trumpets the novel as "a literary masterpiece"; Oprah was delivering for her readers the "best book," the superb work of an author who self-identified as "solidly in the high-art literary tradition."[14]

In a series of interviews in October 2001, Franzen repeatedly made comments that indicated his discomfort with his book being selected for Oprah's Book Club. Being in the "high-art literary tradition," he expressed uneasiness about the mass-marketing of his book, its presence in big-box retail establishments (as opposed to independent or boutique bookstores), and he lamented in an interview on National Public Radio's *Fresh Air* that Oprah's imprimatur would lead to the book being read, and consequently disliked, by people for whom the book was never intended: "First and foremost, it's a literary book. And I think it's an accessible literary book. It's an open question how big the audience is to which it will be accessible, and I think beyond the limits of that audience, there's going to be a lot of, 'What was Oprah thinking?' kind of responses."[15] On 22 October, after having heard multiple disparagements of her program and audience from her chosen author, Oprah had had enough; she released a statement disinviting Franzen from her show and canceling the book group discussion. Franzen frantically began to back-pedal and apologize, but Oprah stood her ground, advising her readers to move on to the next book. The nuances of the Franzen-Oprah feud as it played out among the principals and the critical media have been discussed with much greater detail elsewhere; Kathleen Rooney thoroughly and sensitively parses the class and aesthetic orientations of the two principals, as well as the gender biases of Franzen's statements. Trysh Travis has argued that Oprah's Book Club's New Thought theology is at the root of Franzen's discomfort, and she gracefully summarizes the dustup and the critical fallout.[16] Scholarly consensus seems to be that Franzen was at best clueless, at worst unrepentantly and idiotically snobbish, and that Oprah got the best of the disagreement by asserting her right of refusal and withdrawing her allegiance and the allegiance of her vast and ostensibly loyal audience.

A somewhat different dynamic played out on the Oprah.com message boards that were dedicated to the novel and which were open and fully engaged at the time of the conflict. Between the beginning of October and 15 October, while a vast majority of the posters were primarily concerned with board technicalities such as how to display icons before their usernames, how to make them animated, and how to customize their viewing preferences, some readers did address the novel in preliminary fashion. Posters expressing hesitation about the book quickly asserted their intentions to "stick with it," despite distaste for either the characters or Franzen's style. The 7 October post of "mlnurk" is typical: "As many of you said and a lot of you haven't had trouble with . . . but I sure am having a problem getting into this book. I can't get past chip!! I keep putting it down and wishing I was reading something else. I'm enjoying reading the posts much better than the actual book . . . but I'm not giving up!" (ellipses in original).[17] Posters struggled gamely in the days before Wikipedia to identify Michel Foucault, whose philosophies are espoused by one character. They debate another character's dedication to her family and wonder about the significance of the title.

After Franzen's *Fresh Air* interview, the discussion, unsurprisingly, became focused on his statements, with posters finding varying degrees of justification in what he says. "Stolafgirl" posts that Franzen had "dirty, ungrateful things to say about Oprah and the book club. I found him to be quite egotistical and am looking forward to his appearance on the show at the end of the month to see how he acts with readers as well as Oprah."[18] "Esty105" answers that "[h]e sounds insufferable just like his book. Maybe he should have put a label on it FOR MEN ONLY. Then

I wouldn't have wasted my time reading it."[19] "Rborja76" weighs in that "I didn't come away with the notion that he said anything 'harsh' about Oprah, at least nothing that I felt was an unfair complaint about the show. Then again, I'm a man."[20] And "sabine12" offers, "In reading the reactions of many of the posters to this board: He is dead-on right. This book IS different. It is NOT plot-driven; it is more 'literary' than some of the other picks. And, let's be honest, many of the folks on this board have NOT liked this book."[21] Posting on the boards required registration, and most of these respondents were repeat—and therefore dedicated—posters; while the righteous indignation of many of the responses is perhaps expected, there is also a generous representation of readers who take seriously Franzen's critiques of the book club offerings and suggest that the negative responses to the book might well be a function of its "high-art literary" profile.

Vituperation and celebration intermingled on the board for the next week, followed by more of the same, leavened with confusion, after Oprah announced the cancellation of the show and discussion with Franzen. While many readers made public statements of renunciation ("I'm returning my book!" exclaims "martster" on 24 October),[22] others lamented the loss of an opportunity to talk about the book and criticized both Franzen and Oprah for posturing that does a disservice to the readers, and to literature in general. Sabine12 again offers a cogent analysis: "To put it bluntly, I think this stinks."

> I'm disappointed in both sides—the author for making such elitist and ill-considered comments and, honestly, I'm a little disappointed in the show for not taking this opportunity to engage in a very interesting discussion about what seems to be a recurring issue. I would love to have a chance to talk to Mr. Franzen and show him that women who watch daytime television CAN appreciate "literature."[23]

Enough readers wrote in to disagree with Oprah's move that the board, which had previously been a place of gentle agree-to-disagree rhetoric, became tense, with moderators needing to remind posters to discuss the book, not one another. "Instead of condemning Oprah," one reader writes, "I want to thank her for practicing what she preaches to her audience, the importance of demanding to be treated respectfully. Also by canceling the show Oprah has sent a message that no one is allowed to insult the viewers of her show."[24] But readers also argued that Oprah "has an obligation to us her readers and book club participants. Even I did not like the current selection of the month, I always watched the show and enjoy it [sic]. I end up usually getting something out of reading a book I did not care for just from the book club dinner."[25] Many readers were livid because the show was going to be cancelled after they had made a significant financial commitment to the book, which was only available in hardcover and cost up to $40.00 for Canadian readers. As Siouxj writes, "Once I bought the book, it sat there for almost a week. I would pick it up, only to put it back down after the searing burning guilt had fully stained my hand—I had such shame for spending 40 bucks on a book."[26]

Gradually, with no reversal forthcoming from Oprah or her board moderators, a core group of the board members decided to refocus their energies on having the discussion they were clearly going to be denied by the show. By 14 November, they were debating not only the application of the term "Great American Novel" to Franzen's novel in particular, drawing comparisons (both positive and negative) to *The Great Gatsby*, *An American Tragedy*, and *The World according to Garp*. They were likewise debating the concept of the Great American Novel and questioning what they saw as the profit-driven attempts to apply that term to a new novel (by a white male!) every five years or so. Returning to the loss of the dinner show, "zurilaw" comments (with scare quotes around "Great American Novel" to indicate the deepening of the term that resulted from their prior discussion):

> I sigh at the show-discussion that might have been, but then I contemplate the discussion that probably would have been, and I count myself lucky to be spared a trivialization of a "Great American Novel." If the discussion were to have been limited to the most concrete of connections . . . a la What The Corrections Taught Me About Living with a Parkinson's Patient . . . or My Sibling is Sooo Like Chip (or Denise or Gary) . . . or My Mother-in Law Cooks with Grease and Gives Tacky Gifts . . . then I might have been unbearably demoralized, indeed beyond correction. I am enormously grateful to have been spared that particular fate . . . and to have been left instead to ponder the irony of a literary phenomenon that alternately catapults sales and cancels discussion, and a media icon who blithely proclaims a "Great American Novel" yet feels (apparently) uncompelled to sponsor (on air) the recap, reflection and debate that the work that prompted so weighty an appellation demands.[27]

Ironizing both the impulse to hierarchize texts and ham-fisted, literalizing attempts to render a "high-art literary" novel "accessible," this poster identifies and exposes strains of cultural arbitration that stretches all the way back to Mabie, and expresses and enacts her independence from arbiters on either side of the cultural divide.

On 17 September 2010, Oprah Winfrey announced that the first book club offering for her last season on *The Oprah Winfrey Show* would be *Freedom*, Jonathan Franzen's first novel in nine years, the follow-up to *The Corrections*. She declared the new book "exquisite . . . a masterpiece." Noting that she and Franzen "have a little history," Oprah explained that she had cleared the selection with him in advance, and she encouraged her audience to join the virtual discussion on Oprah.com. Unsurprisingly, the first posts are largely preoccupied with the Oprah-Franzen drama rather than with the book itself. While some readers felt that Oprah was affording Franzen publicity and sales that might be more helpful to a less well-established author, more agreed with the sentiments expressed by "sandra194," who was "not surprised that Oprah 'forgave' or moved on with her relationship with Franzen—this is what she talks about all the time—not holding grudges against folks. Go Oprah!"[28] Excited about the possibilities for a redemption arc, posters anticipated an eventful book club telecast.

When discussion turns to the text itself, the responses quickly segregate themselves into fans and defenders of the book and the irritated, bored, and angry haters of the book. Many from the latter group comment that they are typically library-goers who made an exception this time around and purchased the book; like Siouxj in 2001, their irritation is amplified by the thought that they "wasted" such money on a purchase, and now they will not be able to recoup the cost in recreation or pleasure. As "6dinnersid" comments on 15 October:

> I have been an avid reader for years . . . and read all types of novels. After 200 pages of Freedom, I could not stand to read another page. It just seemed like filler to me. And the sentences go on and on and on. I am extremely disappointed in this Oprah book selection and even more so that I spent $28 on this book. Love Oprah and her show![29]

Like this reader, Oprah's readers generally take care to specify that their criticism of the text or the choice did not extend to a personal critique of Oprah herself (by mid-November, there was even a theory afloat that Oprah did not read or choose the book herself, but was coerced into doing so by corporate interests!). But these posters, like Mabie's readers, clearly expected to get a good return on the investment of their time and money. "Filler" in a book, as in a sausage, is unforgiveable.

Readers who liked *Freedom* also expressed their approbation in the language of "value," turning even to address the relative "value" of participating in an online discussion of the text. "Kiki5026" writes, "[I find] the comments that have been posted to be either very positive or extremely negative and I wonder about those who posted all of the negative comments. Sure, we all enjoy reading upbeat books that are interesting and hopeful. But how much more do we get out of a book that makes us think and feel, like Freedom does?"[30] Other defenders write testier responses, frustrated by their philistine fellow-readers who lament the unrelatability of Franzen's characters. One frequent participant, "jgluz," has reached the limit of patience by 29 October: "I'm sorry that this wasn't the usual escapist, empty-calorie, sentimental drivel that keeps the industry afloat. I'm sorry that anybody had to work at it to squeeze out an iota of empathy for this coterie of completely human, fully-voiced, flawed and beautiful characters. I'm sorry that Franzen would be proven right in having worried about exposing this lot to his work the first time around."[31] Jgluz values empathy but anathematizes "sentimental" and "escapist" literature. In language that directly echoes the concerns of high realism's early century defenders, jgluz denigrates a grasping and commercialized publishing industry, interested only in "keeping [itself] afloat," while turning immediately to an assessment of the mass of readers (Oprah readers—"this lot") as constitutionally incapable of appreciating good literature. It is an efficient, thorough, and passionate, if highly conventional, post.

Unlike the 2001 discussion, the 2010 boards were visibly controlled by the guiding voice of Oprah's book club producer, Jill ("producerji"), who offered prompts for discussion every week and who replied to selected posts. As in the case of the reader letters that Mabie "answers" in his columns, we cannot know the extent to which responses on the Oprah discussion boards were selected, edited, or even scripted. Even if we were to assume that all of these responses had actually been written by discrete, individual readers, the degree to which each response was mediated by culturally constructed expectations of readerly attitudes is unknowable. But at the very least, one may read this discussion as a representation of discussions of a book like Jonathan Franzen's *Freedom*, a book celebrated by the *New York Times* and publicly embraced by the nation's highly educated, and self-consciously cerebral, president.[32] And in reading this representation of readership, we can note several things about the ways reading is supposed to work. Some readers will be dissenters who complain of boredom or of lack of identification; many of these readers will insist that they entered into the reading project in good faith, because they were told by a trusted adviser that this book would be good for them. Such responses necessitate the rallying of defenders who rail against the lowbrow tastes of the others and who find "value" in a book's "difficulty." But there are no voices that question reading per se; reading's value has been secured. Even if you do not like *Freedom*, you might like another book; turning away from literature altogether is simply not an option. This presumption of reading's essential value—aesthetic, emotional, social, material—is the enduring legacy of Mabie, the internalization of reading up.

Appendix A: The Mabie Canon

Most Frequently Mentioned Single Works

Title	Number of Mentions
Vanity Fair	16
The Rise of Silas Lapham	14
Hugh Wynne, Free Quaker	13
Anna Karenina	12
The Bible	12
The Virginian	12
The Scarlet Letter	11
Adam Bede	10
David Copperfield	10
The Mill on the Floss	10
The Choir Invisible	9
The Marble Faun	9
Treasure Island	9
Uncle Tom's Cabin	9
The Grandissimes	8
Henry Esmond	8
In Memoriam	8
Ivanhoe	8
Lady Baltimore	8
The Masquerader	8
Old Creole Days	8

Most Frequently Mentioned Single Works (continued)

Title	Number of Mentions
The Spy	8
The Adventures of Huckleberry Finn	7
The House of Mirth	7
The House of the Seven Gables	7
Red Rock	7
Robinson Crusoe	7
A Tale of Two Cities	7

Most Frequently Mentioned Authors

Author	Number of Mentions
Ralph Waldo Emerson	30
William Shakespeare	30
Henry Van Dyke	30
William Makepeace Thackeray	26
William Dean Howells	24
Nathaniel Hawthorne	23
Thomas Carlyle	20
F. Marion Crawford	19
Edgar Allan Poe	19
Oliver Wendell Holmes	18
Thomas Nelson Page	18
Edith Wharton	18
James Lane Allen	17
Henry James	17
Alfred Lord Tennyson	17
Charles Dickens	16
Sarah Orne Jewett	16
Sir Walter Scott	16
Mrs. Humphry Ward	16
Kate Douglas Wiggin	16
Owen Wister	16
Thomas Bailey Aldrich	15
Margaret Deland	15
Henry Wadsworth Longfellow	15
S. Weir Mitchell	15

George E. Woodberry	15
George Eliot	14
Ellen Glasgow	14
F. Hopkinson Smith	14
James Fenimore Cooper	13
Mary E. Wilkins Freeman	13
Rudyard Kipling	13
Matthew Arnold	12
Washington Irving	12
John Greenleaf Whittier	12
George Washington Cable	11
John Fox Jr.	10
Hamlin Garland	10
Mark Twain	10
Honoré de Balzac	9
William Frend De Morgan	9
John Fiske	9
Thomas Hardy	9
Booth Tarkington	9

Appendix B: "Novels Descriptive of American Life" (November 1908)

An interesting and profitable course running parallel with a course in history, sociology, biology, or poetry could be arranged by reading some of the following novels dealing in a serious spirit with American character and life:

Simms's "The Partisan"
Cooper's "The Spy"
Hawthorne's "The House of the Seven Gables"
Cable's "Old Creole Days," "The Grandissimes"
Howells's "The Rise of Silas Lapham," "A Hazard of New Fortunes"
Eggleston's "A Hoosier Schoolmaster"
Bret Harte's "Luck of Roaring Camp and Other Stories"
Mary Hallock Foote's "The Led-Horse Claim"
Octave Thanet's "Heart of Toil," "Stories of a Western Town"
Wister's "The Virginian," "Lady Baltimore"
F. Hopkinson Smith's "The Fortunes of Oliver Horn"
Thomas Nelson Page's Short Stories and "Red Rock"
Mrs. Deland's "Old Chester Tales"
J. L. Allen's "Flute and Violin," "The Choir Invisible"
Frank Norris's "The Octopus," "The Pit"
Garland's "Main Travelled Roads"
Miss Jewett's "Country of the Pointed Firs," "The Tory Lover"
Miss Wilkins's "New England Nun," "Pembroke"
Churchill's "The Crisis," "Coniston," "Mr. Crewe's Career"

Brander Matthews's "His Father's Son"
S. Weir Mitchell's "Hugh Wynne"
Fox's "The Little Shepherd of Kingdom Come"
Mrs. Wharton's "The House of Mirth"
Robert Grant's "Unleavened Bread"
Robert Herrick's "The Common Lot," "The Memoirs of an American
    Citizen"
Grace F. King's "Balcony Stories"

NOTES

Introduction

1. "To-Day's Books and Their Authors," 2.

2. Ibid. In the absence of archival evidence of such reader letters, it is of course impossible to know for certain that hundreds of *Journal* readers actually did request such a feature or that they phrased it in the precise language of this announcement. Still, we can discern a good deal about reading attitudes among *Journal* readers, or at least the editorial perceptions of those attitudes, or perhaps editorial desires to foster such attitudes, from this advertisement of coming attractions.

3. Dreiser, *Sister Carrie*, 393. Subsequent references are parenthetically cited as *SC*.

4. M. H. Dunlop argues that Dreiser does not simply evoke this "mechanically-produced" popular fiction to critique the "multiply produced" popular tastes of the day but that he specifically mentions these novels because they can function so effectively as oblique commentary on his own heroine's story. Plot and character parallels make it possible to read Carrie's life either as a version of the Ross novel (and thus a "sensation" novel) or as a variation on the Clay novel (a "sentimental" novel) (Dunlop, "Carrie's Library," 201–15). Dunlop seems, though, to undercut her own nuanced readings by emphasizing Dreiser's disdain of the popular novel and downplaying Dreiser's apparent attention to and communion with the specifics of popular texts, however "multiply produced" or hackneyed. Dreiser's careful selection of these texts in fact works to the allusive advantage of the reader who would have been familiar not just with the reputations of these works as "trash" but with the details of these texts: in other words, with readers like Carrie who were delving into Dreiser's text in the same ways, and potentially for the same reasons, that Carrie pursued Balzac—because someone said it was better for them. Dreiser unfortunately would have to wait for some time to gain this kind of popular support—the book of course did not sell in 1900—yet because the "alterations" between the initial typescript and the final 1900 edition were made in the interest of attracting and keeping a female audience, we can

imagine that he had this readership in mind when reworking this portion of the novel (as he did, substituting Ross's novel for an earlier, and, Dunlop argues, less appropriate, work). For a discussion of the textual history of the novel, see Lehan, "The City, the Self, and Narrative Discourse," 81–82.

5. On Marden, see Hart, *The Popular Book*, 160–61. Carl Bode in his introduction to Alger's *Ragged Dick and Struggling Upward* (xxi) discusses the author's cyclical popularity: "When he died [in 1899], the obituaries were more or less dismissive. On the other hand, by a turn of events so remarkable that even Alger wouldn't have dared to use it in his books, the early twentieth century took up those books and transformed them into a vogue. During the euphoric years before World War I, the Alger myth was perfected and his fiction sold better—by hundreds of thousands of copies—than it ever had while he was alive."

6. The consideration of women's moral education and of the problem of women's susceptibility to literature has been a particularly rich area of study; see, e.g., Flint, *The Woman Reader*.

7. Ohmann, *Selling Culture*, 75. This group was not exclusively urban and suburban; as Ohmann points out (74–75), the transportation and communication infrastructure in place by the beginning of the twentieth century enabled similar consumption patterns and expectations in rural areas as well.

8. Mabie, *Books and Culture*, 18–19.

9. Scanlon, *Inarticulate Longings*, 13. On department stores, see Leach, *Land of Desire*; on marketing and print advertising, see Ohmann, *Selling Culture*, and Garvey, *Adman in the Parlor*, among others.

10. *Ladies' Home Journal*, February 1902, 6, 14–15.

11. Radway, *A Feeling for Books*, 142–43.

12. Christopher P. Wilson, looking at the marketing of Sinclair Lewis's *Main Street* in the 1920s, notes that "the growing consensus in the teens was that the 'book-buying habit' was not secure enough among the general public and that book promotion needed to focus instead on 'opinion makers,' notably critics, discriminating booksellers, or influential community figures, and, in [Charles] Doran's words, be more 'impartial,' professional, even academic" (Wilson, *White Collar Fictions*, 216). Writing in the first decade of the twentieth century, Mabie was still trying to see that that "habit" was well established in his readers.

13. Hutner, *What America Read*, 22.

14. Radway, *A Feeling for Books*, 152–53.

15. This history has been told many times, but perhaps most influentially for this project by Chartier, *A History of Private Life*, vol. 3, and, specific to the American context, in Kaestle, "The History of Readers."

16. Machor, "Introduction: Readers/Texts/Contexts," xi.

17. Certeau, *Practice of Everyday Life*, 166.

18. Rose, "Rereading the English Common Reader," 55; Gilmore, *Reading Becomes a Necessity of Life*, 163 (cited in Rose).

19. Adam Smith's famous formulation of the process of identification, Howard argues in "What Is Sentimentality?" (224), offers a "resolution of the dilemma posed by the increasingly individualist topography of the self":

As we have no immediate experience of what other men feel, we can form no idea of the manner in which they are affected, but by conceiving what we ourselves should feel in the like situation. Though our brother is upon the rack, as long as we ourselves are at our ease, our senses will never inform us of what he suffers. They never did, and never can, carry us beyond our own person, and it is by the imagination only that we can form any conception of what are his sensations. Neither can that faculty help us to this any other way, than by representing to us what would be our own, if we were in his case. It is the impressions of our own senses only, not those of his, which our imaginations copy. By the imagination we place ourselves in his situation, we conceive ourselves enduring all the same torments, we enter as it were into his body, and become in some measure the same person with him, and thence form some idea of his sensations, and even feel something which, though weaker in degree, is not altogether unlike them. (Smith, *The Theory of Moral Sentiments*, 1:9)

Smith's discussion of the imagination's role in identification paved the way for the mode of sentimentality in literature, and for the use of sympathy as a training ground for the emotions.

20. Hartman, *Scenes of Subjection*, 19–20. The substitution of self for other becomes, literarily, the process of escapism that Jürgen Habermas identifies as an adjunct to the identificatory moment. Through identification, anyone may "enter into the literary action as a substitute for his own, to use the relationships between the figures, between the author, the characters, and the reader as substitute relations for reality" (Habermas, *Structural Transformation of the Public Sphere*, 50). As Glenn Hendler notes, citing this same passage, Habermas sees the evocation of sentimental identification as a moment in which the novel "mediates between private personality and public sociality because it enacts the division of public and private in each reader" (Hendler, *Public Sentiments*, 115). Hendler goes on to trace the ways in which sentimental identification, which he reads as a process of Althusserian interpellation, was variously deployed to mold public spheres that could be heteronormative, antislavery, pro-temperance, or politically feminist, finally arguing that "it is not so much a particular identity or subject position that is reproduced in the reader's act of identification as it is the transformative process of identification itself," that in fact the thing produced by sentimental identification is "affect itself" (217, 218). Such production of affect, though it engages in the "fantasy that affect can be the ground and site of noncoercive communicative exchange in the public sphere," in effect ends up as one of the most potentially influential means of communication available (218).

21. Bennett, *What Books Can Do* FOR YOU, 147.

22. Hochman, *Getting at the Author*, 4. Hochman observes that the "fictional narrator that could merge with both the author and the characters became a particular favorite. Imagined as an inhabitant not only of the represented world within the text but also of the world outside it, such a narrator was a fertile source of reader identification—a composite human figure, exemplary but not distant" (38).

23. Sicherman, "Sense and Sensibility," 213.

24. Ibid., 215.

25. My use of the terms *highbrow* and *middlebrow* throughout this project follows the historical arc of a literary work's acceptance, according to the class in which it was placed by a majority of critics at the time of its publication and initial popularity.

On middlebrow culture as it arose in response to literary realism at the end of the nineteenth century, see Kammen, *American Culture, American Tastes*; and Hutner, *What America Read*.

26. In her recent expansion of this study, Sicherman notes more generally the ways that reading fostered intellectual and professional aspirations in women like the Hamiltons, Jane Addams, and Ida B. Wells-Barnett throughout the later nineteenth century. See Sicherman, *Well-Read Lives*.

27. See Fish, *Is There a Text in This Class*; Mailloux, *Rhetorical Power*; and Bennett, "Texts in History."

28. Bennett, "Texts in History," 10.

29. Ibid., 11.

30. See Wilson, *White Collar Fictions*.

31. Wharton, "The Vice of Reading," 513. Subsequent references are parenthetically cited as "VR."

32. Dunn, "A Plea for the Shiftless Reader," 133.

33. Ibid., 132.

34. Bell, *The Problem of American Realism*, 4.

35. Glazener, *Reading for Realism*, 14. As Glazener suggests, and my analysis bears out, the "romantic revival" provides even more evidence for the influence of market pressures on elite determinations of aesthetic quality. While writers in the *Atlantic* group of magazines came, by the 1890s, to distance themselves from elements of literary realism because they found the mode either too far distanced from the real problems of real people or too unmarketable, their biases against the mode's ostensible "elitism" were not shared by people who wanted to become—or at least to seem like—members of the elite. The cultural cachet that had attached to realism in the 1880s had not evaporated in the eyes of the public, even well into the 1910s; realism was still highbrow literature and, as such, was highly desirable cultural capital.

36. Ibid., 96, 145–46. The messiness here seems akin to what Hartman calls the "violence of identification," in which "in making the other's suffering one's own, this suffering is occluded by the other's obliteration" (*Scenes of Subjection*, 20, 19).

37. While I take Bell's caveat to heart, that we should move beyond "the question of the relation of 'American realism' to the tradition of Continental realism or to some ideal model of realistic mimesis" (*The Problem of American Realism*, 5), I do not read it as indicating that we should ignore the ways that the relative "acceptability" of various Continental realists was one of the key battlegrounds on which William Dean Howells, Henry James, and others contested their definitions of realism. I also accept Bill Brown's critique of Bell as too easily dismissing the contradictions between Howells's fiction and his criticism (Brown, review of *The Problem of American Realism*). Again, I am interested less in trying to figure out what "realism" really was than in thinking about how it was being constructed vis-à-vis Balzac—and then suggesting that Dreiser purposefully evokes Balzac in *Sister Carrie* as a shorthand for people who would be "in the know" about this particular debate.

38. Howells, *Criticism and Fiction*, 20.

39. Ibid., 25.

40. "Howells differentiates the realist taste that he endorses from another taste mode by which members of the middle and upper classes might—and indeed did—aesthetically engage what he positioned as the rawer aspects of American life: by

rendering them exotically picturesque" (Barrish, *American Literary Realism*, 25). This kind of taste was importantly equivalent for Howells to a taste for "high culture" aesthetic preferences like written (as opposed to performed) Shakespeare or Italianate architecture—part of the constellation of tastes that the truly refined would share.

41. Howells, *The Rise of Silas Lapham*, 193. Subsequent references are parenthetically cited as *SL*.

42. See Hartman, *Scenes of Subjection*.

43. Wharton, *The Writing of Fiction*, 8. Subsequent references are parenthetically cited as *WF*.

44. James, "The Lesson of Balzac," 132. Subsequent references are parenthetically cited as "LB."

45. Radway, *A Feeling for Books*, 285, 288.

46. Ibid., 283.

47. Ibid., 284.

1 / Mr. Mabie Tells What to Read

1. Rascoe, *Titans of Literature*, 363.

2. Morse, *Life and Letters*, 3.

3. Scanlon, *Inarticulate Longings*, 2. Frank Luther Mott, for one, contended that "there can be little doubt that men comprised a considerable proportion of the reading audience of *Ladies' Home Journal* from the start" (*A History of American Magazines*, 4:551). Mott even notes that, during World War I, the *Journal* ranked third among magazines requested by soldiers at the front (550). Whether this was for a touch of home to relieve homesickness or because of the *Journal*'s male-targeted editorial content, it speaks to the connections so many Americans in the first quarter of the twentieth century had to this magazine, how close it was to their sense of both home and nation.

4. While the *Journal* did not leave men entirely out of the equation, it did not make much room, editorially or otherwise, for African American readers, for newly arrived immigrants, or for women who were not involved in or in search of a socially sanctioned heterosexual marriage. Although diversity was neither represented in nor validated in the pages of the magazine, however, we cannot assume that women who belonged to or sympathized with these groups did not read, or were not influenced by, the *Journal*'s content.

5. Bok, "Fifteen Years of Mistakes," 18.

6. By some estimates, $1.00 in 1902 had the same "purchasing power" as $24.86 had in 2007, and $1.50 in 1912 would translate to $33.09. If one measures by the nominal gross domestic product per capita, arguably a better sense of the "affordability" of the subscription for an average person, the cost of a subscription becomes a bit more onerous: $150.55 in 1902, and $175.04 in 1912 (www.measuringworth.com). Given the articles I cite below about salaries in the $7.00 a week range, we can see that, in fact, the *Journal* would be a fairly prized commodity for any subscriber.

7. Steinberg, *Reformer in the Marketplace*, xv, quoted in Scanlon, *Inarticulate Longings*, 14.

8. Scanlon, *Inarticulate Longings*, 13.

9. Curtis quoted in ibid., 14.

10. Both Jennifer Scanlon and Helen Damon-Moore have discussed the *Journal*'s

lack of inclusivity, and both find the magazine equally unwelcoming to lower- and working-class women (see especially Scanlon, *Inarticulate Longings*, 13–25).

11. The story about the Minnesota family is found in the August 1903 installment, "From Practically Nothing to Their Own Homes." The teaser for September promises an article titled "Some More Houses Saved for on Less than $15 a Week Salary." The series published the editors' selections of stories sent in to the *Journal* for a prize competition; the author of the winning story received a $100 prize. The prize-winning entry, published in the October 1903 issue, does not tell the story of an unusually strapped family (many others tell of salaries of $7 a week or less, and most have more than this couple's one child), but it does end with an interesting moral twist: "As for myself, before my marriage I never knew the value of money, as I was the petted daughter of a rich man" ("How Some Families Have Saved for Homes," 22).

12. "I learned in that dingy cupboard my first lesson in what to do with wearisome hours, for recurrent work faithfully performed becomes sensitized into proper mechanical ability and leaves the brain free to fill with other things, sometimes far freer than if the body were idling" ("The Joy to Be Found in Work," 59).

13. Bok, Literary Leaves, November 1889, 11.

14. Ramsey, Books and Bookmakers, June 1889, 11.

15. For the history of *Scribner's*, see Mott, *A History of American Magazines*, vol. 4; Glazener, *Reading for Realism*; and John, *The Best Years of the "Century."*

16. Damon-Moore, *Magazines for the Millions*, 63. In his autobiography, Bok describes an exchange with Curtis that sets up the situation of competing columns:

> Mr. Curtis told Bok he had read his literary letter in the *Philadelphia Times*, and suggested that perhaps he might write a similar department for the *Ladies' Home Journal* [*sic*]. Bok saw no reason why he should not, and told Mr. Curtis so, and promised to send over a trial instalment. The Philadelphia publisher then deftly went on, explained editorial conditions in his magazine, and, recognizing the ethics of the occasion by not offering Bok another position while he was already occupying one, asked him if he knew the man for the place.
> "Are you talking at me or through me?" asked Bok.
> "Both," replied Mr. Curtis.
> This was in April of 1889. (Bok, *Americanization*, 155–56)

Perhaps Curtis did not know that his longtime household hints columnist would be interested in writing about books; perhaps he did not think he would be able to snare the talents of Bok. At any rate, Ramsey's column began appearing in June 1889, and Bok's new column two months later.

17. Bok, Literary Leaves, September 1889, 11.

18. Ibid.

19. Ramsey, Books and Bookmakers, October 1889, 11; Bok, Literary Leaves, October 1889, 11.

20. "Romance Reduced to Figures," 13.

21. Bok, *Americanization*, 291.

22. Ibid.

23. [Bridges], Droch's Literary Talks, December 1896, 23. Subsequent references to columns in this series are parenthetically cited by date.

24. Bok is similarly unforthcoming in his autobiography. While he notes that a

books column was a key component of his project of "making the American public more conversant with books and authors," Mabie's work is almost an afterthought: "Accordingly, he [Bok] engaged Robert Bridges (the present editor of *Scribner's Magazine*) to write a series of conversational book-talks under his nom de plume of 'Droch.' Later, this was supplemented by the engagement of Hamilton W. Mabie, who for years reviewed the newest books" (Bok, *Americanization*, 291). Not only is this account of what Mabie's columns addressed completely inaccurate, but it renders Mabie's work subordinate to "Droch's" twelve columns, which appeared five years earlier, from December 1896 to November 1897.

25. Morse, *Life and Letters*, 211.

26. Jeanette Mabie to Grace King, 6 February 1917, quoted in Rife, "Hamilton Wright Mabie," 256n48.

27. Hamilton Wright Mabie to Mrs. E. D. North, 28 August 1908, quoted in Morse, *Life and Letters*, 213.

28. Morse, *Life and Letters*, 211–12.

29. Mabie, "Mr. Mabie's Talk about New Books," October 1906, 22. Subsequent references to Mabie's columns in *The Ladies' Home Journal* are parenthetically cited by date.

30. "To-Day's Books and Their Authors," 2.

31. The caption of the accompanying illustration actually specifies that the woman pictured is "Mary Eleanor Wilkins, who recently became Mrs. Charles M. Freeman," but Mabie refers to her as "Miss Wilkins" throughout this column.

32. "Empathic response," as Judith Fetterley and Marjorie Pryse argue, is one of the elements that "distances regionalism from an uncritical adoption of realist representation" (*Writing out of Place*, 107). For the complex relationship between New England regionalist writing and sentimentality, see Fleissner, *Women, Compulsion, Modernity*.

33. Welch, "Miss Wilkins at Home," 69.

34. Berkson, "A Goddess behind a Sordid Veil," 150.

35. As Glenn Hendler has demonstrated, sentimentality was a mode that cut across genders, despite its representation as a feminizing mode; Mabie's tack of gendering sentiment as feminine was directly aligned with a realist critical practice. For a discussion of the masculinity of sentiment as it was deployed in the nineteenth century, see Hendler, *Public Sentiments*.

36. Norris, "A Plea for Romantic Fiction," 214–15.

37. Glazener, *Reading for Realism*, 230.

38. Ibid., 171.

39. James, "The Art of Fiction," 507.

40. Kett, *The Pursuit of Knowledge under Difficulties*, 83.

41. For the range of warnings offered to female readers in both Europe and America during the first half of the nineteenth century, see Lyons "New Readers in the Nineteenth Century."

42. Clarke, "The Novel-Reading Habit," 670–71.

43. Howells quoted in Trachtenberg, *The Incorporation of America*, 185.

44. Glazener, *Reading for Realism*. Glazener coins this phrase to describe the reception formations being promulgated by elite *Atlantic*-group literary arbiters during the era of American literary realism. I deliberately invoke her phrase as a shorthand for her nuanced and compendious project.

2 / The Compromise of *Silas Lapham*

1. Mabie, "A Typical Novel," 423.

2. Alan Trachtenberg cited Mabie's review in his magisterial *Incorporation of America* (182) to set up a discussion of literary realism as the welcome anodyne to overweening nineteenth-century romanticism and sentimentality. Warner Berthoff styled Mabie an "old-guard critic"; while praising Mabie for his "literate and reasoned polemic," he notes that Mabie "carelessly lumps James and Howells together" (*The Ferment of Realism*, 51, 52n1). Edwin Harrison Cady is a bit kinder to Mabie in *The Road to Realism* (241), calling him "a gifted man," if a "neo-romantic opponent," who "took trouble to estimate Howells accurately and fairly . . . understood Howells beautifully, knew exactly what he disagreed with and why, and made his points with candor and force."

3. See Santayana, *Genteel Tradition*. Lewis, "The American Fear of Literature," 15. Lewis's invective is only one of many that he leveled against Howells in the Nobel lecture; he also accused Howells of "effusively seeking to guide America into becoming a pale edition of an English cathedral town," and indicted his realism as a sham: "In his fantastic vision of life, which he innocently conceived to be realistic, farmers, and seamen and factory hands might exist, but the farmer must never be covered with muck, the seaman must never roll out bawdy chanteys, the factory hand must be thankful to his good kind employer, and all of them must long for the opportunity to visit Florence and smile gently at the quaintness of the beggars" (Lewis, 16, 15).

4. Cowley, *After the Genteel Tradition*, 10.

5. Rascoe, *"Smart Set" History*, 14.

6. Bok, *Americanization*, 128.

7. Ibid., 135–36.

8. Ibid., 143.

9. Eller, "Critical Edition," lxxvi.

10. Howells was able to command princely sums for his writings wherever they appeared, but rarely a lump sum like $10,000 for one serial. In 1891, he earned $15,000 for works published under an exclusive contract with *Harper's*; once he became a literary free agent, he was able to earn much more, $30,000 in 1893. This was the year of *My Literary Passions* and *The Coast of Bohemia*; as a point of comparison, the remaining $15,000 that year came from another serialized novel, a book publication, three plays, one children's book, two autobiographical essays and one autobiographical book, and some miscellaneous shorter pieces (Crowley, *Black Heart's Truth*, 32–33).

11. Eller, "Critical Edition," lxxvi. That Howells was not indifferent to the remuneration he received is evident from a letter he wrote to his daughter Mildred in June 1895: "The wolf will have to gnaw through contracts for $30,000 before it reaches the door" (Goodman and Dawson, *William Dean Howells*, 335).

12. Howells, "The Coast of Bohemia," December 1892, 4, 3.

13. Howells, "The Coast of Bohemia," October 1893, 4.

14. Ibid.

15. Ibid., 32.

16. Cooke, *Howells*, 208–9.

17. Howells, "The Coast of Bohemia," June 1893, 3–4.

18. Ibid., 4.

19. Eller, "Critical Edition," xl.

20. Boyeson, "Mr. Howells at Close Range," 7.

21. Ibid., 7.

22. Howells, *My Literary Passions*, ix.

23. The documentary evidence for this negotiation from Howells's side is unfortunately no longer extant, but the details have been pieced together by Jonathan R. Eller from the letters in Harvard's Houghton Library. I am reliant on his account, and on my own reading of these letters, for my narrative here.

24. Edward Bok to William Dean Howells, 24 September 1892.

25. Ibid.

26. Howells originally broke the manuscript into subtitled sections; he mentions sixty-one authors by name in that typescript (Eller, "Critical Edition," lxxvi–vii).

27. Boyeson, "Mr. Howells at Close Range," 7.

28. Ibid.

29. Ibid., 8.

30. Ibid.

31. Howells writes in his Editor's Study for May 1886 (973):

> At the beginning of this century . . . romance was making the same fight against effete classicism which realism is making today against effete romance. . . . The romance of that day and the realism of this are in certain degree the same. Romance then sought, as realism seeks now, to widen the bounds of sympathy, to level every barrier against aesthetic freedom, to escape from the paralysis of tradition. It exhausted itself in this impulse, and it remained for realism to assert that fidelity to experience and probability of motive are essential conditions of a great imaginative literature.

Howells's own appropriation of the terms of sympathy and imagination demonstrate the imprecision of all such debates in the U.S. context.

32. Boyeson, "Mr. Howells at Close Range," 7.

33. Howells's Editor's Study columns appeared in *Harper's New Monthly Magazine* from January 1886 to March 1892. Boyeson's reminiscences seem to date from the period 1872–73, when Winifred would have been ten or eleven; John Mead, five or six; and Mildred, an infant of one or two. When Howells began his stint in the Editor's Study, the children would have been twenty-three, eighteen, and fourteen; by the time Howells was writing for the *Journal*, John Mead was twenty-five and Mildred twenty-one; Winifred had died prematurely in 1889 (Goodman and Dawson, *William Dean Howells*, xxi–xxvi).

34. Howells, "My Literary Passions," December 1893, 10.

35. Ibid.

36. Howells, "My Literary Passions," April 1894, 15.

37. Howells, "My Literary Passions," August 1894, 14.

38. Howells, "My Literary Passions," May 1894, 13.

39. "Detached intimacy" is the phrase coined by Lisa Spiro to describe a reading position exemplified by readers of Marvel, "in which the reader, though swept over by feeling, still keeps fantasy at arm's length, wrapped up between the boards of a book." Contrary to the escapist stance, "detached intimacy suggests that the reader can engage in a profound identification with the book even as she remains conscious

that she is actively constructing a fantasy" (Spiro, "Reading with a Tender Rapture," 61). Howells's retreat to the woods perfectly models "detached intimacy."

40. Howells, "My Literary Passions," October 1894, 15.

41. Howells, "My Literary Passions," August 1894, 14.

42. Howells, "My Literary Passions," October 1894, 15.

43. Howells, "My Literary Passions," March 1894, 13.

44. Howells, "My Literary Passions," June 1894, 15.

45. Howells, "My Literary Passions," February 1894, 17.

46. Ibid.

47. Oxley, "Literary Improvement Clubs," 16.

48. Bok to Howells, 24 September 1892.

49. Hochman, *Getting at the Author*. The attractions of "knowing" or "befriend-ing" an author in the early nineteenth century are also discussed in Zboray and Zboray, *Literary Dollars and Social Sense*.

50. Howells, "My Literary Passions," April 1894, 15.

51. Howells, "My Literary Passions," November 1894, 15.

52. "The Writers for *The Ladies' Home Journal* for 1895."

53. Howells, "My Literary Passions," February 1895, 14.

54. Howells, "My Literary Passions," August 1894, 14.

55. Bok, *Americanization*, 375.

56. Mabie, "A Typical Novel," 422.

57. Ibid., 423.

58. Kar, "Archetypes of American Innocence."

59. Wasserstrom, "William Dean Howells: The Indelible Stain," 487; Crowley, *The Black Heart's Truth*, 85.

60. Crowley, *The Black Heart's Truth*, 79.

61. Howells, *A Hazard of New Fortunes*, 388. Subsequent references are denoted parenthetically as *HNF*.

62. Crowley, *The Dean of American Letters*, 25.

63. Howells, Editor's Study, January 1890, 323.

64. One example of such wishful thinking may be found in Everett Carter's introduction to the Indiana University Press edition of *Hazard*. Many other critics have seen Howells as ultimately complicit with the consumer capital model of publication (see, e.g., Kaplan, *The Social Construction of American Realism*; Borus, *Writing Realism*; and Bell, *The Problem of American Realism*, among others). Reading *Hazard* through the lens of the late-nineteenth-century insurance industry, Jason Puskar argues that *Every Other Week* becomes a model of mutuality through which Howells "attempts to imagine not a retreat from the marketplace entirely but the construction of a new kind of marketplace with which realism might make its peace" (Puskar, "William Dean Howells and the Insurance of the Real," 53).

3 / James for the General Reader

1. Henry James to William James, 23 July 1890, in *The Letters of Henry James*, 170.

2. Jacobson, *Henry James and the Mass Market*, 18.

3. Henry James to William Dean Howells, 4 May 1898, in *The Letters of Henry James*, 309; quoted also in Johanningsmeier, "Real American Readers," 96.

4. Johanningsmeier, "Real American Readers," 97.

5. Ibid., 87.

6. James, *Literary Criticism*, 2:1082.

7. Henry James to James B. Pinker, 10 June 1906, quoted in Anesko, *"Friction with the Market,"* 364n28.

8. There were already plenty of extant copies of the original versions of all of James's novels—indeed, the expense and relative scarcity of the New York Edition versions mean that they would have been the more difficult to obtain. The initial edition was limited to only 156 copies, with handmade papers and gilt lettering, among other blandishments. A cheaper, unlimited edition was made soon after from the same plates, thus perpetuating the practice that had led to lawsuits in other cases, where the cheaper printings had lessened the resale value of the first (Leuschner, "Utterly, Insurmountably, Unsaleable," 31, 34).

9. The validation of readers' letters is of course nearly impossible—there is no telling whether Mabie reproduced an actual reader letter, or whether he produced a composite of several letters he had received, or whether this issue was just one that had been bothering him, or that he suspected had bothered his audience, and he decided to manufacture a reader letter as a pretext for discussing it at greater length—perhaps so as not to look like someone who was daunted by James. The letter both reassures a James-phobic reader that he or she is not alone in feeling that way and maintains Mabie's authority as a reader of high culture, and a helpful gatekeeper for his *Journal* readers.

10. Though Mabie does not recommend *Hudson* in the pages of the *Journal* after the December 1907 appearance of the revised version of the text as the first volume of James's New York Edition, he does not forget the novel altogether, listing it as a representative James text in his 1911 promotional tie-in pamphlet for the Globe-Wernicke bookcase company, *The Blue Book of Fiction: A List of Novels Worth Reading Chosen from Many Literatures*; one assumes that here, too, he is thinking of the 1875–78 versions.

11. [Review of *Roderick Hudson*, by Henry James], *Chicago Tribune*, 1; [Powell], [Review of *Roderick Hudson*, by Henry James], *New York Herald*, 3.

12. [Powell], [Review of *Roderick Hudson*, by Henry James], 3.

13. [Review of *Roderick Hudson*, by Henry James], *Chicago Tribune*, 1.

14. James, preface to *Roderick Hudson*, 1047.

15. James, *Roderick Hudson*, 63. Subsequent references are parenthetically cited as *RH*.

16. Buzard, "The Uses of Romanticism," 42.

17. Murray, *A Handbook of Rome*, 59.

18. Glazener, *Reading for Realism*, 176–77.

19. [Review of *The Princess Casamassima*], *Lippincott's Monthly Magazine*, 359.

20. Bell, *The Problem of American Realism*, 104–5.

21. Jacobson, *Henry James and the Mass Market*, 48.

22. James, *The Princess Casamassima*, 334.

23. Ibid., 333.

24. Fuller, "Latest Novel of Henry James," 4.

25. "Mr. James's Latest Novel," 5.

26. [Hay], "James's *The Portrait of a Lady*," 8.

27. [Review of *The Portrait of a Lady*, by Henry James, and *A Laodicean*, by Thomas Hardy], *New York Herald*, 5.

28. [Review of *The Portrait of a Lady*, by Henry James], *Chicago Tribune*, 10.

29. "Mr. James's Latest Novel," 5.

30. James, *The Portrait of a Lady*, 33. Subsequent references to the text of the 1908 New York Edition are denoted parenthetically as *PL*. The Norton edition I used here includes a textual appendix mapping the variations between the 1881 and 1908 editions (493–575). References to the language used in the 1881 edition are indicated parenthetically as *PL* 1881, and the page number where that variation appears in the textual appendix is cited.

31. "Mr. James's Latest Novel," 5.

32. [Review of *The Portrait of a Lady*, by Henry James, and *A Laodicean*, by Thomas Hardy], 5.

33. Oliphant, [Review of Henry James's *Portrait of a Lady*], 382.

34. Henry James to Charles Scribner's Sons, 27 January 1908, quoted in Anesko, *"Friction with the Market,"* 149.

35. James, Preface to *Portrait of a Lady*, 13.

36. Fuller, "Latest Novel of Henry James," 4.

37. "Mr. James's *Portrait of a Lady*," 474. Baym, "Revision and Thematic Change in *The Portrait of a Lady*," 627.

38. Baym, "Revision and Thematic Change in *The Portrait of a Lady*," 634.

39. "Mr. James's *Portrait of a Lady*," 474.

40. Brownell, [Review of Henry James's *Portrait of a Lady*], 103.

41. Pilkington, *Francis Marion Crawford*, i.

42. Crawford, *Saracinesca*, 4. Subsequent references are denoted parenthetically as *S*.

43. Crawford, *The Novel: What It Is*, 11. Subsequent references are denoted parenthetically as *NWI*. On Crawford's writing *The Novel: What It Is* in response to Howells's *Criticism and Fiction*, see Pilkington, *Francis Marion Crawford*, 110–12.

4 / Misreading *The House of Mirth*

1. Shari Benstock, in *No Gifts from Chance* (155), attributes this story to an article in the *Detroit Post*, 17 November 1906. The *Post* was actually not in press at that time, and I have been unable to locate the story in any other Detroit paper from the time; the search for the source is ongoing.

2. See Wolff, introduction to *The House of Mirth*, by Edith Wharton, vii. Further references to *The House of Mirth* are to the Penguin 1993 edition and are cited parenthetically as *HM*. See also "Books in Demand," *New York Times Saturday Review of Books*, 18 November 1905.

3. The book's enormous sales figures, along with the circulation records from public libraries, strongly suggest that middle-class readers made up a sizable portion of the audience for *The House of Mirth*; the upper class alone was not large enough to account for these numbers. For historical definitions of social classes in the early twentieth century, see Ohmann, *Selling Culture*.

4. Wharton, *A Backward Glance*, 207.

5. Jauss, *Toward an Aesthetic of Reception*.

6. Wharton's abiding interest in the sales of her books is well known and well documented. For a lively discussion of this aspect of her authorial personality, see Lee,

Edith Wharton; regarding her dissatisfaction with Scribner's distribution and marketing of *Ethan Frome*, see especially 422–25.

7. Certeau, *Practice of Everyday Life*, 174.

8. Ibid., 166.

9. Peattie, "Mrs. Wharton's House of Mirth"; Peattie, "Best Fiction of the Year."

10. "Dust and Ashes."

11. Ibid.

12. Bentley, *The Ethnography of Manners*, 184.

13. Ibid., 190.

14. Walter Benn Michaels, to whom Bentley's readings of *The House of Mirth* and, more primarily, *Custom of the Country*, are in part addressed, reads this scene as a moment in which the risk-addicted Lily becomes "only a stand-in for another person who is impersonating her, the person of the writer" (*The Gold Standard and the Logic of Naturalism*, 240). Candace Waid argues that "the *tableau vivant* represents the scene of a triumphant woman writing letters, spelling out a word," and "anticipating or rather scripting the audience's response as she poses as the self-portrait of the author" (*Edith Wharton's Letters*, 43).

15. Shuman, *How to Judge a Book*, 69.

16. Montgomery, *Displaying Women*, 165.

17. Ibid., 166.

18. "The House of Mirth," *New York Times Saturday Review of Books*, 4 November 1905. When the readers' forum was devoted to discussion of *The House of Mirth*, it frequently had the novel's title as its headline; at other times, there was a different heading, such as "From Readers" or "The Average Reader."

19. "The House of Mirth," 18 November 1905.

20. "The House of Mirth," 25 November 1905.

21. This stance exactly opposes the position Selden takes when he tells Lily that society is a "show" in which the actors are blind to the illusion but the audience can see clearly: ". . . [T]he queer thing about society is that the people who regard it as an end are those who are in it, and not the critics on the fence. It's just the other way with most shows—the audience may be under the illusion, but the actors know that real life is on the other side of the footlights" (*HM*, 70).

22. "Topics of the Week," 25 November 1905.

23. "The House of Mirth," 25 November 1905.

24. Ibid.

25. Elinor Glyn was a London socialite whose society novels were best-selling *succès des scandales* in the United States (Mott, *Golden Multitudes*, 249–51). *Three Weeks* was published in England in 1907 and became an American best seller in 1908.

26. "The House of Mirth," 9 December 1905.

27. "Mrs. Wharton's Novel," 30 December 1905.

28. "The Average Reader," 6 January 1906.

29. Ibid.

30. "The House of Mirth," 20 January 1906.

31. Cawelti, *Apostles of the Self-Made Man*, ix.

32. Barbara Hochman and I offered this reading nearly simultaneously in 2002–3; I in my unpublished dissertation, "Reading Up: Middle Class Readers and Narratives

of Success from the 1890s to the 1920s" (Cornell University), and Hochman in her "Highbrow/Lowbrow: Naturalist Writers and the 'Reading Habit.'"

33. Merish, *Sentimental Materialism*, 24.

34. Waid reads Lily's flight from Bertha Dorset as her flight from sexual knowledge, marriage, and childbirth, and presents this as a key passage in her overall reading of the novel as Lily's attempt to escape the "underworld" of dangerous eroticism for which Bertha Dorset stands (*Edith Wharton's Letters*, 46–47).

35. Edith Wharton to Edward Burlingame, 23 November 1905, in *The Letters of Edith Wharton*, 98.

36. Advertisement, *Chicago Herald Tribune*, 18 November 1905, 9; Edith Wharton to Charles Norton, 31 October 1905, quoted in Benstock, *No Gifts from Chance*, 150.

37. Edith Wharton to Francis Kinnicutt, 26 December 1904, in the private collection of Amy Beckwith.

38. McGrath, "Wharton Letter Reopens a Mystery."

39. Kaplan, *The Social Construction of American Realism*, 85.

40. Wharton, *A Backward Glance*, 206.

41. Dawson, "Lily Bart's Fractured Alliances," 22.

42. Lidoff, "Another Sleeping Beauty," 239, 255.

43. "Mrs. Wharton's 'Sanctuary,'" BR9.

44. "Edith Wharton's New Novel," 2933–35.

45. Lee, *Edith Wharton*, 171.

5 / The Comforts of Romanticism

1. Kaplan, "Romancing the Empire," 667.

2. See Glazener, *Reading for Realism*.

3. Allen, "Two Principles in Recent American Fiction," quoted in Campbell, "In Search of Local Color," 70–71.

4. Campbell, "In Search of Local Color," 63.

5. Warner quoted in ibid., 66. Campbell offers a thorough reading of an extended excerpt from this essay.

6. See Johanningsmeier, "Sarah Orne Jewett and Mary E. Wilkins Freeman."

7. Petrie, *Conscience and Purpose*, 79.

8. Brodhead, *Cultures of Letters*; Zagarell, "Troubling Regionalism."

9. Jewett, *Deephaven*, 248. Subsequent references are indicated parenthetically by *D*. At one point Kate reminisces about Uncle Jack, who she had thought was old but "really was just out of college and not so old as I am now" (*D*, 136).

10. Zagarell, "Troubling Regionalism," 647.

11. Ibid., 646.

12. See Koepflmacher, *Ventures into Childland*, 274; and Sorby, *Schoolroom Poets*, 176.

13. Romines, "In *Deephaven*," 44–45.

14. Ibid., 44.

15. Cable, *The Grandissimes*, 6–7. Subsequent references are indicated parenthetically as *G*.

16. Ringe, "Narrative Voice in Cable's *The Grandissimes*," 13.

17. Ibid.

18. Kreyling, introduction to *The Grandissimes*, by George Washington Cable, ix.

19. James David Hart considers it the second best-selling book of 1898 (*The*

Popular Book, 203), as it came in second on the *Bookman* bookstore best-seller list for that year; however, it only appears on Frank Luther Mott's "better seller" list (*Golden Multitudes*, 324).

20. Howells, "The New Historical Romances," 939.

21. Matthews, "The Historical Novel," in *The Historical Novel and Other Essays*, 19. Matthews's essay originally appeared in *Forum*, September 1897.

22. "Dr. Mitchell's 'Hugh Wynne,'" BR5.

23. Cather is scathing in her critique of Hugh:

As to Hugh Wynne himself, I am afraid I do not altogether admire him. The book is written in the first person, thus giving the young hero a great opportunity to talk about himself, which he does with a vengeance. He is forever telling how brave and how strong and how handsome he is, all of which had much better be left to the imagination. I do not like the man Hugh Wynne as well as I like the boy who took the schoolmaster's flogging so bravely and was so tender with his mother. (Cather [Delay], "Old Books and New," 12)

24. [Edmunds], "Some Thoughts on Hugh Wynne."

25. ["Similia Similibus"], "'Richard Carvel and 'Hugh Wynne.'"

26. [Young], "'Hugh Wynne,' 'Richard Carvel,' 'Janice Meredith.'"

27. ["Desdichado"], "Another View of 'Richard Carvel.'"

28. [Review of *Richard Carvel*].

29. ["L."], "Coincidences in Fiction."

30. ["A.U."], "An Appeal to Our Readers."

31. [Moore], "Why 'Richard Carvel' Is Preferred."

32. ["Veritas"], "Wants More like 'Janice Meredith.'"

33. ["J.T.H."], "The Toss of a Cent, for All Are Good."

34. [Middleton], "'Richard Carvel' beyond Question."

35. ["L.A.M"], "'Hugh Wynne' and 'Richard Carvel' Side by Side."

Epilogue

1. Kirkpatrick, "'Oprah' Gaffe by Franzen."

2. Winfrey, *The Oprah Winfrey Show*, 17 September 2010.

3. Glazener, *Reading for Realism*, 150.

4. For more on Chautauqua and the self-culture and self-education movements in America more generally, see Kett, *The Pursuit of Knowledge under Difficulties*.

5. Rubin, *The Making of Middlebrow Culture*, 28.

6. Advertisement, *New York Times*, 23 January 1921, 50.

7. Advertisement, *New York Times*, 27 February 1921, BR9.

8. Advertisement, *New York Times*, 5 February 1922, 44.

9. On the Modern Library, see Satterfield, *The World's Best Books*. For the Book-of-the-Month Club, see Radway, *A Feeling for Books*. For the Reader's Subscription, see Krystal, Barzun, and Trilling, *A Company of Readers*.

10. From Richard Lacayo's appropriately metatextual, quasi-postmodern review in *Time* magazine:

Here's how you know you have written one of the year's most anticipated novels. In the spring your publisher, Farrar, Straus & Giroux, distributes 3,500 advance copies to reviewers and booksellers. Each comes with a note from your celebrated editor, Jonathan Galassi, the head of Farrar, Straus, who calls your book one of the best that his house, also home to Tom Wolfe, Scott Turow and the poet Seamus Heaney, has issued in 15 years. Next there's a movie deal from the producer Scott Rudin, whose credits include *Wonder Boys* and *A Civil Action*. Then you get a dust-jacket photo lit in a way that turns your facial bones into Alpine escarpments. You also get a good-size spread—this one—in TIME, the magazine your late father always wanted to see you in. And in that story you get a sentence he would have loved: *The Corrections* is one of the great books of the year. (Lacayo, "Books: Great Expectations")

11. Franzen quoted in Rooney, *Reading with Oprah*, 41.

12. Jonanna, 2 October 2001, http://boards.oprah.com (accessed 23 May 2002).

13. Prose, "Shot through the Heart," 214.

14. Rooney, *Reading with Oprah*, 41.

15. Franzen quoted in ibid., 43.

16. See Travis, "It Will Change the World If Everybody Reads This Book."

17. Mlnurk, 7 October 2001, http://boards.oprah.com (accessed 23 May 2002).

18. Stolafgirl, 15 October 2001, http://boards.oprah.com (accessed 23 May 2002).

19. Esty105, 15 October 2001, http://boards.oprah.com (accessed 23 May 2002).

20. Rborja76, 15 October 2001, http://boards.oprah.com (accessed 23 May 2002).

21. Sabine12, 15 October 2001, http://boards.oprah.com (accessed 23 May 2002).

22. Martster, 24 October 2001, http://boards.oprah.com (accessed 23 May 2002).

23. Sabine12, 24 October 2001, http://boards.oprah.com (accessed 23 May 2002).

24. Vcmcmullen, 26 October 2001, http://boards.oprah.com (accessed 23 May 2002).

25. Tonifoster, 25 October 2001, http://boards.oprah.com (accessed 23 May 2002).

26. Siouxj, 26 October 2001, http://boards.oprah.com (accessed 23 May 2002).

27. Zurilaw, 16 November 2001, http://boards.oprah.com (accessed 31 May 2002).

28. Sandra194, 20 September 2010, http://www.oprah.com/oprahsbook-club/Oprahs-Book-Club-Reading-Calendar-Freedom-by-Jonathan-Franzen/1|3#comments_top (accessed 4 November 2010).

29. 6dinnersid, 15 October 2010, http://www.oprah.com/oprahsbookclub/Oprahs-Book-Club-Producer-Jills-Freedom-Discussion-1#comments (accessed 4 November 2010).

30. Kiki5026, http://www.oprah.com/package_pages/freedom/book-club-discussion.html (accessed 4 November 2010).

31. Jgluz, 29 October 2010, http://www.oprah.com/oprahsbookclub/Oprahs-Book-Club-Reading-Calendar-Freedom-by-Jonathan-Franzen/1|3#comments_top (accessed 4 November 2010).

32. See Kakutani, "A Family Full of Unhappiness, Hoping for Transcendence."

Bibliography

Advertisement. *Chicago Herald Tribune*, 18 November 1905, 9.

Advertisement. *New York Times*, 23 January 1921, 50.

Advertisement. *New York Times*, 27 February 1921, BR9.

Advertisement. *New York Times*, 5 February 1922, 44.

Allen, James Lane. "Two Principles in Recent American Fiction." *Atlantic Monthly*, October 1897, 433–43.

Anesko, Michael. *"Friction with the Market": Henry James and the Profession of Authorship*. New York: Oxford University Press, 1986.

["A.U."]. "An Appeal to Our Readers." *New York Times Saturday Review of Books*, 3 February 1900.

"The Average Reader." *New York Times Saturday Review of Books*, 6 January 1906.

Barrish, Phillip. *American Literary Realism, Critical Theory, and Intellectual Prestige, 1880–1995*. New York: Cambridge University Press, 2001.

Baym, Nina. "Revision and Thematic Change in *The Portrait of a Lady*." In Henry James, *The Portrait of a Lady*, 2nd ed., edited by Robert D. Bamberg, 620–34. New York: W. W. Norton, 1995.

Bell, Michael Davitt. *The Problem of American Realism: Studies in the Cultural History of a Literary Idea*. Chicago: University of Chicago Press, 1993.

Bennett, Jesse Lee. *What Books Can Do FOR YOU: A Sketch Map of the Frontiers of Knowledge, with Lists of Selected Books*. New York: George H. Doran, 1923.

Bennett, Tony. "Texts in History: The Determinations of Readings and Their Texts." *Journal of the Midwest Modern Language Association* 18, no. 1 (Spring 1985): 1–16.

Benstock, Shari. *No Gifts from Chance: A Biography of Edith Wharton*. New York: Penguin, 1995.

Bentley, Nancy. *The Ethnography of Manners: Hawthorne, James, Wharton.* New York: Cambridge University Press, 1995.

Berkson, Dorothy. "'A Goddess behind a Sordid Veil': The Domestic Heroine Meets the Labor Novel in Mary E. Wilkins Freeman's *The Portion of Labor.*" In *Redefining the Political Novel: American Women Writers, 1797–1901,* edited by Sharon M. Harris, 149–68. Knoxville: University of Tennessee Press, 1995.

Berthoff, Warner. *The Ferment of Realism: American Literature, 1884–1919.* New York: Cambridge University Press, 1981.

Bode, Carl. Introduction to *Ragged Dick and Struggling Upward,* by Horatio Alger. New York: Penguin, 1985.

Bok, Edward. *The Americanization of Edward Bok: An Autobiography.* New York: Charles Scribner's Sons, 1973.

———. "Fifteen Years of Mistakes." *Ladies' Home Journal,* November 1898, 18.

———. Letter to William Dean Howells, 24 September 1892. Howells Family Papers. Houghton Library, Harvard University, Cambridge, MA.

———. Letter to William Dean Howells, 1 October 1892. Howells Family Papers. Houghton Library, Harvard University, Cambridge, MA.

———. Literary Leaves. *Ladies' Home Journal,* September 1889, 11.

———. Literary Leaves. *Ladies' Home Journal,* October 1889, 11.

———. Literary Leaves. *Ladies' Home Journal,* November 1889, 11.

"Books in Demand." *New York Times Saturday Review of Books,* 18 November 1905.

Borus, Daniel H. *Writing Realism: Howells, James, and Norris in the Mass Market.* Chapel Hill: University of North Carolina Press, 1989.

Bourdieu, Pierre. *Distinction: A Social Critique of the Judgement of Taste.* Cambridge, MA: Harvard University Press, 1984.

Boyeson, Hjalmar Hjorth. "Mr. Howells at Close Range." *Ladies' Home Journal,* November 1893, 7–8.

[Bridges, Robert]. Droch's Literary Talks. *Ladies' Home Journal,* December 1896, 23.

———. Droch's Literary Talks. *Ladies' Home Journal,* January 1897, 15.

———. Droch's Literary Talks. *Ladies' Home Journal,* March 1897, 16.

———. Droch's Literary Talks. *Ladies' Home Journal,* September 1897, 15.

———. Droch's Literary Talks. *Ladies' Home Journal,* November 1897, 15.

Brodhead, Richard. *Cultures of Letters: Scenes of Reading and Writing in Nineteenth-Century America.* Chicago: University of Chicago Press, 1993.

Brown, Bill. Review of *The Problem of American Realism,* by Michael Davitt Bell. *Modern Philology* 94 (February 1997): 262–67.

Brownell, W. C. [Review of Henry James's *Portrait of a Lady*]. *Nation,* 2 February 1882, 102–3.

Buzard, James. "The Uses of Romanticism: Byron and the Victorian Continental Tour." *Victorian Studies* 35, no. 1 (Autumn 1991): 29–50.

Cable, George Washington. *The Grandissimes*. New York: Charles Scribner's Sons, 1907.

Cady, Edwin Harrison. *The Road to Realism: The Early Years, 1837–1855, of William Dean Howells*. Syracuse, NY: Syracuse University Press, 1956.

Campbell, Donna M. "'In Search of Local Color': Context, Controversy, and *The Country of the Pointed Firs*." In *Jewett and Her Contemporaries: Reshaping the Canon*, edited by Karen L. Kilcup and Thomas S. Edwards, 63–76. Gainesville: University Press of Florida, 1999.

Carrington, George C., Jr. Introduction to *The Kentons*, by William Dean Howells. Bloomington: Indiana University Press, 1971.

Cather, Willa [Helen Delay, pseud.]. "Old Books and New." *Home Monthly* 7 (January 1898): 12. Willa Cather Archive, http://cather.unl.edu/nf038.html.

Cawelti, John G. *Apostles of the Self-Made Man*. Chicago: University of Chicago Press, 1965.

Certeau, Michel de. *The Practice of Everyday Life*. Translated by Steven Rendall. Berkeley: University of California Press, 1984.

Channing, William Ellery. "On the Elevation of the Laboring Classes." In *Essays, English and American*, edited by Charles W. Eliot, 321–80. Harvard Classics. New York: P. F. Collier and Son, 1938.

Chartier, Roger. *A History of Private Life*. Vol. 3, *Passions of the Renaissance*. Translated by Arthur Goldhammer. Cambridge, MA: Harvard University Press, 1989.

Clarke, George. "The Novel-Reading Habit." *Arena*, May 1898, 670–79.

Cooke, Delmar Gross. *William Dean Howells: A Critical Study*. New York: E. P. Dutton, 1922.

Cowley, Malcolm. *After the Genteel Tradition: American Writers, 1910–1930*. Carbondale: Southern Illinois University Press, 1964.

Crawford, F. Marion. *The Novel: What It Is*. New York: Macmillan and Co., 1893.

———. *Saracinesca*. New York: Macmillan, 1887.

Crowley, John W. *The Black Heart's Truth: The Early Career of W. D. Howells*. Chapel Hill: University of North Carolina, 1985.

———. *The Dean of American Letters: The Late Career of William Dean Howells*. Amherst: University of Massachusetts Press, 1999.

Damon-Moore, Helen. *Magazines for the Millions: Gender and Commerce in the "Ladies' Home Journal" and the "Saturday Evening Post," 1880–1910*. Albany: State University of New York Press, 1994.

Davidson, Cathy N. *Reading in America: Literature and Social History*. Baltimore: Johns Hopkins University Press, 1989.

Dawson, Melanie. "Lily Bart's Fractured Alliances and Wharton's Appeal to the Middlebrow Reader." *Reader* 41 (Spring 1999): 1–30.

["Desdichado"]. "Another View of 'Richard Carvel.'" *New York Times Book Review*, 2 December 1899.

"Dr. Mitchell's 'Hugh Wynne.'" *New York Times Book Review*, 2 October 1897.

Dreiser, Theodore. *Sister Carrie*. Edited by Donald Pizer. 2nd ed. New York: W. W. Norton, 1990.

Dunlop, M. H. "Carrie's Library: Reading the Boundaries between Popular and Serious Fiction." In *Theodore Dreiser: Beyond Naturalism*, edited by Miriam Gogol, 201–15. New York: New York University Press, 1995.

Dunn, Martha Baker. "A Plea for the Shiftless Reader." *Atlantic Monthly*, January 1900, 131–36.

"Dust and Ashes: American Fashionable Life in a New Novel by Mrs. Wharton." *New York Daily Tribune*, 14 October 1905.

"Edith Wharton's New Novel." *Independent*, 10 December 1903, 2933–35.

[Edmunds, Frederica]. "Some Thoughts on Hugh Wynne." *New York Times Book Review*, 23 April 1898.

Eller, Jonathan R. "A Critical Edition of W. D. Howells' *My Literary Passions*." Ph.D. diss., Indiana University, 1985.

Fetterley, Judith, and Marjorie Pryse. *Writing out of Place: Regionalism, Women, and American Literary Culture*. Urbana: University of Illinois Press, 2003.

Fish, Stanley. *Is There a Text in This Class? The Authority of Interpretive Communities*. Cambridge, MA: Harvard University Press, 1980.

Fleissner, Jennifer. *Women, Compulsion, Modernity: The Moment of American Naturalism*. Chicago: University of Chicago Press, 2004.

Flint, Kate. *The Woman Reader, 1837–1914*. New York: Oxford University Press, 1993.

Freeman, Mary E. Wilkins. *The Portion of Labor*. New York: Harper and Brothers, 1901.

"From Practically Nothing to Their Own Homes." *Ladies' Home Journal*, August 1903, 27.

Fuller, Henry B. "Latest Novel of Henry James Is a Typical Example of His Art." *Chicago Evening Post*, 30 August 1902, 4.

Garvey, Ellen Gruber. *The Adman in the Parlor: Magazines and the Gendering of Consumer Culture, 1880s to 1910s*. New York: Oxford University Press, 1996.

Gilmore, William J. *Reading Becomes a Necessity of Life: Material and Cultural Life in Rural New England, 1780–1835*. Knoxville: University of Tennessee Press, 1989.

Glazener, Nancy. *Reading for Realism: The History of a U.S. Literary Institution, 1850–1910*. Durham, NC: Duke University Press, 1997.

Gogol, Miriam. *Theodore Dreiser: Beyond Naturalism*. New York: New York University Press, 1995.

Goodman, Susan, and Carl Dawson. *William Dean Howells: A Writer's Life*. Berkeley: University of California Press, 2005.

Habermas, Jürgen. *The Structural Transformation of the Public Sphere: An Inquiry into a Category of Bourgeois Society*. Translated by Thomas Burger and Frederick Lawrence. Cambridge, MA: MIT Press, 1989.

Hart, James David. *The Popular Book: A History of America's Literary Taste.* New York: Oxford University Press, 1950.

Hartman, Saidiya V. *Scenes of Subjection: Terror, Slavery, and Self-Making in Nineteenth-Century America.* New York: Oxford University Press, 1997.

[Hay, John]. "James's *The Portrait of a Lady.*" *New York Tribune,* 25 December 1881, 8.

Hendler, Glenn. *Public Sentiments: Structures of Feeling in Nineteenth-Century American Literature.* Chapel Hill: University of North Carolina Press, 2001.

Hochman, Barbara. *Getting at the Author: Reimagining Books and Reading in the Age of American Realism.* Amherst: University of Massachusetts Press, 2001.

————. "Highbrow/Lowbrow: Naturalist Writers and the 'Reading Habit.'" In *Twisted from the Ordinary: Essays on American Literary Naturalism,* edited by Mary E. Papke, 217–36. Knoxville: University of Tennessee Press, 2003.

"The House of Mirth." *New York Times Saturday Review of Books,* 4 November 1905.

————. *New York Times Saturday Review of Books,* 18 November 1905.

————. *New York Times Saturday Review of Books,* 25 November 1905.

————. *New York Times Saturday Review of Books,* 9 December 1905.

————. *New York Times Saturday Review of Books,* 20 January 1906.

"How Some Families Have Saved for Homes." *Ladies' Home Journal,* October 1903, 22.

Howard, June. "What Is Sentimentality?" In *Publishing the Family,* 213–56. Durham, NC: Duke University Press, 2001.

Howells, William Dean. "The Coast of Bohemia." *Ladies' Home Journal,* December 1892, 4.

————. "The Coast of Bohemia." *Ladies' Home Journal,* January 1893, 3.

————. "The Coast of Bohemia." *Ladies' Home Journal,* June 1893, 3–4.

————. "The Coast of Bohemia." *Ladies' Home Journal,* October 1893, 4.

————. *Criticism and Fiction.* New York: Harper and Brothers, 1891.

————. The Editor's Study. *Harper's New Monthly Magazine,* May 1886, 973.

————. The Editor's Study. *Harper's New Monthly Magazine,* January 1890, 323.

————. *A Hazard of New Fortunes.* Bloomington: Indiana University Press, 1976.

————. "My Literary Passions." *Ladies' Home Journal,* December 1893, 10.

————. "My Literary Passions." *Ladies' Home Journal,* February 1894, 17.

————. "My Literary Passions." *Ladies' Home Journal,* March 1894, 13.

————. "My Literary Passions." *Ladies' Home Journal,* April 1894, 15.

————. "My Literary Passions." *Ladies' Home Journal,* May 1894, 13.

————. "My Literary Passions." *Ladies' Home Journal,* June 1894, 15.

————. "My Literary Passions." *Ladies' Home Journal,* August 1894, 14.

————. "My Literary Passions." *Ladies' Home Journal,* October 1894, 15.

————. "My Literary Passions." *Ladies' Home Journal,* November 1894, 15.

——. "My Literary Passions." *Ladies' Home Journal*, February 1895, 14.

——. *My Literary Passions and Criticism and Fiction*. New York: Harper and Brothers, 1910.

——. "The New Historical Romances." *North American Review*, December 1900, 935–48.

——. *The Rise of Silas Lapham*. Bloomington: Indiana University Press, 1971.

Hutner, Gordon. *What America Read: Taste, Class, and the Novel, 1920–1960*. Chapel Hill: University of North Carolina Press, 2009.

Ingersoll, Robert Sturgis. *Open That Door!* Philadelphia: J. B. Lippincott Co., 1916.

Jacobson, Marcia. *Henry James and the Mass Market*. Birmingham: University of Alabama Press, 1983.

James, Henry. "The Art of Fiction." *Longwood's Magazine*, September 1884.

——. "The Lesson of Balzac." In *Literary Criticism*, vol. 2, edited by Leon Edel, 115–39. New York: Library of America, 1984.

——. Letter to William Dean Howells, 4 May 1898. In *Letters, Fictions, Lives: Henry James and William Dean Howells*, edited by Michael Anesko. New York: Oxford University Press, 1997.

——. Letter to William James, 23 July 1890. In *The Letters of Henry James*, edited by Percy Lubbock, 170. New York: Charles Scribner's Sons, 1920.

——. *The Portrait of a Lady*. 2nd ed. Edited by Robert D. Bamberg. New York: W. W. Norton, 1995.

——. Preface to *Portrait of a Lady*. In *Literary Criticism*, vol. 2, edited by Leon Edel, 1070–85. New York: Library of America, 1984.

——. Preface to *Roderick Hudson*. In *Literary Criticism*, vol. 2, edited by Leon Edel, 1039–52. New York: Library of America, 1984.

——. *The Princess Casamassima*. New York: Harper and Row, 1964.

Jauss, Hans Robert. *Toward an Aesthetic of Reception*. Translated by Timothy Bahti. Minneapolis: University of Minnesota Press, 1982.

Jewett, Sarah Orne. *Deephaven*. Boston: Houghton Mifflin Co., 1905.

Johanningsmeier, Charles. "How Real American Readers Originally Experienced James's 'The Real Thing.'" *Henry James Review* 27, no. 1 (2006): 75–100.

——. "Sarah Orne Jewett and Mary E. Wilkins Freeman: Two Shrewd Businesswomen in Search of New Markets." *New England Quarterly* 70, no.1 (March 1997): 57–82.

John, Arthur. *The Best Years of the "Century": Richard Watson Gilder, "Scribner's Monthly," and the "Century Magazine," 1870–1909*. Urbana: University of Illinois Press, 1981.

"The Joy to Be Found in Work." *Ladies' Home Journal*, November 1904, 59.

["J.T.H."]. "The Toss of a Cent, for All Are Good." *New York Times Book Review*, 24 February 1900.

Kaestle, Carl F. "The History of Readers." In *Literacy in the United States: Read-*

ers and Reading since 1880, 33–72. New Haven, CT: Yale University Press, 1993.

Kakutani, Michiko. "A Family Full of Unhappiness, Hoping for Transcendence." *New York Times*, 16 August 2010.

Kammen, Michael. *American Culture, American Tastes: Social Change and the Twentieth Century*. New York: Knopf, 1999.

Kaplan, Amy. "Romancing the Empire: The Embodiment of American Masculinity in the Popular Historical Novel of the 1890s." *American Literary History* 2, no. 4 (Winter 1990): 659–90.

———. *The Social Construction of American Realism*. Chicago: University of Chicago Press, 1988.

Kar, Annette. "Archetypes of American Innocence: Lydia Blood and Daisy Miller." *American Quarterly* 5 (Spring 1953): 31–38.

Kett, Joseph F. *The Pursuit of Knowledge under Difficulties: From Self-Improvement to Adult Education in America, 1750–1990*. Stanford, CA: Stanford University Press, 1994.

Kilcup, Karen L., and Thomas S. Edwards, eds. *Jewett and Her Contemporaries: Reshaping the Canon*. Gainesville: University Press of Florida, 1999.

Kirkpatrick, David D. "'Oprah' Gaffe by Franzen Draws Ire and Sales." *New York Times*, 29 October 2001. http://www.nytimes.com/2001/10/29/books/oprah-gaffe-by-franzen-draws-ire-and-sales.html.

Koepflmacher, U. C. *Ventures into Childland: Victorians, Fairy Tales, and Femininity*. Chicago: University of Chicago Press, 1998.

Kreyling, Michael. Introduction to *The Grandissimes*, by George Washington Cable. New York: Penguin, 1988.

Krystal, Arthur, Jacques Barzun, and Lionel Trilling. *A Company of Readers: Uncollected Writings of W. H. Auden, Jacques Barzun, and Lionel Trilling from the Readers' Subscription and Mid-Century Book Clubs*. Edited by Arthur Krystal and Wystan Hugh Auden. New York: Free Press, 2001.

["L."]. "Coincidences in Fiction." *New York Times Book Review*, 23 December 1899.

Lacayo, Richard. "Books: Great Expectations." *Time*, 10 September 2001. http://www.time.com/time/magazine/article/0,9171,1000729,00.html?internalid=atb100#ixzzocucIrYpa.

["L.A.M."]. "'Hugh Wynne' and 'Richard Carvel' Side by Side." *New York Times Book Review*, 24 February 1900.

Larned, J. N. *Books, Culture, and Character*. Boston: Houghton, Mifflin Co., 1906.

Leach, William. *Land of Desire: Merchants, Power, and the Rise of a New American Culture*. New York: Vintage, 1994.

Lee, Hermione. *Edith Wharton*. New York: Knopf, 2007.

Lehan, Richard. "The City, the Self, and Narrative Discourse." In *New Essays* on *Sister Carrie*, edited by Donald Pizer, 65–86. Cambridge and New York: Cambridge University Press, 1991.

Leuschner, Eric. "'Utterly, Insurmountably, Unsaleable': Collected Editions, Prefaces, and the 'Failure' of Henry James's New York Edition." *Henry James Review* 22 (2001): 24–40.

Lewis, Sinclair. "The American Fear of Literature." In *The Man from Main Street: A Sinclair Lewis Reader; Selected Essays and Other Writings, 1904–1950*, edited by Harry E. Maule and Melville Cane, 3–17. New York: Random House, 1953.

Lidoff, Joan. "Another Sleeping Beauty: Narcissism in *The House of Mirth*." In *American Realism: New Essays*, edited by Eric J. Sundquist, 238–58. Baltimore: Johns Hopkins University Press, 1982.

Lorimer, George C. *What I Know about Books and How to Use Them*. Boston: J. H. Earle, 1892.

Lyons, Martyn. "New Readers in the Nineteenth Century." In *A History of Reading in the West*, edited by Guglielmo Cavallo, Roger Chartier, and Lydia G. Cochrane, 313–44. Oxford, UK: Polity Press, 1999.

Mabie, Hamilton Wright. "A Typical Novel." *Andover Review*, November 1885, 417–29.

———. "My Study Fire: Concerning Culture." *Outlook*, 9 December 1893, 1072–73.

———. *Books and Culture*. New York: Dodd, Mead and Co., 1896.

———. Mr. Mabie's Literary Talks. *Ladies' Home Journal*, March 1902, 17.

———. Mr. Mabie's Literary Talks. *Ladies' Home Journal*, April 1902, 17.

———. Mr. Mabie's Literary Talks. *Ladies' Home Journal*, May 1902, 17.

———. Mr. Mabie's Literary Talks. *Ladies' Home Journal*, June 1902, 17.

———. Mr. Mabie's Literary Talks. *Ladies' Home Journal*, July 1902, 19.

———. Mr. Mabie's Literary Talks. *Ladies' Home Journal*, September 1902, 17.

———. Mr. Mabie's Literary Talks. *Ladies' Home Journal*, October 1902, 17.

———. Mr. Mabie's Literary Talks. *Ladies' Home Journal*, November 1902, 17.

———. "Mr. Mabie's Christmas Book Talk." *Ladies' Home Journal*, December 1902, 19.

———. Hamilton W. Mabie's Literary Talks. *Ladies' Home Journal*, January 1903, 15.

———. Hamilton W. Mabie's Literary Talks. *Ladies' Home Journal*, March 1903, 17.

———. Hamilton W. Mabie's Literary Talks. *Ladies' Home Journal*, May 1903, 15.

———. "Mr. Mabie's Literary Talk to Girls." *Ladies' Home Journal*, June 1903, 15.

———. Mr. Mabie's Literary Talks. *Ladies' Home Journal*, July 1903, 14.

———. Mr. Mabie's Literary Talks. *Ladies' Home Journal*, September 1903, 15.

———. "Mr. Mabie's Literary Talks: Travels at Home." *Ladies' Home Journal*, January 1904, 17.

———. "A Literary Talk by Mr. Mabie." *Ladies' Home Journal*, March 1904, 16.

———. "Mr. Mabie Answers Some Questions." *Ladies' Home Journal*, May 1904, 24.

———. "Mr. Mabie on Sunday-School Books." *Ladies' Home Journal*, September 1904, 18.

———. "Mr. Mabie Answers Some Literary Questions." *Ladies' Home Journal*, November 1904, 20.

———. "Some Books of the Season." *Ladies' Home Journal*, December 1904, 19.

———. "Mr. Mabie Tells about the Books." *Ladies' Home Journal*, January 1905, 20.

———. "Mr. Mabie Talks about Poetry." *Ladies' Home Journal*, March 1905, 21.

———. "Mr. Mabie Answers Some Questions." *Ladies' Home Journal*, May 1905, 18.

———. "Mr. Mabie Talks of the New Novels." *Ladies' Home Journal*, June 1905, 28.

———. "Mr. Mabie Answers Some Questions." *Ladies' Home Journal*, September 1905, 18.

———. "Mr. Mabie on Self-Culture." *Ladies' Home Journal*, October 1905, 20.

———. "Mr. Mabie Answers Some Questions." *Ladies' Home Journal*, November 1905, 20.

———. "Mr. Mabie Tells of the Christmas Books." *Ladies' Home Journal*, December 1905, 21.

———. "Mr. Mabie Comments on Books of the Season." *Ladies' Home Journal*, January 1906, 30.

———. "Mr. Mabie Answers Some Questions." *Ladies' Home Journal*, March 1906, 20.

———. "Mr. Mabie's Answers to Questions." *Ladies' Home Journal*, April 1906, 26.

———. "Mr. Mabie Talks about Helpful Books." *Ladies' Home Journal*, May 1906, 18.

———. "Mr. Mabie Tells of Summer Books." *Ladies' Home Journal*, July 1906, 18.

———. "Mr. Mabie's Talk about New Books." *Ladies' Home Journal*, October 1906, 22.

———. "Mr. Mabie on the Home as a School." *Ladies' Home Journal*, November 1906, 22.

———. "Mr. Mabie's Talk on Current Books." *Ladies' Home Journal*, March 1907, 22.

———. "Should the Young Read Novels?" *Ladies' Home Journal*, September 1907, 28.

———. "Mr. Mabie on Books for Young People." *Ladies' Home Journal*, October 1907, 24.

———. "Mr. Mabie Tells of the World's Greatest University." *Ladies' Home Journal*, November 1907, 28.

———. "Mr. Mabie Talks about the New Books." *Ladies' Home Journal*, January 1908, 28.

———. "When a Club Can Do Good Work." *Ladies' Home Journal*, October 1908, 38.

———. "Mr. Mabie Suggests Courses for Private Reading." *Ladies' Home Journal*, November 1908, 36.

———. "Mr. Mabie Tells about Edgar Allan Poe." *Ladies' Home Journal*, January 1909, 30.

———. "Literary Sheep and Ghosts." *Ladies' Home Journal*, March 1909, 42.

———. "Courses of Novel-Reading." *Ladies' Home Journal*, September 1909, 28.

———. "The Book as a Christmas Gift." *Ladies' Home Journal*, December 1909, 32.

———. "Books about Europe for Home Reading and Travel." *Ladies' Home Journal*, June 1910, 34.

———. "How to Live on 24 Hours a Day." *Ladies' Home Journal*, 1 November 1910, 36.

———. "New Books Worth Reading." *Ladies' Home Journal*, March 1911, 30.

———. "Are the American Novelists Deteriorating?" *Ladies' Home Journal*, September 1911, 24.

———. "Are the Best-Sellers Worth Reading?" *Ladies' Home Journal*, November 1911, 30.

———. "The New Books as Christmas Gifts." *Ladies' Home Journal*, December 1911, 30.

———. "Living Novelists Best Worth Reading." *Ladies' Home Journal*, February 1912, 42.

———. "Which Way Is Literature Going?" *Ladies' Home Journal*, April 1912, 42.

———. *The Blue Book of Fiction: A List of Novels Worth Reading Chosen from Many Literatures*. Cincinnati: Globe-Wernicke Co., 1911.

Machor, James L. "Introduction: Readers/ Texts/ Contexts." In *Readers in History: Nineteenth-Century American Literature and the Contexts of Response*, edited by James L. Machor, vii–xxix. Baltimore: Johns Hopkins University Press, 1993.

Machor, James L., and Philip Goldstein. *Reception Study: From Literary Theory to Cultural Studies*. New York: Routledge, 2001.

Mailloux, Steven. *Rhetorical Power*. Ithaca, NY: Cornell University Press, 1989.

Matthews, Brander. *The Historical Novel and Other Essays*. New York: Charles Scribner's Sons, 1901.

McGrath, Charles. "Wharton Letter Reopens a Mystery." *New York Times*, 21 November 2007. http://www.nytimes.com/2007/11/21/books/21wharton.html.

Merish, Lori. *Sentimental Materialism: Gender, Commodity Culture, and Nineteenth-Century American Literature*. Durham, NC: Duke University Press, 2000.

Michaels, Walter Benn. *The Gold Standard and the Logic of Naturalism*. Berkeley: University of California Press, 1987.

[Middleton, George]. "'Richard Carvel' beyond Question." *New York Times Book Review*, 10 March 1900.

Montgomery, Maureen. *Displaying Women: Spectacles of Leisure in Edith Wharton's New York*. New York: Routledge, 1998.

[Moore, Mrs. E. J.]. "Why 'Richard Carvel' Is Preferred." *New York Times Book Review*, 4 March 1900.

Morse, Edmund W. *The Life and Letters of Hamilton W. Mabie*. New York: Dodd, Mead, 1920.

Mott, Frank Luther. *Golden Multitudes: The Story of Best Sellers in the United States*. New York: Macmillan, 1947.

——. *A History of American Magazines*. Vol. 4. 1938. Cambridge, MA: Harvard University Press, 1968.

"Mr. James's Latest Novel [Review of Henry James's *Portrait of a Lady*]." *New York Times*, 27 November 1881, 5.

"Mr. James's *The Portrait of a Lady*." *Literary World*, 17 December 1881, 474.

"Mrs. Wharton's Novel: Further Contributions to the Discussion of the Ethical and Artistic Import of 'The House of Mirth.'" *New York Times Saturday Review of Books*, 30 December 1905.

"Mrs. Wharton's 'Sanctuary.'" *New York Times Saturday Review of Books*, 21 November 1903.

Murray, John. *A Handbook of Rome and its Environs*. 12th ed. London: John Murray, 1875.

Norris, Frank. "A Plea for Romantic Fiction." In *The Responsibilities of the Novelist, and Other Literary Essays*, 214–15. New York: Doubleday, Page and Co., 1903.

Officer, Laurence, and Samuel Williamson. MeasuringWorth. http://www.measuringworth.com (accessed 9 September 2009).

Ohmann, Richard M. *Selling Culture: Magazines, Markets, and Class at the Turn of the Century*. New York: Verso, 1996.

Oliphant, Margaret. [Review of Henry James's *Portrait of a Lady*]. *Blackwood's Edinburgh Magazine*, March 1882, 374–83. Reprinted in *The Portrait of a Lady*, by Henry James, 2nd ed., edited by Robert D. Bamberg, 668–76. New York: W. W. Norton, 1995.

Oxley, J. Macdonald. "Literary Improvement Clubs." *Ladies' Home Journal*, January 1894, 16.

Peattie, Elia W. "Best Fiction of the Year." *Chicago Daily Tribune*, 2 December 1905.

——. "Mrs. Wharton's House of Mirth: Remarkably Fine Work by the Author." *Chicago Daily Tribune*, 28 October 1905.

Petrie, Paul R. *Conscience and Purpose: Fiction and Social Consciousness in Howells, Jewett, Chesnutt, and Cather*. Tuscaloosa: University of Alabama Press, 2005.

Pilkington, John, Jr. *Francis Marion Crawford*. New York: Twayne Publishers, 1964.

Pizer, Donald. *New Essays on Sister Carrie*. New York: Cambridge University Press, 1991.

[Powell, Thomas]. [Review of *Roderick Hudson*, by Henry James]. *New York Herald*, 26 December 1875, 3.

Prose, Francine. "Shot through the Heart." *O: The Oprah Magazine*, September 2001, 214.

Puskar, Jason. "William Dean Howells and the Insurance of the Real." *American Literary History* 18, no. 1 (2006): 29–58.

Radway, Janice. *A Feeling for Books: The Book-of-the-Month Club, Literary Taste, and Middle-Class Desire*. Chapel Hill: University of North Carolina Press, 1997.

———. *Reading the Romance: Women, Patriarchy, and Popular Literature*. Chapel Hill: University of North Carolina Press, 1984.

Ramsey, A. R. Books and Bookmakers. *Ladies' Home Journal*, June 1889, 11.

———. Books and Bookmakers. *Ladies' Home Journal*, October 1889, 11.

———. Books and Bookmakers. *Ladies' Home Journal*, November 1889, 10.

Rascoe, Burton. *"Smart Set" History: The Smart Set Anthology*. New York: Reynal and Hitchcock, 1934.

———. *Titans of Literature, from Homer to the Present*. New York and London: G. P. Putnam's Sons, 1932.

[Review of *Richard Carvel* by Winston Churchill]. *New York Times Saturday Review of Books*, 9 December 1899.

[Review of *Roderick Hudson*, by Henry James]. *Chicago Tribune*, 11 December 1875, 1.

[Review of *The Portrait of a Lady*, by Henry James]. *Chicago Tribune*, 10 December 1881, 10.

[Review of *The Portrait of a Lady*, by Henry James, and *A Laodicean*, by Thomas Hardy]. *New York Herald*, 12 December 1881, 5.

[Review of *The Princess Casamassima*, by Henry James]. *Lippincott's Monthly Magazine*, February 1887, 359.

Rife, David James. "Hamilton Wright Mabie: A Critical Biography." Ph.D. diss., Southern Illinois University, 1975.

Ringe, Donald A. "Narrative Voice in Cable's *The Grandissimes*." In *The Grandissimes: Centennial Essays*, edited by Thomas J. Richardson, 13–22. Jackson: University Press of Mississippi, 1981.

"Romance Reduced to Figures." *Ladies' Home Journal*, March 1890, 13.

Romines, Ann. "In *Deephaven*: Skirmishes near the Swamp." In *Critical Essays on Sarah Orne Jewett*, edited by Gwen L. Nagel, 43–57. Boston: G. K. Hall and Co., 1984.

Rooney, Kathleen. *Reading with Oprah: The Book Club That Changed America*. Fayetteville: University of Arkansas Press, 2005.

Rose, Jonathan. "Rereading the English Common Reader: A Preface to a History of Audiences." *Journal of the History of Ideas* 53, no. 1 (1992): 47–70.

Rubin, Joan Shelley. *The Making of Middlebrow Culture*. Chapel Hill: University of North Carolina Press, 1992.

Santayana, George. *The Genteel Tradition: Nine Essays by George Santayana.* Edited by Douglas Wilson. Cambridge, MA: Harvard University Press, 1967.

Satterfield, Jay. *The World's Best Books: Taste, Culture, and the Modern Library.* Amherst: University of Massachusetts Press, 2002.

Scanlon, Jennifer. *Inarticulate Longings: "Ladies' Home Journal," Gender, and the Promises of Consumer Culture.* New York: Routledge, 1995.

Shuman, Edwin L. *How to Judge a Book: A Handy Method of Criticism for the General Reader.* Boston: Houghton Mifflin, 1910.

Sicherman, Barbara. "Sense and Sensibility: A Case Study of Women's Reading in Late-Victorian America." In *Reading in America: Literature and Social History,* edited by Cathy N. Davidson, 201–25. Baltimore: Johns Hopkins University Press, 1989.

———. *Well-Read Lives: How Books Inspired a Generation of American Women.* Chapel Hill: University of North Carolina Press, 2010.

["Similia Similibus"]. "'Richard Carvel and 'Hugh Wynne." *New York Times Book Review,* 11 November 1899.

Smith, Adam. *The Theory of Moral Sentiments.* Vol. 1. Oxford: Clarendon Press, 1976.

Sorby, Angela. *Schoolroom Poets: Childhood, Performance, and the Place of American Poetry, 1865–1917.* Lebanon: University of New Hampshire Press, 2005.

Spiro, Lisa. "Reading with a Tender Rapture: *Reveries of a Bachelor* and the Rhetoric of Detached Intimacy." *Book History* 6 (2003): 57–93.

Steinberg, Salme Harju. *Reformer in the Marketplace: Edward W. Bok and "Ladies' Home Journal."* Baton Rouge: Louisiana State University Press, 1979.

"To-Day's Books and Their Authors." *Ladies' Home Journal,* February 1902, 2.

"Topics of the Week." *New York Times Saturday Review of Books,* 25 November 1905.

Trachtenberg, Alan. *The Incorporation of America: Culture and Society in the Gilded Age.* 1st ed. New York: Hill and Wang, 1982.

Travis, Trysh. "'It Will Change the World If Everybody Reads This Book': New Thought Religion in Oprah's Book Club." *American Quarterly,* September 2007, 1017–41.

["Veritas"]. "Wants More like 'Janice Meredith.'" *New York Times Book Review,* 24 February 1900.

Waid, Candace. *Edith Wharton's Letters from the Underworld: Fictions of Women and Writing.* Chapel Hill: University of North Carolina Press, 1991.

Wasserstrom, William. "William Dean Howells: The Indelible Stain." *New England Quarterly* 32 (December 1959): 486–95.

Welch, Margaret Hamilton. "Miss Wilkins at Home." *Harper's Bazar,* 27 January 1900, 69.

Wharton, Edith. *A Backward Glance.* New York: Charles Scribner's Sons, 1933.

———. *The House of Mirth*. New York: Penguin, 1993.

———. Letter to Edward Burlingame, 23 November 1905. In *The Letters of Edith Wharton*, edited by R. W. B. Lewis and Nancy Lewis. New York: Macmillan, 1988.

———. Letter to Francis Kinnicutt, 26 December 1904. http://www.nytimes.com/slideshow/2007/11/20/books/wharton-slideshow_2.html.

———. *The Uncollected Critical Writings*. Edited by Frederick Wegener. Princeton, NJ: Princeton University Press, 1996.

———. "The Vice of Reading." *North American Review*, October 1903, 513–21.

———. *The Writing of Fiction*. 1925. New York: Simon and Schuster, 1997.

Wilson, Christopher P. *White Collar Fictions: Class and Social Representation in American Literature, 1885–1925*. Athens: University of Georgia Press, 1992.

Wilson, Douglas, ed. *The Genteel Tradition: Nine Essays by George Santayana*. Cambridge, MA: Harvard University Press, 1967.

Winfrey, Oprah. *The Oprah Winfrey Show*, 17 September 2010. http://www.oprah.com/oprahshow/Oprahs-Book-Club-Announcement-Video.

Wolff, Cynthia Griffin. Introduction to *The House of Mirth*, by Edith Wharton. New York: Penguin, 1993.

"The Writers for *Ladies' Home Journal* for 1895." *Ladies' Home Journal*, December 1894, cover.

[Young, Charles H.]. "'Hugh Wynne,' 'Richard Carvel,' 'Janice Meredith.'" *New York Times Book Review*, 2 December 1899.

Zagarell, Sandra A. "Troubling Regionalism: Rural Life and the Cosmopolitan Eye in Jewett's *Deephaven*." *American Literary History* 10, no. 4 (Winter 1998): 639–63.

Zboray, Ronald J., and Mary Saracino Zboray. *Literary Dollars and Social Sense: A People's History of the Mass Market Book*. New York: Routledge, 2005.

Index

Aeschylus, 162–63
aesthetics, language of, 1–3, 25, 56, 57–59, 63
African American readers, 215n4
Alcott, Louisa May, 10
Alden, Henry Mills, 62
Aldrich, Thomas Bailey, 206
Alger, Horatio, 4, 116, 212n5
Allen, James Lane, 81, 102, 117, 174, 206;
    The Choir Invisible, 102, 172, 186, 205,
    209; *Flute and Violin*, 209
Andover Review, 61, 81, 83–84
Arena, 59
Arnold, Matthew, 206; *Culture and
    Anarchy*, 195; *Essays in Criticism*, 195
Atlantic Monthly, 13–14, 24, 29, 50, 62, 64,
    69, 99, 105, 171, 174, 185, 195, 214n35,
    217n44
Austen, Jane, 82, 102, 118; *Northanger
    Abbey*, 179–80
authorship: anxieties about misreading,
    12–19; construction of, 14; intention
    and, 11; realism and, 14–15

Baedeker's, 113
Balzac, Honoré de, 15–17, 206, 214n37;
    characters in, 17–18; *Eugénie Grandet*,
    115; *Père Goriot*, 2, 15–17
Barrish, Phillip, 16
Baym, Nina, 126
Bell, Michael Davitt, 14, 116, 214n37

Bennett, Arnold, 170
Bennett, Emerson, 73–74
Bennett, Jesse Lee, *What Books Can Do
    For You*, 10
Bennett, Tony, 11–12
Bentley, Nancy, 223n14
Berkson, Dorothy, 47
Besant, Walter, 116
best-sellers, 48, 54, 137, 138, 166–67
The Bible, 205
biography, 41
Blackwood's, 122
Bode, Carl, 212n5
Bok, Edward, 25–26, 29–33, 35, 38, 41, 63–
    64, 69–71, 77–80, 216n16, 216–17n24,
Bok Syndicate Press, 29
book clubs. *See under* literature
Book-of-the-Month Club, 5, 7, 8, 19, 197
(Boston) Literary World, 126
Bourdieu, Pierre, 155
Boyeson, Hjalmar Hjorth, 68, 69, 70, 71,
    72, 219n33
Bridges, Robert, 32–35, 57, 216–17n24;
    "Droch" columns, 44 (*see also*
    "Droch"); "Heroines in Fiction," 34–35
Brodhead, Richard, 176
Brontë sisters, 10
Brown, Bill, 214n37
Bulwer-Lytton, Edward, *The Last Days of
    Pompeii*, 191

Burlingame, Edward, 163–64
Burnett, Frances Hodgson, *Little Lord Fauntleroy*, 31
Buzard, James, 113
Byron, George Gordon, "Manfred," 113

Cable, George Washington, 21, 31, 81, 104, 117, 173, 184, 206; *The Cavalier*, 182; *Doctor Sevier*, 181; *The Grandissimes*, 102, 172, 181–86, 193, 205, 209, 224–25n19; 1907 edition, 183–84; genre of, 185; identification in, 184; illustrations in, 183–84; *John March, Southerner*, 181; as literary tourism, 185; "local color" in, 185; *Old Creole Days*, 81, 182, 205, 209; readership of, 184; as romance, 185
Cady, Edwin Harrison, 218n2
Campbell, Donna M., 174
canonicity, 84–85, 87
capital, 8, 20, 54–55. *See also* cultural capital
Carleton, Will, 31
Carlyle, Thomas, 206
Carter, Everett, 220n64
Cather, Willa, 188, 225n23
Cawelti, John G., 160
The Century, 24, 62, 186
Certeau, Michel de, 9, 149–50, 162
Cervantes, Miguel de, *Don Quixote*, 75
Channing, William Ellery, 54
characters, 17–18, 52–53, 59, 61, 83–84, 103, 123–26, 134, 175
Charles Scribner's Sons, 29, 103, 163–64
Chautauqua movement, 195
Chicago Daily Tribune, 150
Chicago Evening Post, 119, 126
Chicago Tribune, 106, 120
Churchill, Winston: *Coniston*, 209; *The Crisis*, 186, 209; *Mr. Crewe's Career*, 209; *Richard Carvel*, 186, 190–91, 192
Clarke, George, 59
Clarke, James Freeman, *Self-Culture*, 195
class, 26–27, 38, 149–56, 165, 177–78, 213–14n25, 215–16n10, 222n3. *See also* status; upward mobility
Clay, Bertha M., *Dora Thorne*, 2
Colby, Frank Moore, 23–24
Collier, P. F., 195, 197
consumer culture, 3–4, 6, 8–9, 12, 26, 60, 139–40, 143, 150, 172, 198

Cooke, Delmar Gross, *William Dean Howells: A Critical Study*, 66–67
Cooper, James Fenimore, 34, 50, 118, 206; *The Deerslayer*, 102; *The Last of the Mohicans*, 84, 102; *The Spy*, 206, 209
Copeland, Stephanie, 164
Cowley, Malcolm, 62
Crawford, F. Marion, 104, 127–36, 193, 206 (*see also* Crawford, F. Marion, works of); characterization and, 134; *Corleone*, 128; genre and, 135; literary marketplace and, 135; readership of, 130–31, 134; reading as leisure, 135–36; realism and, 134–35; resemblance and, 134; romance and, 134–35
Crawford, F. Marion, works of: *Cecilia*, 128; *The Cigarette-Maker's Romance*, 128; *The Novel: What It Is*, 99, 134; *A Roman Singer*, 128; *Saracinesca*, 127, 128–34; *Stradella*, 128; *Via Crucis*, 128
The Critic, 174
critics/criticism: "genteel critics," 36, 62; Mabie and, 43–44; professional status of, 14–15; realism and, 14–15. *See also* specific critics
cultural capital, 20, 40, 54–59
Cummins, Maria Susanna, *The Lamplighter*, 167
Curtis, Cyrus, 26, 29, 64, 216n16
Curtis Publishing Company, 25, 26, 64

Damon-Moore, Helen, 215–16n10
Dawson, Melanie, 165–66
Defoe, Daniel, *Robinson Crusoe*, 206
Deland, Margaret, 31, 206; *The Awakening of Helena Ritchie*, 167; *Old Chester Tales*, 209
De Morgan, William Frend, 206
Dickens, Charles, 10, 34, 102, 167, 206; *David Copperfield*, 81, 115, 172, 205; *A Tale of Two Cities*, 206
discipline, versus talent, 108–9
Dixon, Thomas, *The Clansman*, 167
Doyle, Arthur Conan, *The Hound of the Baskervilles*, 43
Dreiser, Theodore, 19; *An American Tragedy*, 201; *Sister Carrie*, 2–3, 15, 211–12n4, 214n37
"Droch," 32–35, 37–38, 44, 57, 216–17n24. *See also* Bridges, Robert
"The Duchess," 31

Dumas, Alexandre, 34; *Pitou, Ange*, 191
Dunlop, M. H., 211–12n4
Dunn, Martha Baker, 13, 15; "A Plea for the Shiftless Reader," 13–14

economics, language of, 1–3, 20, 25, 56–59. *See also* capital
Edgworth, Maria, 118
"Edmunds, Frederica," 190
education, 53–56, 86, 108–9. *See also* self-culture; self-education, 53–56
Eggleston, Edward, *A Hoosier Schoolmaster*, 209
Eliot, George, 102, 117–18, 206; *Adam Bede*, 117, 205; *The Mill on the Floss*, 115, 117, 205
elite culture. *See* highbrow culture
Eller, Jonathan R., 68, 219n23
Emerson, Ralph Waldo, 50, 56, 206
empathy, 15–16, 217n32
escapism, 57, 59, 142, 161, 186, 192, 213n20
Everyman's Library, 195

Farrar, Straus, and Giroux, 198, 225–26n10
Fetterly, Judith, 217n32
Fish, Stanley, 11
Fiske, John, 206
Fitzgerald, F. Scott, *The Great Gatsby*, 201
Five-Foot Shelf of Books, 195–97
Foote, Marly Hallock, *The Led-Horse Claim*, 209
Ford, Paul Leicester, *Janice Meredith*, 191, 192
Forum, 186–88
Foucault, Michel, 199
Fox, John Jr., 206; *The Little Shepherd of Kingdom Come*, 210
Franzen, Jonathan, 195; *The Corrections*, 197–204, 225–26n10; *Freedom*, 202–3
Fresh Air, 198

Galassi, Jonathan, 225–26n10
Garland, Hamlin, 127, 174, 206; *Main Travelled Roads*, 209
gender, reading and, 34–35, 48–49, 59, 70–71, 193, 199–200, 214n26, 215n4, 217n35
genre, 45, 50–51, 53, 135, 182. *See also* specific genres
Gibbon, Edward, 41
Gilder, Richard Watson, 62, 185

Gilmore, William J., 9
Gissing, George, 116
Gladstone, William, 116, 142, 172
Glasgow, Ellen, 173, 206
Glazener, Nancy, 14–15, 50, 214n35, 217n44
Glyn, Elinor, *Three Weeks*, 158, 223n25
Grant, Robert, *Unleavened Bread*, 210
Gras, Felix, *Reds of the Midi*, 191
Great American Novel, 201
Green, Anna Katharine, *The Millionaire Baby*, 167
Greenwood, Grace, 29–30
Griffith, D. W., *Birth of a Nation*, 167

Habermas, Jürgen, 213n20
Haggard, Rider, 136
Hamerton, Philip Gilbert, *Intellectual Life*, 195
Hamilton family, 10–11
Hardy, Thomas, 206; *Far from the Madding Crowd*, 117; *Under the Greenwood Tree*, 117
Harland, Henry, 158
Harper's Bazar, 46–47
Harper's Monthly, 11, 174, 218n10, 219n33; Editor's Study columns, 72, 219n31
Hart, James David, 224–25n19
Harte, Bret, *Luck of Roaring Camp and Other Stories*, 209
Hartman, Saidiya V., 10
Harvard Classics, 195–97
Hawthorne, Nathaniel, 34, 50, 78, 102, 118, 206; *The House of Seven Gables*, 81, 168, 175, 206, 209; *The Marble Faun*, 49, 102, 112, 205; *The Scarlet Letter*, 84, 172, 182, 205
Hay, John, 119
Heine, Heinrich, 74, 75
Hendler, Glenn, 213n20, 217n35
Herrick, Robert: *The Common Lot*, 56, 210; *The Memoirs of an American Citizen*, 210
Herter, Albert, 184
Hichens, Robert Smythe, *The Garden of Allah*, 167
highbrow culture, 20, 139–40, 143, 151–56, 165, 171, 175, 213–14n25, 214–15n40, 217n44. *See also* upper class
high society. *See* upper class
historical fiction, 186–87, 189–92

Hochman, Barbara, 10, 16, 213n22, 223–24n32

Holmes, Joseph, 158

Holmes, Oliver Wendell, 118, 206; *Elsie Venner*, 175

The Home Monthly, 188

Houghton Mifflin, 105

Howard, June, 9–10, 212–13n19

Howells, John Mead, 219n33

Howells, Mildred, 219n33

Howells, William Dean, 15, 18–20, 24, 49–50, 59, 118, 127, 171, 173, 176, 185–86, 193, 218n2, 219n23. *See also* Howells, William Dean, works of; biography of, 68–69; correspondence with Bok, 70–71; earnings of, 218n10, 218n11; as exemplary, 70–71, 80; family and, 70–73, 219n33; identification and, 18–19; imagination and, 219n31; James and, 100; *The Ladies' Home Journal* and, 62, 63–98; lightness of, 82–84; literary marketplace and, 94; readership of, 74, 79, 85–86, 87–90; reading and, 70–71, 75–77, 80; realism and, 8, 68, 71, 73–74, 77–78, 97, 214n37, 214–15n40, 219n31, 220n64; on reviewing, 76–77; romance and, 95–96, 219n31; romanticism and, 74, 87; sentimentality and, 95–96; on Spanish literature, 75; success of, 70–71; sympathy and, 96; taste and, 214–15n40

Howells, William Dean, works of: autobiography of, 64; *A Chance Acquaintance*, 93; *The Coast of Bohemia*, 64, 65–68, 69, 80, 89–90, 93, 94, 218n10; *Criticism and Fiction*, 15–16, 134; Editor's Study columns, 72, 219n31; *A Hazard of New Fortunes*, 20, 31–32, 63, 81, 83, 91, 93–97, 209, 220n64; *The Kentons*, 83–84, 93; *The Lady of Aroostook*, 20, 63, 81, 83, 91–93; *A Modern Instance*, 83; "My Book Friends" idea, 69, 77; *My Literary Passions*, 68–81, 218n10; *The Rise of Silas Lapham*, 16–17, 20, 22, 52, 55, 61–98, 102, 168, 171, 186, 205, 209; Mabie's review of, 81–91; reading in, 85–86; realism of, 83–84; *Their Wedding Journey*, 32, 93

Howells, Winifred, 219n33

Hugo, Victor, 34

Hutner, Gordon, *What America Read*, 7

identification, 7–12, 15, 17, 46, 61, 72, 85–86, 166, 204, 212–13n19, 213n20; Cable and, 184; Howells and, 18–19; James and, 103, 111–12, 114; Jewett and, 174–81; readers and, 219–20n39; reading up and, 161–63; Wharton and, 162–63

imagination, 10, 212–13n19, 219n31

impressionism, 116

Independent, 169

Ingelow, Jean, 178–79; "The Days without Alloy," 178–79; *Mopsa the Fairy*, 178

Ingersoll, Robert Sturgis, *Open That Door!*, 4

instrumentalism, 71

intentions, authorial, 11

interiority of characters, 18

interpretation. *See also* misreading: author anxieties about misreading, 12–19; interpretive communities, 11; interpretive violence, 12

Irving, John, *The World According to Garp*, 201

Irving, Washington, 34, 50, 206; *Sketch Book*, 181

Jacobson, Marcia, 116

James, Henry, 15, 19–21, 99–127, 136, 157, 171–73, 193, 206. *See also* James, Henry, works of; accessibility of, 100; on Balzac, 17, 18; characters and, 103, 106; Howells and, 100; identification and, 103, 111–12, 114; involvement with syndication, 100; literary status of, 100; pessimism of, 126; popularity and, 99–100; psychology and, 104; publication in periodicals, 99–100; readership of, 100, 120, 122–24, 221n9; realism and, 116, 214n37; romance and, 114–27; sympathy and, 106–14

James, Henry, works of: *The Ambassadors*, 101, 104; *The American*, 20, 21, 101, 104; "The Art of Fiction," 52, 104; *Bostonians*, 81; *Daisy Miller*, 92; *The Golden Bowl*, 100, 101; *Guy Domville*, 116; *A Hazard of New Fortunes*, 115; "The Lesson of the Master," 104; "The Lesson on Balzac," 18; New York Edition, 20–21, 101, 103–6, 121–23, 126, 221n8; *The Outcry*, 101; *The Passionate Pilgrim*, 104; *The Portrait of a Lady*,

20–21, 66, 81, 100–105, 118–27, 128, 136, 160–61, 171–72, 182; as bildungsroman, 122; characterization in, 123–26; reception of, 119–23, 126; revisions of, 123–24; romance and, 118–27; success of, 126; *The Princess Casamassima*, 100, 103, 114–18, 126, 132; "The Real Thing," 104; *Roderick Hudson*, 20–21, 100–114, 117–18, 126, 129, 171, 221n10; identification in, 114; publication of, 105; reviews of, 106; *The Spoils of Poynton*, 116; *The Tragic Muse*, 99; *The Turn of the Screw*, 100; *What Maisie Knew*, 116; *The Wings of the Dove*, 101, 104, 119, 126

James, William, 99
Jewett, Sarah Orne, 21, 45, 81, 168, 173–74, 184, 206. *See also* Jewett, Sarah Orne, works of; readership of, 177, 178
Jewett, Sarah Orne, works of: *A Country Doctor*, 175; *The Country of the Pointed Firs*, 175, 176, 177, 209; *Deephaven*, 102, 175–81; class in, 177–78; identification in, 175–81; reading in, 180–81; reception of, 175–76; sympathy in, 178; "The Dulham Ladies," 177; *The Queen's Twin*, 177; *Tales of New England*, 177; *The Tory Lover*, 47–48, 174, 175, 209
Johanningsmeier, Charles, 100
Johnson, Samuel, 40
Johnston, Mary, 173, 186

Kaplan, Amy, 165, 172
Keats, John, 34
King, Grace F., *Balcony Stories*, 210
Kingsley, Charles, *Westward Ho*, 181
Kinnicutt, Francis, 164
Kipling, Rudyard, 63–64, 206; *Just-So Stories*, 84

Lacayo, Richard, 225–26n10
Ladies' Home Journal, 1, 5–8, 12, 19–20, 22–35, 45–46, 84, 171–75, 193, 195, 197, 216n16. *See also under* Mabie, Hamiliton Wright, works and columns of; African American readers and, 215n4; Books and Bookmaking column, 28–29, 30–31; circulation of, 25, 79; class and, 26, 215–16n10; columns in, 25; cost of, 215n6; eclecticism of, 65; as a family magazine,

25–26; female readership of, 215n4; Howells and, 62, 63–98; illustrations in, 66, 67, 82; impact of, 25; James and, 100–101, 123, 126; lack of inclusivity, 215–16n10; letters in, 143–44; Literary Leaves column, 29–31; Literary Talks column, 33; male readership of, 25–26, 215n3; reader letters in, 211n2; readership of, 2–3, 25–28, 35–38, 42–43, 47, 53–55, 70–71, 74, 79–87, 112, 121, 177, 184, 211n2; reading advice in, 28, 32–33, 37–44; as taste maker, 26–27; Wharton and, 139, 141, 144, 150, 169
Lamb, Charles, *Essays of Elia*, 181
Larned, J. N., *Books, Culture, and Character*, 4
Lathrop, George Parsons, 185
Lee, Hermione, 169
Lewis, Sinclair, 62, 218n3; *Main Street*, 212n12
Lidoff, Joan, 166
Lincoln, Abraham, 116
Lippincott's Monthly Magazine, 116
literature. *See also specific genres*: as capital, 4; contemporary, 22; elite, 3, 4, 7–8; friendship with books, 75, 77–78; instrumentalism of, 71; literariness, 192; literary classification, 50–51, 53, 94–95; literary clubs, 31, 76–77, 172, 193; literary hierarchies, 13, 94–95; literary magazines, 172, 174; literary marketplace, 3, 19, 24, 40, 54, 94, 135, 140, 174, 198, 214n35; literary standards, 40; literary status, 3–4, 7–8, 13, 24, 33, 40, 42–43, 54–55, 64, 84–85, 94–95, 139–40; literary value, 1–2; marketing of, 140; as pleasurable, 33–34; popular, 138–39, 140, 147; Spanish, 75; utility of, 136
"local color," 172, 173, 175, 176–77, 185
Longfellow, Henry Wadsworth, 206
Lorimer, George C., *What I Know about Books and How to Use Them*, 4
Lowell, James Russell, 71

Mabie, Hamilton Wright, 1, 5–8, 11–13, 15, 19–60, 171–72, 174, 181–82, 193, 195, 216–17n24. *See also* Mabie, Hamilton Wright, works and columns of; advice of, 38–39; aesthetic goals of, 44; approach of, 38, 44–45, 56–57; on best-sellers, 48, 166–67; biography of, 23, 36, 37–38; Cable and, 185–86; on canonicity, 84–85, 205–7; character and, 175; columns of, 39, 100–101, 172–73 (*see also specific columns*); compared to Bridges's "Droch" columns, 44–45; correspondence of, 36–37; Crawford and, 127–36; criticism and, 43–44; generic classifications and, 45, 50–51, 53, 182; historical fiction and, 187, 192; holiday books column, 55; Howells and, 61–98; James and, 100–127, 136, 221n9; Jewett and, 174–81; literary classification of, 50–51, 53; on magazines, 40–41; Mitchell and, 186–92; pessimism and, 126; philosophy of, 39–40; reader queries and, 114–15, 143–44, 186, 203, 221n9; readership of, 37–43, 53–55, 59–60, 78, 86–87, 91, 95, 102, 107, 112, 115, 118, 136–40, 173–74, 177–78, 182, 185–86; reading habit and, 141–45, 148, 212n12; reading up and, 197; realism and, 45–51, 53, 61, 63, 81–85, 91, 168, 173, 181–82, 193, 218n2; on reception, 50–51; regionalism and, 117, 169–70, 172–81; reviewing philosophy of, 39–44; romance and, 115, 117, 173, 186; romanticism and, 49, 97, 170; selection process of, 43–44; self-culture and, 195; "Self-Culture Is Possible through Books," 53–54; sentimentality and, 175, 217n35; on sexual morality, 48; "six rules for those who read," 144–45; on successful novels, 187–88; sympathy and, 110, 175, 181; terminological imprecision of, 45, 53; three tests of a good novel, 52; Wharton and, 138–44, 148, 150, 151–52, 167, 168–70

Mabie, Hamilton Wright, works and columns of: "The American Romance," 115, 116; "Are the American Novelists Deteriorating?," 49–50, 173; "Are the Best-Sellers Worth Reading?," 48, 137, 166–67; "Are the Later Poets Worth Reading?," 101; "A Beginning in the Best Fiction," 105, 117, 175; "Best American Novels," 105; "Books about Europe for Home Reading and Travel," 128; *Books and Reading; or, What Books Shall I Read and How Shall I Read Them?*, 5; "Courses of Novel-Reading," 51, 175; "Courses of Reading for Summer Moods," 81; "How to Form the Reading Habit," 141–42; "How to Live on 24 Hours a Day," 57; "Living Novelists Best Worth Reading," 101; March 1909 column, 187; Mr. Mabie Answers Some Questions, 39; "Mr. Mabie Comments on Books of the Season," 42; "Mr. Mabie on Sunday-School Books," 50; "Mr. Mabie on the Home as a School," 108; Mr. Mabie's Literary Talks, 39; "Mr. Mabie Suggests Courses for Private Reading," 171, 193; "Mr. Mabie Tells about the Books," 60; "Mr. Mabie Tells What to Read," 39; "New Books Worth Reading," 44; "New Novels of Incident," 44; "Novels Descriptive of American Life," 168, 209–10; "Novels for Summer Reading," 84; "Novels of Realism," 81; October 1905 column, 182; October 1908 column, 187; reading lists for women's clubs, 193; "Read What You Like," 40–41; "The Relation of Books and Wealth," 55; "A Short Course in Fiction," 81; "Should the Young Read Novels," 161–62; "Should the Young Read Novels?," 169; "Some Standard Novels" list, 175; "A Typical Novel," 61–98; "When a Club Can Do Good Work," 193; "Which Way Is Literature Going?," 101, 169–70; writings in *The Outlook*, 45

Mabie, Jeanette, 36

Machor, James L., 11; *Readers in History*, 8

Macmillan, 105

magazines. *See* periodicals; *specific magazines*

Mailloux, Steven, 11

Marden, Orison Swett, *Pushing to the Front*, 4

Marvel, Ik, 74; *Tears, Idle Tears*, 87–88

mass culture. *See* consumer culture

mass-market magazines, 6, 7, 8, 24–25

Matthews, Brander, 174, 186–88; *His Father's Son*, 210

McCutcheon, George Barr: *Beverly of Graustark*, 84, 167; *Graustark*, 84

men. *See* gender, reading and

Meredith, George, 34

Michaels, Walter Benn, 223n14
middlebrow culture, 3, 5, 7–8, 19, 165–66, 167, 213–14n25
middle class, 3, 4, 5, 7–12, 19, 26, 38
Middleton, George, 192
Milton, John, 79–80; "Il Penseroso," 79; "Ode on Christ's Navitity," 79–80; *Paradise Lost*, 79
misreading, 11, 12–21, 160, 162–63, 171. *See also* interpretation
Mitchell, S. Weir, 173, 206; dismissal from the Society of Friends, 189; *Hugh Wynne, Free Quaker*, 172, 186–92, 205, 210; as genre-bending, 188; as historical fiction, 187; as a metaphor for the new nation, 189–90; realism in, 188
modernism, 53, 62, 172
Modern Library, 197
Modjeska, Helena, 6
Montgomery, Maureen, 155
Morse, Edwin W., 36
Mott, Frank Luther, 215n3, 224–25n19
The Mount, 164
Murfree, Mary Noailles, 117; *The Prophet of the Great Smoky Mountains*, 102
Murray, John, *Guide to Rome*, 113–14

National Public Radio, 198
naturalism, 13, 14–15, 48, 50, 51, 53, 101, 116, 170, 172
newspapers. *See* periodicals; *specific newspapers*
New Thought theology, 199
New York Daily Tribune, 150–51
New York Globe, 23–24
New York Herald, 106, 120, 122
New York Public Library, 137
New York Times, 119, 120, 122–23, 164, 169, 187–92, 196, 203. *See also New York Times Book Review*
New York Times Book Review, 21, 155–59, 163, 189–92, 196–97, 223n18
New York Tribune, 119–20
Norris, Frank, 49–51, 62, 118, 127; *The Octopus*, 50, 168, 170, 209; *The Pit*, 50, 168, 170, 209; "A Plea for Romantic Fiction," 49
North, Mrs. E. D., 37, 38, 59
The North American Review, 43, 139, 171, 174
Norton, Charles, 164

novels of manners, 17, 20

Ohmann, Richard M., 5, 212n7
Oliphant, Margaret, 122
Oprah, 22, 197–204
Oprah.com message boards, 199–203
Oprah's Book Club, 22, 197–204
Osgood, J. R., 105
O: The Oprah Magazine, 198
The Outlook, 37, 45, 62
Oxley, J. Macdonald, "Literary Improvement Clubs," 76–77

Page, Thomas Nelson, 81, 117, 206; *Red Rock*, 81, 206, 209; short stories of, 209
Paul R. Petrie, 176
periodicals, 6–8, 40–41, 196. *See also specific periodicals*; elite, 24, 172, 175; literary, 11, 172, 174; literary content of, 40–41; literary magazines, 172, 174; literary status of, 40–41; mass-market, 6, 7, 8, 24–25; as medium of literary fineness, 40; newspapers, 196; readership of, 40–41, 172
Philadelphia Times, 216n16
Poe, Edgar Allan, 34, 103, 206
Porter, Noah, *Books and Reading; or, What Books Shall I Read and How Shall I Read Them?*, 4, 7, 195
professionalism, 5, 12
Prose, Francine, 198
Pryse, Marjorie, 217n32
psychological novels, 17
psychology, 17, 104
publishers, 3, 4, 13. *See also specific publishers*
Puskar, Jason, 220n64

Radway, Janice, 3, 7, 8, 19
Ramsey, A. R. (Annie), 28–32, 38, 216n16
Rascoe, Burton, 62
"Rborja76," 200
readers, 2–3, 18, 24, 134, 159, 204, 219–20n39. *See also* under *specific authors and works*; African American, 215n4; ambitious, 142–43; born, 146–47; elite, 143; female, 34–35, 48–49, 59, 70–71, 193, 214n26, 215n4; identification and, 219–20n39; male, 215n4; mechanical, 13, 139–48, 159, 164; middle-class, 3–5, 7–12, 38, 140–43, 149–50, 165–66;

misreading by, 12–22; orientation of, 136; "sense-of-duty," 138–40; upwardly mobile, 85–86, 148, 149–56

Reader's Subscription, 197

reading, 8, 10–11, 75–76, 154; benefits of, 193–94; books vs. newspapers, 196; friendly, 75, 77–78; as information, 46, 47; as information gathering, 7; as leisure, 135–36; leisured, 75–76; middle-brow, 7–12; phenomenology of, 149; as pleasurable, 46, 47; popularization of, 24; self-interested, 76–77; sentimentality and, 47; success and, 196–97; sympathy and, 161–62, 166; utility of, 135–36

reading advice, 2–5, 24–25, 28, 32–33, 37–44, 140–41, 165–66

reading culture, Victorian, 10–11

reading formations, 11–12

reading habit, 139–48, 212n12

reading manuals, 4–7, 59, 140, 154, 165–66

reading up, 2–4, 19–20, 38, 40, 44, 57, 63, 85, 107, 129, 136, 148–56, 161–62, 171, 193–94, 196–97, 204; contemporary literature, 22; identification and, 161–62

realism, 170, 172–73, 203, 214n35, 214n37, 217n44, 218n2, 219n31, 220n64; as advice manual, 71; aesthetics of, 12; authorship and, 14–15; Crawford and, 134–35; critics and, 14–15; critics/criticism and, 14–15; as cultural capital, 20; high, 173, 182, 193, 195, 203; Howells and, 8, 63, 68, 71–74, 77–78, 83–84, 97, 116, 214n37, 214–15n40, 219n31, 220n64; James and, 116, 134–36, 214n37; Mabie and, 8, 10, 17, 19–20, 24, 33, 35, 44–53, 60–61, 63, 81–85, 91, 168, 173, 181–82, 193, 218n2; mass culture and, 3–4; Mitchell and, 188; realist criticism, 15; transition to, 181

reception, 7–12, 44, 50–51, 146–47

regionalism, 20–22, 46, 47, 53, 102, 115, 117, 169–70, 172–81, 209–10, 217n32

Repplier, Agnes, 195

respectability, 6–7

Revolutionary War novels, 189–90, 191

Rice, Alice Hegan, *Mrs. Wiggs of the Cabbage Patch*, 84

Riis, Jacob: *How the Other Half Lives*, 33; *Making of an American*, 142

Ringe, Donald A., 185

romance, 12, 14–15, 17, 19–20, 22, 35, 44–47, 49–50, 52–53, 60, 182, 186–92, 219n31; American, 116; Cable and, 185; of chivalry, 115; comforts of, 171–74; Crawford and, 128, 134–35; Howells and, 63–64, 74, 90, 95–97, 219n31; James and, 114–27; Mabie and, 115, 116, 117, 173, 186; transcendentalist, 102; of the workshop, 115

romanticism, 51, 60, 62, 71–72, 103, 169–70, 171–94, 214n35; Howells and, 74, 87; Mabie and, 49, 97, 170

Romines, Ann, 179

Rooney, Kathleen, 199

Roscoe, William, *Leo the Tenth*, 112

Rose, Jonathan, 9

Ross, Albert, *Moulding a Maiden*, 2

Rossetti, Christina, 178

Rowson, Susanna, *Charlotte Temple*, 167

Rubin, Joan Shelley, 3, 196; *The Making of Middlebrow Culture*, 7, 28

Rudin, Scott, 225–26n10

Ruskin, John, 178

Santayana, George, 62

Saturday Evening Post, 25

Scanlon, Jennifer, 215–16n10

Scherman, Harry, 8

Scott, Walter, 10, 13–14, 17, 34, 50, 102, 117–18, 167, 206; *Ivanhoe*, 81, 117, 205; *Quentin Durward*, 49, 115; *Waverly*, 117

Scribner's [Monthly] Magazine, 29, 32, 33, 164, 185, 216–17n24

self-culture, 53–54, 56, 59, 82, 107, 118, 161, 172, 182, 195

self-education, 53–56

self-help books, 4

self-possession, 57, 59

sentimentality, 9–12, 14–15, 17, 19–20, 30, 46–49, 52–53, 173, 192, 203, 213n20; Howells and, 63, 90, 95–96; Mabie and, 175, 217n35; reading and, 47; Wharton and, 154

Shakespeare, William, 34, 74, 78, 206

Shuman, Edwin L., *How to Judge a Book*, 154

Sicherman, Barbara, 10–11, 19, 214n26

Sienkiewicz, Henryk, *Quo Vadis*, 191

Simms, William Gilmore, *The Partisan*, 209

Sinclair, May, 53
Sinclair, Upton, *The Jungle*, 167
Sismondi, J.-C.-L. Simonde de, *History of
Italian Republics*, 112
Smith, Adam, 10
Smith, F. Hopkinson, 82, 206, 212–13n19;
The Fortunes of Oliver Horn, 209;
Kennedy Square, 169
Spiro, Lisa, 219–20n39
Staël, Madame (Anne Louise Germaine)
de, 112; *Corrine*, 112
status, 2–3, 6–8, 13, 24, 26–27, 33. *See also*
class; literary status
Stendhal, 17
Stevenson, Robert Louis, 28–29; *Treasure
Island*, 81, 205
Stowe, Harriet Beecher, 118; *Minister's
Wooing*, 175; *Oldtown Folks*, 175; *Uncle
Tom's Cabin*, 48–49, 102, 167, 172, 187,
205
success, 70, 108, 136, 142, 161, 196–97;
morality and, 91; success culture, 24,
54, 57
Swift, Jonathan, *Gulliver's Travels*, 73
sympathy, 9–10, 15–17, 22, 59, 72, 96,
219n31; Howells and, 96; James and,
106–14; Jewett and, 178; Mabie and,
110, 175, 181; reading and, 161–62, 166

talent, discipline and, 108
Tarkington, Booth, 7–8, 52–53, 206;
Conquest of Canaan, 167
taste, 15, 40, 56–57, 94–95, 214–15n40;
culture of, 4–5, 10–11, 26–27; education
and, 86; language of, 20; taste-making
ventures, 197
Tennyson, Alfred, 34, 206; *Idylls of the
King*, 181
Tennyson, Alfred Lord, *In Memoriam*, 205
Thackeray, William Makepeace, 18, 34, 74,
102, 167, 193, 206; *Henry Esmond*, 74,
115, 205; *Vanity Fair*, 20, 63, 81–82, 115,
186, 205; *The Virginians*, 187, 191
Thanet, Octave: *Heart of Toil*, 209; *Stories
of a Western Town*, 209
Thurston, Katherine Cecil: *The
Masquerader*, 43–44, 167, 205; *Max*,
43–44
Time magazine, 225–26n10
Tolstoy, Leo, *Anna Karenina*, 205
Trachtenberg, Alan, 218n2

transportation, public, 142–43
Travis, Trysh, 199
Trollope, Anthony, *Barchester Towers*, 81
Twain, Mark, 127, 173, 206; *The Adventures
of Huckleberry Finn*, 102, 121, 206

upper class, 151–56, 158, 165, 178. *See also*
highbrow culture
upward mobility, 2, 4, 19, 57, 60, 171,
193–94, 196–97. *See also* reading up;
Howells and, 81, 85; James and, 103,
107; Wharton and, 137, 140–41, 148–56,
161–62

Van Dyke, Henry, 206
"Veritas," 192
Virgil, *Georgics*, 79

Waid, Candace, 162–63, 223n14, 224n34
Ward, Mrs. Humphry, 118, 168, 206;
Eleanor, 112; *Robert Elsmere*, 29
Warner, Charles Dudley, 174
Warner, Susan, *The Wide, Wide World*, 167
Washington, Booker T., *Up from Slavery*,
142
Watts, Mary, 173
Wharton, Edith, 15, 19, 20, 53, 171, 173,
193, 206. *See also* Wharton, Edith,
works of; on Balzac, 17–18; on born
readers, 146–47; correspondence
of, 163–64; criticism of society
journalists, 155; identification and,
18–19; marketing and, 140; on the
"mechanical reader," 140, 145–46, 147,
159; misreading of, 140; popularity and,
147–48; publication and, 148; readerly
hierarchies and, 146–47; readership
of, 21, 137–48, 149, 155, 159, 163; on
reception, 146–47; *Sanctuary*, 168–69
Wharton, Edith, works of: *A Backward
Glance*, 165; *Custom of the Country*,
223n14; *Ethan Frome*, 169, 170, 172;
The House of Mirth, 21, 81, 94, 137–70,
171–72, 206, 210, 223–24n32, 224n34;
controversy over, 189–90; ending of,
139; identification in, 162–63; letters to
Wharton about, 163–64; misreading
of, 150–51, 160; negative reviews of,
150; popularity of, 137–38, 150–51,
164; readership of, 164–65, 166, 222n3;
reading in, 153–54, 160–61; reception

of, 155–59, 223n18; sales of, 222n3, 222–23n6,; success and, 161, 222n3, 222–23n6; *tableau vivant* scene in, 152–54, 223n14; *The Valley of Decision*, 168; "The Vice of Reading," 13, 21, 43, 139–40, 142–43, 145–48; *The Writing of Fiction*, 17

Whittier, John Greenleaf, 206; "Snow-Bound," 181

Wiggin, Kate Douglas, 100, 193, 206

Wilkins Freeman, Mary E., 21, 46, 53, 81, 168, 174, 176, 184, 206; *The Heart's Highway: A Romance of Virginia in the Seventeenth Century*, 174; *A New England Nun*, 45, 209;

Pembroke, 102, 209; *The Portion of Labor*, 45–47, 174

Wilson, Christopher P., 12, 212n12

Winfrey, Oprah, 5, 22, 195

Wister, Owen, 173, 206; *Lady Baltimore*, 205, 209; *The Virginian*, 168, 172, 186, 205, 209

women, 34–35, 48–49, 59, 70–71, 193, 214n26, 215n4; education of, 212n6; reading and, 214n26; women's clubs, 172, 193; working, 26, 215–16n10

Woodberry, George E., 206

Wright, Mary Tappan, 82

Zagarell, Sandra A., 176, 177, 178

Zola, Émile, 48, 49, 51, 101, 170

About the Author

Amy L. Blair is Assistant Professor of English at Marquette University in Milwaukee.